GOVERNMENT AND PEOPLE
IN HONG KONG
1841–1962

A Constitutional History

1. The Legislative Council in session

1. The Hong Kong Legislative Council in session with Sir Robert Black presiding, 1960. By courtesy of the Hong Kong Government Information Services.

Frontispiece

Government and People
in Hong Kong
1841-1962

A Constitutional History

G. B. ENDACOTT

The English Constitution is not and cannot be in force in Hong Kong.—SIR JAMES STEPHEN

HONG KONG UNIVERSITY PRESS

1964

THE OXFORD UNIVERSITY PRESS, AMEN HOUSE, LONDON, E.C.4
AND 417 FIFTH AVENUE, NEW YORK 16, ARE THE EXCLUSIVE
AGENTS FOR ALL COUNTRIES EXCEPT ASIA EAST OF BURMA

Printed in Hong Kong by
CATHAY PRESS
31 Wong Chuk Hang Road, Aberdeen

PREFACE

THE Colony of Hong Kong was long regarded as different from all other colonies, as a phenomenon unique even in the many-sided story of British overseas expansion. The dispatches to and from the Colonial Office abound with references to its special character and there was some doubt if it could be regarded as a colony at all. At the outset, Lord Stanley told Sir Henry Pottinger that 'methods of proceeding unknown in other British colonies, must be followed in Hong Kong',[1] and he went on to say that it was founded 'not with a view to colonization, but for diplomatic, commercial and military purposes'. Sir Hercules Robinson, Governor 1859–1865, remarked 'Indeed, Hong Kong is totally unlike any other British dependency and its position is in many respects so grotesquely anomalous'.[2] His successor, Sir Richard Graves MacDonnell also observed 'there is however no parallel between this and any other British settlement',[3] and on a later occasion, referred to the 'special, exceptional circumstances of this very peculiar place, its very peculiar inhabitants and most peculiar geographical position'.[4] Phineas Ryrie, member of the Legislative Council from July 1867 until his death in February 1892, used to describe Hong Kong as *sui generis*.

Yet essentially not only was Hong Kong not peculiar or exceptional, its founding was typical of the forces that moulded the form of British overseas activity in early and mid-Victorian times. Hong Kong was not placed under British control because of territorial acquisitiveness, nor because a handful of Britons wanted to found a new home for themselves on a comparatively uninhabited island off the China coast, but because a trading post or 'factory' was thought to be needed there, equipped with the requisite means of maintaining law and order, dispensing justice impartially and providing military and naval protection. Only under such conditions could trade prosper, and the British merchants thought, not

---

[1] Lord Stanley to Sir Henry Pottinger, 3 June 1848, No. 8, Colonial Office Records, Series 129, Vol. 2, in the Public Record Office. Hence forward abbreviated in the form CO 129/2.

[2] *Annual Report 1859*.

[3] *Annual Report 1866*.

[4] Sir R. G. MacDonnell to Earl Granville, 12 May 1869, No. 701.

unjustifiably, that China was not ready to furnish them herself. That merchants should take this view is not strange, for they naturally seek security against commercial hazards such as arbitrary fiscal exactions, piracy at sea, robbery on land, and breaches of contract. Moreover in China the merchant class was held in low repute, at the bottom of the social order. British merchants, who occupied an honoured position in their own country, were then making similar demands everywhere. Arrogant though the claim must seem, the aim was a commercial *pax britannica*, not from any idealism, though it was liberal enough to allow all nations to share its benefits, but because of the financial rewards of the improved flow of trade. In this world-wide system, Hong Kong played its part.

Yet the charge that Hong Kong was peculiar had some substance. For long its people had no permanent roots there, and did not look upon it as home. The merchants and those who ministered to their needs, aimed to take advantage of the economic opportunities of East-West trade which had brought them to the Island, and then retire to their own homelands. The expectation of life in Hong Kong of the average inhabitant was thus relatively short, though it was long enough to build up a tradition of corporate life. But the chief cohesive factor binding men to the settlement was common economic interest.

Hong Kong was given a Crown Colony form of constitution in 1843, which it still retains. This fact naturally gives rise to doubts as to whether there can be a constitutional history of Hong Kong and must create some misgiving as to the necessity for this book.

As one more case-history in the wider story of British expansion in the 19th and 20th centuries, Hong Kong's constitutional history well illustrates the dominant ideas of the Colonial Office in London, even if it adds little to what is already known about them. Demands for self-government have been made from time to time, and it is of interest to see the arguments used on these various occasions. Further, it is not true that there has been no constitutional development in Hong Kong. The conspicuous absence of political agitation in Hong Kong in contrast to an emergent Asia cannot be explained away; in fact many administrative and constitutional agencies have been created over the year by which the system of Crown Colony rule is modified to enable the Government's actions to be discussed and broadly supported with little electoral machinery.

A further interesting feature of the Hong Kong constitutional development has been the application of British ideas of government to an overwhelmingly Chinese community. In this Hong Kong was unique. The Straits Settlements had large Chinese communities, but were much more multi-racial than Hong Kong. The Chinese were accustomed to political despotism at the centre coupled with —in theory at least—benevolent local administration by the scholar official, and so they did not fret over the absence of the Western forms of political liberty in Hong Kong. At first the Chinese and foreign communities lived side by side with little intercourse, but the development of government services has meant bringing the Chinese more within the purview of government, a process which has taxed the British genius for the application of empirical methods to the solution of political problems. Broadly the overwhelming Chinese character of Hong Kong and the need to protect their interests have been the main factors in the delaying the introduction of essentially Western ideas of political freedom.

A third interesting feature in the constitutional history of Hong Kong was the attempt to adapt colonial institutions set up in Hong Kong to meet the administrative needs of British communities living in the treaty ports. The Home Government in 1843 insisted that its Plenipotentiary and Superintendent of Trade in China should reside at, and be Governor of, Hong Kong. The British position in China was looked at as a whole, and the object of an island under the flag was to serve as a military, administrative and commercial headquarters. The British communities in the treaty ports were subject to the Hong Kong Legislative Council in legislation, to the Hong Kong Supreme Court in the matters of appeals, and were protected by the Hong Kong garrison. The Colonial Treasurer was also responsible for the accounts of the consular offices in the treaty ports.

When these arrangements were made after the Nanking Treaty, the future pattern of the foreign settlements on the China coast was not clearly foreseen. Hong Kong was expected to become the unrivalled emporium for the China trade. Hong Kong did in fact become the headquarters of the largest firms, but the exaggerated hopes at first entertained were unfulfilled. The growth of a teeming city in the International Settlement at Shanghai made it clear that the main weight of British commercial interests had shifted to the mouth of the Yangtze.

The result was that since Hong Kong did not secure its intended position of dominance in British commercial interests in the Far East, the needed administrative institutions could not in the long run be identified with those of the Colony; the phenomenal growth of Shanghai demanded that the administrative arrangements for the British communities in the treaty ports of China should be divorced from those of the Colony.

Yet curiously enough, the wheel has turned full circle, and with the renunciation of treaty rights in China, Hong Kong has since 1945 played the role that its founders had envisaged for it just over a century before.

The materials for this work have come largely from the Public Record Office, London, and from the Hankow Collection in the Library of the University of Hong Kong and I acknowledge with gratitude my debt to the staff of the Research Department of the Public Record Office and of the Hong Kong University Library for unfailing helpfulness. I am grateful for valuable assistance received from the Institute of Historical Research, London University, from the officials of the Hong Kong Supreme Court Library and Hong Kong General Chamber of Commerce, and from Dr J. R. Jones of The Hongkong and Shanghai Banking Corporation who undertook to read the script and whose comments were valuable and illuminating. The script was also read, to its great advantage, by my Publisher, M. Henri Vetch, for which service I am much indebted. I am very appreciative of the ready co-operation of the Hong Kong Government in entertaining and replying as far as possible to the many questions I raised, and of my great gain as result. I wish to thank Miss Munsie Man Kam Yip of the History Department at the University for assistance with typing. The Chinese characters have been supplied by colleagues in the History Department and by the Hong Kong University Press.

Unpublished Crown Copyright material in the Public Record Office has been used with the permission of the Controller of Her Majesty's Stationery Office. The Section on the failure of the municipal scheme is reproduced, by permission of the Hong Kong University Press, from the *Journal of Oriental Studies* (Vol. III, 1956), but in amended form.

G. B. ENDACOTT

CONTENTS

PART III

THE CONSTITUTION IN THE POST-WAR PERIOD, 1945–62

ILLUSTRATIONS

In the Text

Part I

INTRODUCTION

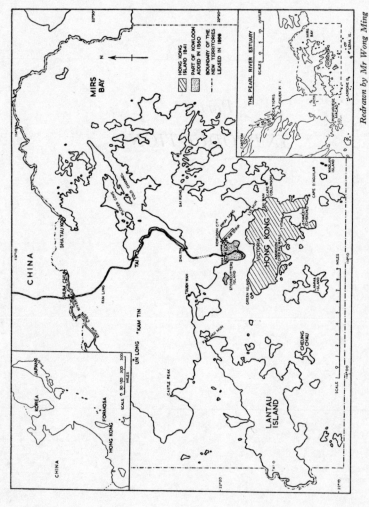

Map of Hong Kong and The New Territories reproduced by permission of the
Oxford University Press, London. Revised by Prof. S. G. Davis, 1964.

Redrawn by Mr Wong Ming

CHAPTER I

INTRODUCTION

The Colony of Hong Kong

THE Colony of Hong Kong is situated on the coast of Kwangtung, the southernmost province of China, at the eastern extremity of the mouth of the Pearl Estuary. The Portuguese Colony of Macao occupies a corresponding position on the west. This broad estuary receives the waters of the most important river system of South China which has been from time immemorial, and still is, the chief commerical link with the interior. The city of Canton, which is the administrative and economic centre of this region, lies some 37 miles up river from the northern end of the estuary and is about 95 miles north-west of Hong Kong. Hong Kong was born of the trading relations between Britain and China and its growth has in the main been determined by geographical and economic factors. Its relations with Canton have been particularly close, and the Chinese in Hong Kong have been traditionally sensitive to opinion in the provincial capital.

The Colony consists of three parts: the first is the Island of Hong Kong, 29 square miles, one of many thousands which are a feature of the China coast, ceded by the Treaty of Nanking in 1842. Next there is the small peninsula of Kowloon on the mainland opposite, which, with Stonecutters Island, was acquired by the Convention of Peking in 1860; it is 3½ square miles. Thirdly, there is the area, usually referred to as the New Territories, which was leased from China in 1898 for 99 years, and which covers 365½ square miles of the mainland from the Pearl Estuary on the west to Mirs Bay on the east, together with some 235 islands in the surrounding waters.

The total area of the Colony is therefore 398 square miles. Much of it is rocky, hilly and barren; peaks of over three thousand feet in height rise abruptly from the sea with little cultivable land along the margin of the sea, and the soil, largely of decomposed granite, is infertile. Yet Chinese skill and industry succeeds, despite these unfavourable conditions, in utilizing the mountain streams to produce rice and vegetables on terraced slopes. Though the New Territories offer more favourable opportunities to the agriculturalist, probably not more than 16% of the total area is cultivable. The rice locally produced would last the Colony only about one month, and so the bulk of its food has to be imported.

A census taken early in 1961 showed a total population of 3,128,044. In 1962 the population increased by 300,000 of which 91,581 was due to a natural increase and the remainder to a net balance of immigration, legal or illegal, giving an estimated total of 3,526,500.[1] The people of Hong Kong have certain well-defined characteristics which bear closely upon the problem of their government. First, the population is predominantly urban; the rural New Territories, excluding New Kowloon, supported no more than 456,404 people in 1961 while on the Island itself only a comparative handful live outside the urban area, in the few scattered hamlets in outlying areas; but pressure of population is threatening these with urbanization. Secondly, Hong Kong is overwhelmingly Chinese who constitute over 98 per cent of the total; the great majority come from Kwangtung Province and speak Cantonese; but many villages in the New Territories are Hakka (literally, Guest Families) and some of the fishing communities are from Fukien Province; others are political refugees particularly from Shanghai, fleeing from the Communist régime on the mainland. Thirdly, the people are polyglottish and heterogeneous. It was estimated that in 1961 there were 33,140 British and Commonwealth subjects in Hong Kong, excluding the armed forces and their families, and 16,607 other non-Chinese residents; there were 2,103 Americans, 1,863 Portuguese, 652 Japanese, 422 Filipino, 386 Dutch, 329 Indonesian, 323 French, 302 Italian, and 300 German. It would be difficult to find any nationality not represented. Hong Kong is not one community but an aggregation of communities.

A striking feature of the population is that comparatively few belong to Hong Kong. The Colony's function as an entrepôt drew to it men from east and west, coming to trade and in due course returning to their homeland on retirement. This was as true of the Chinese artisan as of the European trader. This feature has been accentuated by Hong Kong's role as an important centre of migration. In 1948 for example, the last year before the Communist take-over created a different situation, two million people entered

---

[1] *Hong Kong Annual Report, 1962.* Hong Kong Government Press, p. 36. Hereafter referred to in the form *Annual Report*.

the Colony and two million left[1] a coming and going of nearly 11,000 per day, and even in 1957 the number of journeys made both ways across the frontiers was said to be equal to or greater than the total population.[2] If it has been true of Hong Kong that throughout its history few of its inhabitants have had their roots there, how much more true is it in the post-war period in which over one million refugees have fled to the Colony from the mainland. This human flood of newcomers put such a strain on the Colony's resources that the century-old policy of the open frontier with China could not be maintained, and immigration restrictions were applied to Chinese travellers in 1950, although illegal immigration has continued. With the frontier closed, Hong Kong people are beginning to take root, for other new Asian countries are also restricting Chinese immigrants.

To feed its dense population, the Colony imports most of its food and the mainland is naturally the chief source, supplying 36% of its foodstuffs in 1962.[3] With its present population, Hong Kong would face a serious food problem if it were isolated from China. In the past Hong Kong got much of its livelihood from being the headquarters of the most important merchant houses trading in the Far East and much business was transacted in Hong Kong though the actual goods concerned may never have touched the Colony. As the clearing house of trade between the East and the rest of the world, it naturally developed specialized associated services such as shipping, banking, insurance, accountancy and legal services, and special market facilities such as the gold market. With shipping came the related industries of shipbuilding, and repairing, victualling and wharfage and warehousing. After the First World War of 1914–18, the entrepôt trade with China began to decline relative to the total trade of the Colony, but the area of the entrepôt trade grew to cover much of the Far East and South-East Asia. Since the establishment of the People's Republic of China on the mainland in 1949, the economic dependence on China, already less marked, virtually disappeared. The political refugees after the Second World War 1939–45, increased the Colony's resources of capital and labour, and began to develop

[1] *Annual Report 1948*, p. 9
[2] *Annual Report 1957*, p. 36
[3] *Annual Report 1962*, p. 76

its industry, chiefly textiles and other light industry. The Colony's commercial and financial facilities have helped to market its own products, and to distribute the products of the west Pacific region. The success of Hong Kong as an important commercial centre has been its stability; there has been no ruinous currency inflation as in China; Chinese customs and usage have been respected; British law courts have had the confidence of the population, Chinese and foreign alike. As a free port, it attracted merchants of every nation. The present cosmopolitan complexion of Hong Kong is rooted in its history and in the liberal character of British rule.

British Trading Communities on the China Coast and the Birth of the Colony

British contacts with China began in the seventeenth century with the founding by royal charter in 1600, of 'The Governor and Merchants of London trading into the East Indies', more generally referred to as the East India Company, which was granted a monopoly of English trade to the east of the Cape of Good Hope.[1] These contacts long remained almost entirely commercial. Various factors, including Dutch rivalry, unsettled political conditions in England, and the prior claims of the Company's interests in India, held back the expansion of the China trade until the 18th century. The first British ship to trade successfully with China was the *Macclesfield* in 1699, at Canton. Subsequent attempts to extend the trade to Amoy and Ningpo with which the Portuguese, Dutch and the Company itself had earlier had connections, failed because of excessive exactions, and the trade gravitated to Canton, which in 1755, secured the monopoly of foreign trade by imperial decree.

At first, each ship employed on the Company's service carried its own supercargo who was responsible for the commercial side of the voyage. After 1715, with the increase in the number of ships sent to Canton and the need of greater co-ordination of commercial relations, the supercargoes were grouped into two councils, each resident at Canton during the trading season. In 1786 the councils

---

[1] Some competition was allowed in 1698 when, as a result of Parliamentary jealousy of the royal prerogative, a rival East India Company, chartered by Parliament, was given a share of the trade. Monopoly was restored in 1709 when the two companies were united as the Honourable United East India Company.

were merged and a select committee of six under a president managed the affairs of the Company in Canton until its monopoly was abolished by a revision of its Charter in 1833. Canton became the seat of a factory, similar to the Company's factories in India.

The second half of the 18th century saw a great expansion of British commerce in the East. This was due, amongst other things, to the successes of the Seven Years' War (1756–63), to the loss of the American Colonies which stimulated greater interest in commerce in the Far East, and to the expansion of British influence in India which ensured the opportunity of a dominant place for Britain in India's trade with China and the East Indies. As a result of the participation by the Dutch in the American War of Independence the British broke the Dutch monopoly of the East Indies Trade. It is not surprising therefore that by the last quarter of the century, British commerce at Canton had outstripped that of all other European nations. During the Napoleonic Wars, Britain's position was further strengthened by her naval supremacy which temporarily made her mistress of oceanic trade and placed the colonies of all European nations at her disposal.

The trade between India and China, called the 'country trade', increased in importance and was handled by private British and Parsee merchants in India, under licence from the Company whose monopoly and control were thus technically preserved. From about 1770 onwards the Company confined itself to the tea trade, and came to rely on the 'country traders' to assist it in finding the necessary funds for the purchase of tea. The private merchants naturally wished to reside in Canton during the trading season, and to overcome the Company's reluctance to permit this, they adopted the subterfuge of acting as consuls for foreign states, taking out foreign papers and placing their ships under foreign flags, until the Company was forced to recognize what it was powerless to prevent. In any case the Company could not hinder the coming of Americans (after 1783) or of other European nationals. The Chinese restricted residence in the factories at Canton to males and for the duration of the trading season only. The Europeans normally rejoined their families at Macao in the off-trading season during the summer months. Macao was therefore the social and recreational centre.[1]

---

[1] Portuguese trade was also centred at Macao.

On the Chinese side, a group or guild of some thirteen Chinese merchants,[1] The Co-hong, operating individually and not corporately, held a monopoly of trade with the Westerners similar to that theoretically held by the Company. They paid heavily for this privilege and besides acting as security merchants for all the Western traders, they were held responsible for their general conduct. Trade with the West was supervised by an official called the Hoppo, appointed by the Emperor and removed from the control of the provincial hierarchy, who was able to see that a share of the profits of this lucrative trade accrued to the Imperial treasury.

The foreign traders prospered and the Company's factory at Canton and its house in Macao were noted for their luxurious appointments. There was mutual trust in commercial dealings and as long as the Company's control remained, there were no written contracts. Yet there were many grievances.

Chinese regulations[2] imposed upon the Foreign Devils[3] a comprehensive series of restrictions which they found vexing and humiliating. Entry into the walled city of Canton was forbidden and residence was restricted to the factory area except for occasional supervised visits to the *fati* or flower gardens across the river. The possession of firearms, the employment of Chinese servants, the use of sedan chairs, and the learning of the Chinese language were all banned. Communication with Chinese officials was allowed only through the medium of the Co-hong, and then only in the form of a petition, normally used in China in addressing a person of superior status. This Chinese assumption of superiority was a source of constant irritation. The port charges and ship measurement fees were not publicly promulgated and were arbitrarily varied so that the merchants were unable to calculate their costs. In the fixing of commodity prices the foreign merchants were largely in the hands of the Co-hong because of its monopoly.

The Select Committee at Canton made many unavailing attempts to negotiate directly with the local provincial officials to modify

[1] Known as the Hong merchants, or Co-hong. It had a chequered history; it was founded in 1720 and became an essential part of the Canton system when it was given a monopoly of Western trade in 1755. It was dissolved in 1771 because many of its members became insolvent, and re-formed by imperial decree in 1782. The membership varied in number from time to time.

[2] These were the Eight Regulations, but their number varied with each promulgation and they were not all applied all the time.

[3] The general term used by the Chinese for all Europeans was then *fan-kuei-tzu*.

the conditions under which foreigners lived and conducted business at Canton; it also complained to the Court of Directors of the Honourable Company in London. The British Government was sympathetic and even supported the Company's plans for the acquisition of an island off the North Borneo coast or in the Philippines as an entrepôt for an extended British trade in the Far East.[1] Two diplomatic missions to Peking, Lord Macartney's in 1793 and Lord Amherst's in 1816, succeeded in reaching the capital[2] but failed to secure any concession and their failure was interpreted by the traders in Canton as proving that it was futile to appeal to the Emperor for redress. Neither was the lesson lost upon the Chinese provincial hierarchy.

An uneasy *modus vivendi* was gradually established, partly by mutual threats to stop the trade, a step which both sides were really anxious to avoid. This game of commercial poker favoured the Chinese because it was the West that sought a trade which the Chinese could forego with no great harm, for China was largely self-sufficient.

One further problem was that of jurisdiction. Chinese law courts did not inspire confidence because they were not free from interference by executive officials, used torture to extract confessions without which under Chinese law no prisoner could be condemned, and were prepared to punish as a substitute the person who was responsible in law for the behaviour of the accused if the latter could not be found. Again the distinction between murder and homicide was not so clearly drawn to Chinese minds as to British; for example, in 1784 a gunner of the ship *Lady Hughes* accidentally killed a Chinese in the course of firing a salute; his surrender was demanded and after some demur agreed to, with the result that he was condemned to death and strangled. Following this incident the British refused to hand over any of their own nationals for trial and the Chinese officials in practice did not dispute this measure of extraterritoriality, though they never explicitly recognized it as a right.

Conditions at Canton became increasingly irksome as mercantilist ideas with which they were to some extent consonant, gave

---

[1] Vincent T. Harlow, *The Founding of the Second British Empire 1763–83*, London 1952, pp. 103–146.

[2] Lt.-Colonel Charles Cathcart was sent on an embassy to Peking in December 1787, but he died off the Java coast on his way there.

way in England to Adam Smith's doctrines of freeing trade from unnecessary restrictions. In 1833 the Company's monopoly at Canton was abolished by act of Parliament,[1] and British commercial interests there were placed under a Chief Superintendent of Trade responsible to the Foreign Office.

The first Chief Superintendent of Trade, Lord Napier, arrived off Macao in August 1834. His instructions to reside at Canton and communicate with the Chinese Viceroy direct, were unfortunately at variance with the Chinese regulations, and the local mandarins were unwilling to recognize his diplomatic status until they had referred to Peking. He himself was too anxious to impress the Chinese with his own importance and dignity, and the result was an impasse. The Viceroy stopped the trade, which was the normal Chinese response in case of dispute, and Napier, believing that the foreign community was threatened, ordered two British warships up the river to Canton for protection. This display of force failed to induce the Chinese to recognize his mission. Napier, now a very sick man, retired to Macao; his journey there was subjected to deliberate and humiliating delays and he died soon after, on 11 October 1834. His mission had lasted barely three months.

His two successors, J. F. Davis and Sir George Robinson made no attempt to force the issue, and then in December 1836 Captain Charles Elliot, R.N., became Superintendent of Trade. He adopted a policy of conciliation, particularly in the use of the customary word 'petition', *pin*, in writing to the Viceroy and so secured official Chinese recognition of his position but when the Foreign Secretary, Lord Palmerston, refused to allow Elliot to act in this or any other way which compromised the British claim to equality, Elliot could make no headway and retired to Macao. The attempt to remove grievances by negotiation therefore failed.

The ending of the Company's monopoly brought an increasing flow of foreign residents. In 1837 they numbered 308,[2] of which 158 were British, 62 Parsee, 44 American, 28 Portuguese and the remaining 16 of various nationalities. Except for the few missionaries and the officials of the British Mission, most of them were attached to the 57 'agency houses', which were the normal type of merchant firm in Canton.

---

[1] 3 & 4 William IV, c 93. See also below p. 64 ff.
[2] *The Chinese Repository*, January 1837.

In spite of the restrictions, or rather because of them, the foreign residents enjoyed a vigorous social life and evinced much public spirit. They set up a Chamber of Commerce to give concerted support to the Superintendent of Trade, and launched two societies aimed at the regeneration of the Chinese, the Society for the Diffusion of Useful Knowledge and the Morrison Education Society. British doctors in the service of the Company and, after 1834, attached to the Superintendent of Trade, conducted a small hospital for the treatment of Chinese; the American Dr Peter Parker treated Chinese in a much-needed hospital for eye diseases, and a hospital for seamen was founded by the merchants at the nearby anchorage of Whampoa.

The rapid growth of the 'country trade' reflected the growing Chinese demand for opium. Opium had certainly been known in China since the T'ang Dynasty (618–906) as a medicinal herb with valuable anti-biotic qualities. Opium smoking was a more recent (17th century) importation, similar to that of tobacco, and when this practice became widespread the Emperors tried to curb it by a number of edicts beginning with that of 1729. They proved ineffectual and in 1800 an absolute prohibition of the import and local production of the drug was decreed. Nevertheless opium continued in demand and found a ready sale, the trade therefore persisted, not without official connivance. The fact that the trade was illegal was a factor in its prosperity because it became a cash trade in which port formalities, restrictions and fees were avoided. By 1800, the annual import averaged about 4,000 chests,[1] by 1828, the annual average rose to over 10,000 chests, and by 1839 this had nearly quadrupled to some 39,000 chests. The Imperial Court, concerned over the social evil, and perhaps even more over the financial problems consequent upon the drain of silver from China, decided after much debate to take more stringent action to stop the trade. Chinese opium dealers were strangled, and on one occasion in January 1839, the sentence was carried out in the area facing the Factories, as an unmistakable threat to their inmates.

To the Chinese, the issue was the simple one of suppressing a harmful, uneconomic and illegal trade. They did not recognize any problem over the legitimate trade, conducted as it was on such terms as they chose to dictate; they argued that if foreign merchants

[1] Chests varied in weight. A chest of Malwa and of Persian opium weighed about 133 lb.; a chest of Bengal opium weighed 160 lb.

came to China they must expect to obey the laws of China. The British Government demanded equality with China and her recognition of its Superintendent of Trade as necessary pre-condition of any official discussion of difficulties. It placed the onus of suppressing the contraband trade on the Chinese Government and not on the British officials, who were bound by British law and could take no part in the enforcement of Chinese law without risk of being sued in British courts.

The foreign community at Canton demanded the abolition of personal and commercial restrictions, and the appointment of a plenipotentiary, armed with the necessary powers to negotiate a settlement, and backed by the requisite force, without which, in their view, no concessions could be expected.[1] Merchant opinion was against acquiring Chinese territory, though the view was frequently expressed that an island station might be obtained by negotiation or purchase for the purpose of residence and trade. Lord Macartney had been instructed in 1793 to ask for an island, and Lord Napier again urged this on the British Government in 1834. The advantages of an island station were: it would give greater personal security to the merchants; it would permit courts of law to function under British control and to establish that law and order which the Victorians almost regarded as the equivalent of civilization itself; it would become an emporium of trade if allowed to function freely; and finally it would provide a military and naval base of great strategic value.

The opium trade was much debated among the foreign community at Canton. The missionaries crusaded against it on moral grounds. Its defenders argued that opium did no harm and was even beneficial, and, by a peculiar travesty of Adam Smith's ideas, even that, in opposing the opium trade, the Chinese were opposing the divine will, since God had ordained that all nations should trade freely for their mutual advantage. Undoubtedly the main reasons for the continuance of the trade were the practical ones, that there was a demand for opium and if one nation refused to supply it, then other nations would.

The Chinese appointed a special Commissioner, Lin Tse-hsü, to suppress the evil, and he arrived at Canton in March 1839. He was in a hurry and took immediate and decisive action. Since it

[1] The Merchants' Petition to the King in Council, 9 December 1834. Parliamentary Papers 1840, No. 27, p. xxxvi.

was impossible to set up a preventive service strong enough to match the well-armed and speedy opium ships, he decided to put pressure on the foreign merchants in Canton. Within a week of his arrival he demanded that all opium held by them should be surrendered and that as a condition of trading at Canton, all masters of incoming ships should sign a bond agreeing to the death penalty if they carried opium. In accordance with precedent, trade was stopped, the foreign community was shut up in the factories at Canton and denied food and services until they accepted Lin's conditions. Elliot made his way to Canton at great personal risk and after attempts to bargain with Lin, took upon himself the responsibility of handing over all stocks of opium at the various anchorages. He protested against Lin's acts and refused to renew commercial relations until the British Government had received his report of these proceedings and determined its policy.

Palmerston decided that the time had come for a settlement of the outstanding difficulties at Canton. His chief demands were compensation for the opium given up, the opening of four additional ports to trade, and, as security against the repetition of such actions as Lin had taken, either the cession of an island or the granting of an acceptable commercial treaty. An expedition to back these demands arrived off Macao in the summer of 1840. Rear-Admiral George Elliot and his cousin, Captain Charles Elliot, the Superintendent of Trade, were named as joint plenipotentiaries.

The British plan was to seize the Chusan Islands situated off the mouth of the Yangtze and institute a blockade of the coast as a preliminary to the opening of negotiations which were to be based upon a letter Palmerston had addressed 'To the Minister to the Emperor of China', copies of which the Plenipotentiaries were to attempt to deliver to Chinese officials at Canton, Shanghai and at the mouth of the Peiho River. Chinese envoys were met at the last-named place, and the two Elliots agreed to return to Canton and resume negotiations there. The Admiral now retired through ill-health, leaving Charles Elliot in sole charge.

The negotiations at Canton were punctuated by intermittent hostilities, for the Chinese were obdurate and it was Elliot's policy to restrict the use of force to the minimum. Eventually there resulted the Convention of Chuenpi of 20 January 1841 which provided *inter alia* for the cession of Hong Kong. The Island was accordingly occupied on 26 January 1841. The Convention, however, was repudiated by each side and the principals, Keshen and Elliot, were recalled and their actions disavowed.

Sir Henry Pottinger arrived at Macao in August 1841 as the new British plenipotentiary. His instructions still maintained the principle that security for British trade was to be obtained either by the cession of an insular trading station, or by the negotiation of a commercial treaty giving adequate guarantees. With regard to Hong Kong, Pottinger was told not to give it up except in exchange for another island 'better adapted for the purposes in view' and 'equally defensible'; but he was also informed that the possession of Hong Kong 'would not supersede the necessity for another insular position on the Eastern Coast'.[1] When the Whigs fell from office in September 1841, the new Tory Foreign Secretary, Lord Aberdeen, wrote that he was opposed to the retention of any Chinese territory, and ruled that the desired security for the merchants should take the sole form of a commercial treaty. The demand for an island was therefore dropped.

Under Pottinger the hostilities were conducted with vigour. He occupied the chief ports on the coast, sailed up the Yangtze River and by threatening Nanking and blockading the Grand Canal, forced the Chinese to accept the Treaty of Nanking on 29 August 1842. The Chinese agreed to pay an indemnity of $21 million as compensation for the opium, Hong debts and the war expenses, to open four additional ports, Amoy, Foochow, Ningpo and Shanghai, and to abolish the Co-hong monopoly. There was to be equal status between the official representatives of the two countries and an agreed customs tariff was to be set up. Despite Lord Aberdeen's instructions, Hong Kong was ceded in perpetuity.

In the meantime, Hong Kong had been occupied in January 1841 and Elliot, who was anxious to induce the foreign merchants to transfer their establishments from Macao to the island, had plots of land marked out for sale in the following June, and made the first appointments for the government of the infant colony. His recall was accompanied by a demand from the Home Government to halt all building and to make only the minimum administrative arrangements. The island was thus placed in a curiously anomalous position with some British landholders, and yet without recognized status as a British colony. The British Government refused to

[1] Lord Palmerston to Sir Henry Pottinger, 31 May 1841, No. 16.

acknowledge any cession of territory except in virtue of a treaty, and it was not until the ratifications of the Nanking Treaty were exchanged on 26 June 1843, that a colonial administration was set up in Hong Kong.

As amenities were provided,[1] the Colony began to take the position in the China trade that had formerly been occupied jointly by Macao and Canton. By 1847 its foreign population numbered 618 of whom only 167 were females, with a further 768 'resident aliens'.[2] Canton was too important a trading centre for it to be supplanted by Hong Kong, but the foreign community there never rivalled in number that of Hong Kong. Small communities of traders began to settle at the other four treaty ports but only Shanghai grew to be important.

The foreign community which established itself in Hong Kong after the Treaty of Nanking, was predominantly male, as is evidenced by the population figures just quoted. It was cosmopolitan, for it was the deliberate policy to attract all comers to the port without distinction of race[3] in accordance with the liberal character of British economic policy of this period. The foreigners were from the first heavily outnumbered by the Chinese who in 1847 totalled 20,449, of whom only 4,930 were women.

It was an unruly community. Except for the handful of the most important merchants and government officials, the foreigners were a rough, adventuring, enterprising class, well able to fend for themselves in the absorbing objective of material gain. Hong Kong, with its reputation for fever,[4] attracted only those who saw there the prospect of fairly rapid material success. Many were adventurers from Australia or came from the ranks of deserting seamen.

The opium trade attracted men whose lack of scruple made them difficult to control. One such was James Innes. On 5 May 1839, the Portuguese authorities at Macao seized and handed over to the Chinese eight chests of opium which were found to belong to Innes.

[1] Macao long remained the social centre and until 1852 there was an annual migration thither for the regatta and for horse racing.

[2] Report of Select Committee on Commercial Relations with China, 1847, p. 433 (Appendix No. 1). These figures exclude the British troops who numbered about 1,000.

[3] The Chinese were granted freedom to trade at Hong Kong under Article XIII of the Supplementary Treaty of the Bogue, October 1843.

[4] Deaths from fever among the troops were: 1843, 373; 1844, 216; 1845, 143; 1846, 56. The most serious visitation was in 1842.

Elliot was annoyed because he had just handed over all the opium stocks, and he ordered Innes, who had given trouble before over his opium trading activities, to leave the coast. Innes' reply, dated 30 May 1839, was a point-blank refusal: 'Your order to leave China is waste paper . . . and I give you distinctly to understand, that looking on your order as illegal, I shall land and stay in China whenever I consider it prudent to do so, without any reference to you'. Elliot saw that the chaos produced by the contraband trade might lead to a complete breakdown of law and order, and he was all the more anxious to secure the cession of an island on which British institutions could be set up to control men like Innes. Pottinger wrote to Lord Ellenborough at Calcutta that it would be more difficult to control than to protect British subjects. Davis, who returned to the East in 1844 as Governor of Hong Kong and Superintendent of Trade, declared that it was more difficult to govern the few hundred British than the thousands of Chinese, and in a memorandum to the Foreign Office dated 10 February 1842, he strongly complained of 'the ill-conduct of British subjects in China'. The Anglican missionary, George Smith, described the Hong Kong foreign community in the most scathing terms as rendering the Island unfitted to be the centre of missionary effort in China.[1]

The Chinese in Hong Kong made no better impression; they were originally the villagers and their families and the tanka boat people, some 4,000 in all. But the settlement soon attracted Cantonese and Hakka coolies and artisans from the mainland, amongst whom there were many undesirables. Under pressure from the Chinese officials, respectable Chinese avoided the island. Crime, both petty and serious, became prevalent.

In this unusual heterogeneous population, the urgent problem was to maintain minimal law and order and give protection for person and property.

---

[1] Rev. George Smith, *A Narrative of an Exploratory visit to each of the Consular Cities of China and to the Islands of Hong Kong and Chusan*, Second edition, London 1847, pp. 512 and 513.

Part II

A CENTURY OF
CONSTITUTIONAL DEVELOPMENT
1841 - 1941

CHAPTER II

BIRTH AND EARLY PROBLEMS

Birth of the Constitution

KIYING (or Ch'i-ying), the Manchu Commissioner for Western Affairs, paid a ceremonial visit to Hong Kong in June 1843 for the formal exchange of ratifications of the Treaty of Nanking which had been delayed by the death of his colleague Ilipu.[1] That formality was completed on 26 June 1843 and on the same day, the Island of Hong Kong, 'with its dependencies', was publicly proclaimed a British Colony, with Sir Henry Pottinger, the Plenipotentiary and Superintendent of Trade, as its first governor. The uncertain future of the Island was at last finally resolved after an occupation of two and half years, thus enabling the necessary constitutional arrangements to be brought into force.

The government of a colony acquired by cession was normally set up by Order in Council in the exercise of the royal prerogative, and in the case of Hong Kong this procedure was followed. Hong Kong became a Crown Colony. The form of Crown Colony government varied in detail but usually comprised a governor representing the Crown, assisted by an executive council and a legislative council, each composed at first of officials, with the subsequent addition of a nominated unofficial element which might or might not be in a majority according to local circumstances or the stage of development reached. A later stage was the institution of some form of representative government through elections, which was usually but not necessarily the prelude to full responsibility and self-government.[2] The essence of the system was a flexible combination of central control from the Colonial Office in London with local administration by officials who were expected to supply the initiative and provide the information necessary for the important policy decisions by the Secretary of State. Hong Kong closely followed precedent but there were two problems which caused great discussion. The first was whether the Chinese in Hong Kong should be allowed to live under their own law administered by their own

---

[1] Spelt Elepoo in the English version of the Treaty of Nanking.
[2] See Martin Wight, *The development of the Legislative Council*, London 1946.

officials; and the second referred to the nature of the administrative arrangements for the control of British subjects living in China at the treaty ports. The government of the Colony was not therefore thought of as concerned only with the administration of a ceded island, but rather as a matter embracing the whole British position in the Far East and involving the complex question of relations with the Chinese.

Lord Stanley, who was then Secretary of State for War and the Colonies (1841–45), in a letter to Pottinger in June 1843, recorded his view[1] that the function and purpose of Hong Kong was to serve as a diplomatic, commercial and military post. Pottinger was told that he had three functions: *(i)* to negotiate with the Chinese Emperor; *(ii)* to superintend the trade of British subjects in China; and *(iii)* to regulate the internal economy of the settlement. Stanley went on to say 'Hence it follows that methods of proceeding unknown in other British colonies must be followed at Hong Kong'. Clearly there was to be no slavish copying of precedents. In devising a constitution for the new colony, there was considerable discussion between the two departments involved, the Foreign Office and that of War and the Colonies, as to the arrangements best suited to meet its special conditions.

In the meantime, temporary measures for the administration of the Island were set forth in a series of letters and instruments all dated 4 January 1843, addressed by Lord Aberdeen to Sir Henry Pottinger. The introductory dispatch of this series[2] informed him that the Government intended him to be exclusively in charge in China and that he must assume the government of Hong Kong, exercising his authority by means of proclamations. He was to make the necessary arrangements for defence, including the erection of forts for the protection of shipping in the roads, and of barracks to house the garrison. He was to make grants of land, except that 'H.M. Government would not choose that . . . grants should be made to parties whose object in obtaining such grants would be to dispose of them again with advantage to themselves', to allocate land for public purposes, including roads and streets, and to reserve a part of the shore for a naval establishment. He was

---

[1] Lord Stanley to Sir Henry Pottinger, 3 June 1843, No. 8, CO 129/3. The Departments of War and the Colonies were placed under a single Cabinet Minister, the Secretary of State for War and the Colonies from 1801 to 1854.

[2] Lord Aberdeen to Sir Henry Pottinger, 4 January 1843, No. 4, CO 129/3.

further told that if, as a result of the establishment of a free port and 'the introduction of those liberal arrangements by which foreigners would be encouraged to come, a great commercial entrepôt were created, then H.M. Government would feel justified in securing to the Crown the increased values that the land would then have'.

In one of the letters of this series,[1] Lord Aberdeen asked Pottinger to give his advice 'with the fullest detail' and 'the utmost unreserve' on the future political administration of the island and the judicial arrangements. Regarding the former, after indicating that there would probably be a governor and council and that there would be 'no popular form of government', he mentioned two points on which he particularly wanted Pottinger's opinion: first, how should such a council be chosen, whether wholly or partly from 'official servants of the crown'; and second, whether the governor should, like the Governor-General of India, have the power of overriding the decisions of the council.

Regarding the judicial establishment, Aberdeen thought one resident judge would probably be sufficient for civil and criminal cases; but he pointed out that the main problem was how to frame and administer the law and police regulations so that 'while they satisfied the claims of the British', they might 'best conciliate the respect and fall in with the manners of the Chinese subjects of Her Majesty'. This was a clear recognition of the necessity of adapting institutions to local needs and of respecting Chinese customs. But the problem of dealing with the Chinese was easier to state than to solve and gave rise to prolonged discussion which is summarized below.

Until 26 June 1843, Pottinger therefore temporarily administered the government by proclamation in virtue of his position as Plenipotentiary and Superintendent of Trade. His opinion on the form of the constitution had been asked, but before he could reply, decisions had to be taken by the Home Government, partly because of the slow communications, and partly because some form of constitution had to be ready when the cession of the Island became effective on the exchange of ratifications of the treaty. But the chief need for prompt decision arose from the prevalence of crime in the Island. A. R. Johnston who was in charge of its

---

[1] Lord Aberdeen to Sir Henry Pottinger, 4 January 1843, No. 16, CO 129/3.

administration until Pottinger returned from his negotiations in the North, reported home on 21 October 1842[1] that the jail was full, the magistrate had inadequate powers, police arrangements were inefficient, there were innumerable complaints of burglaries and robberies, gangs attacked isolated houses making good their escape by boat, and acts of piracy were frequent. In view of this disturbing account of the state of the Colony, the setting up of a constitution for the more effective imposition of law and order was regarded as urgent. So in a letter dated 6 April 1843, Lord Stanley informed Pottinger that though it had been intended to have further discussions as to how Hong Kong should be governed, it was now felt that he should have legislative power without delay. A constitution for the colony was therefore drawn up. It was set out in two documents, the Hong Kong Charter dated 5 April 1843, and the Instructions to Sir Henry Pottinger dated the following day, both to come into effect upon his assumption of the office of Governor.

The Hong Kong Charter[2] was a commission 'for erecting the Island of Hong Kong into a separate colony and for the establishing of a Legislative and an Executive Council in the said colony and for granting certain powers and authorities to the governor for the time being of the said colony'. The Charter outlined the constitution in the baldest terms. The Legislative Council was to consist of the Governor and such other persons as were designated to hold places on the Council, at the royal pleasure. The Governor, with the advice of the Legislative Council was given full authority to make laws for the peace, order and good government of the colony subject to three important limitations. It had to be exercised in accordance with any instructions given by the Secretary of State, it was subject to the power of disallowance by the Crown of any ordinance either in whole or part; and Parliament retained the power of concurrent legislation over the Colony. Little was said about the Executive Council except that it was to 'advise and assist' the Governor.

The Governor was given custody of the public seal of the Colony; he was empowered to make grants of land subject to instructions from home; to appoint judges or commissioners of *oyer and terminer*, and justices of the peace for the administration of justice; to remit

---

[1] A. R. Johnston to Lord Aberdeen, 21 October 1842, CO 129/3.
[2] CO 380/91.

fines not exceeding £50, and suspend fines in excess of that amount until the royal pleasure could be made known; to pardon convicted criminals; and to suspend public officials pending a decision by the Crown. If the Governor were absent or incapacitated, these powers were to devolve on the Lieutenant-Governor, or, in his absence, upon the person holding the office of Colonial Secretary. All persons, civil and military, were to be 'obedient and assisting' to the Governor.

The Governor's Instructions of 6 April 1843[1] were based on those provided for the governor of New Zealand,[2] and remained the standard instructions of the governors of Hong Kong until their revision in 1865 on the appointment of Sir Richard Graves MacDonnell as Governor. In them Pottinger was subjected to detailed guidance regarding the working of the constitutional arrangements set out in the Charter; indeed it would be only a slight exaggeration to say that the constitution of Hong Kong must be looked for in the Instructions rather than in the Charter. By them Pottinger was to read the Charter publicly in the presence of the chief officers and principal inhabitants, and to take the oath of allegiance. He was to constitute the Legislative Council by nominating three members for appointment by the Crown to hold office during the royal pleasure, to preside over it and to frame its standing orders.

The Legislative Council was effectively subordinated to the will of the Governor by the instruction that no law was to be passed nor any motion debated unless first proposed by him; but a member had the right to transmit his opinions to the Governor regarding any bill or motion for debate and to have them entered on the minutes. Since these minutes were to be sent half-yearly to the Secretary of State, the latter was thus kept informed of any issues dividing the Governor and his Council, and could decide between them. In practice the Governor himself reported such differences since they normally raised important questions. The Governor was not to propose or assent to, any ordinance repugnant to the Charter or to his Instructions. No ordinance was to be passed, without previous sanction, limiting religious freedom, or permitting bills or paper money or coin (except legal coin of the realm) as legal tender in the Colony, or raising money by the institution of public or

[1] CO 381/35.
[2] *Ibid.*

private lotteries; nor was he, without leave, to propose or assent to any ordinance to which the royal assent had previously been refused. The Governor was to send a signed copy of all ordinances to the Secretary of State, with the Colony's seal attached.

The Governor was given a casting as well as an original vote and he was to have overriding power to make and promulgate laws even against the united opposition of all the members of the Legislative Council.

The Executive Council consisting of three members in addition to the Governor and appointed in the same way as members of the Legislative Council, was to meet only when summoned by the Governor; its quorum was two, exclusive of the presiding member, who was to be the Governor or the senior member present. The Governor was to consult with the Executive Council 'as often as the service may seem to you to require it', and the Council was to be shown instructions from the Secretary of State and similar papers, 'as requisite'. Like the Legislative Council, the Council could discuss only those motions brought before it by the Governor who had full power to act against its advice; it was therefore equally subordinate to him. If a member wished to suggest the discussion of any business he could do so in writing to the Governor and he had the right to have such a request entered on the minutes, copies of which were to be sent home at intervals of six months. In addition, a member who disagreed with the Governor was entitled to have his opinion with his reasons recorded in the minutes; if the Governor acted against the advice of the whole or majority of the Council, he was to supply a full explanation to the Secretary of State.

The Governor was not to make private grants of land for the benefit of individuals except by sale at public auction; and he was to set apart land for roads, towns, villages, churches, schools, health needs, quays and landing places; and he was forbidden to accept any private grant of land for himself. All official appointments were to be temporary, pending the pleasure of the Crown, and if any official were suspended, in accordance with the power given by the Charter, a full report was to be made to the Secretary of State.

These two documents established a Crown Colony constitution following the usual pattern of Governor and Executive and Legislative Councils with control from London exercised by means of instructions to the Governor.

The constitutional arrangements for Hong Kong show evident intention to meet the special conditions of the British position in the Far East where uncertainty over the future, and the absence of precedents, required a greater degree of central control. The essential feature was that the Governor was given overriding powers over the Executive and Legislative Councils, which could discuss only such measures as he chose to place before them, and he could introduce and put into effect legislation contrary to their wishes provided the Secretary of State were informed. The Governor could therefore act at his absolute discretion as long as he could convince the Secretary of State of the desirability of his policy. The Councils were deliberately kept small in number, to enable the Governor to work with a few important officials most closely associated with him in the administration. There could be little formal debate or formality of any sort in a council of three persons, with a quorum of two. The Councils were set up as a matter of form but the reality was firm control by the Secretary of State through the Governor.

There were precedents for these provisions not only in New Zealand but also in the constitutional arrangements for Ceylon and Mauritius, the two eastern colonies which naturally also served to some extent as models.[1] In each case, on the establishment of a new colony, prudence demanded a temporary concentration of authority in the hands of the Governor, and Hong Kong was no exception. But here there were additional reasons. Hong Kong was 'a barren island'[2] with a small indigenous population and with no large or old-established community demanding political representation. It was essentially a military, diplomatic and trading station, and not a settlement in the normal sense and strategic considerations demanded a greater degree of imperial control in Hong Kong than would normally be the case. No popular element

[1] On the assumption of Crown Colony government in Ceylon in 1802, a single undifferentiated council of three officials was set up for consultation on executive and legislative matters, legislative authority being vested in the Governor alone. In 1833, an Executive Council of five was set up, and also a Legislative Council of nine officials and six nominated unofficials, with the provision that the Governor alone should have the power of initiation, and no question could be debated without his approval.

In Mauritius, the Governor was supreme until 1825 when an undifferentiated advisory council of four members was established. Seven years later this was broadened to become a Legislative Council, of seven officials and seven unofficials.

[2] Lord Palmerston to Capt. Charles Elliot, R.N. (Private), 21 April 1841.

in the government could have been expected in Hong Kong in 1843.

In practice this administrative absolutism was much modified. Laissez-faire ideas then dominant meant that the colonial government operated over a very restricted field, covering little more than the maintenance of law and order, and the raising of taxes to meet, or help meet, the cost of the civil establishment and necessary public works. For the rest the individual was left to his own devices. Secondly, it was intended from the start, that the authority of the government should be limited by some form of municipal self-government (see below p. 73) and the special powers of the governor were intended primarily to protect the broader imperial interests. Thirdly, the intention was to place the Chinese subjects of the Queen under their own Chinese law administered by Chinese officials, thus giving them a greater degree of freedom. Fourthly, the Secretary of State was responsible to Parliament in which the vigilance of the opposition could be counted upon to act as a valuable safeguard. Finally, the founding of colonies at this period, often in the teeth of opposition from the generally anti-colonial free traders, had for its aim, the security of commerce and of the merchant, and the creation of those conditions in which commerce should flourish, for example, the suppression of disorder and the settlement of commercial disputes. The normal policy therefore was to interfere with the merchant and with native custom to the minimum consistent with these ends. The constitution set up in Hong Kong should be judged with these considerations in mind, and it may be said that it was not ill-adapted to the purposes in view.

Some time elapsed before the constitutional arrangements could be effectively implemented, mainly because of the lack of suitable candidates for membership of the Councils. Pottinger acted promptly enough and on 24 August 1843, two months after the proclamation of the Charter, the names of the members of the Legislative Council were announced. They were A. R. Johnston, J. R. Morrison and William Caine. Johnston had become deputy Superintendent of Trade upon the reorganization in 1836 of the arrangements regarding the Superintendent of Trade, and he had administered the Island during the temporary absence of Sir Henry Pottinger. Morrison, the son of Robert Morrison, the first protestant missionary to China, became Chinese Secretary and

Interpreter to the Superintendent of Trade on the death of his father in 1834, and played a notable part in the negotiations both before and after the Treaty of Nanking. Caine had come to China with his regiment, the Cameronians, in the 1840 Expedition. He had had experience in India as Deputy Judge-Advocate General and had been selected to serve as civil magistrate of the Island of Chusan during its temporary occupation; in the following year he had been appointed Chief Magistrate in Hong Kong. All were officials in the service of the Crown, two attached to the office of Superintendent of Trade under the Foreign Office and only one was therefore a colonial official. These three were also appointed members of the Executive Council, and an accompanying proclamation allowed them the style of 'Honourable'. That summer in Hong Kong was marked by a serious outbreak of fever and one of the many victims was J. R. Morrison, who died at Macao on 29 August, only a week after the announcement of his nomination to the Council. The following month Johnston returned to England on sick leave. The result was that the Councils as originally nominated by Pottinger never met, and, because there were no local officials considered capable of filling the vacancies, both Councils remained in abeyance. Pottinger himself resided at Macao until October 1843 for the negotiations with Kiying leading to the Supplementary Treaty of the Bogue; and probably he was glad to avoid the fever-ridden Colony. Indeed it was not until January 1844, upon the arrival of Major General D'Aguilar as the General Officer commanding the garrison, that the Councils could be constituted with the bare quorum of two members, D'Aguilar and Caine. Pottinger was unable to find a suitable candidate to take the third seat; hence the instruction that the Councils were always to consist of three members, had to be disregarded. The Legislative Council in this attenuated form thus came into existence and the first Hong Kong ordinance, declaring slavery illegal in the Colony, was passed on 26 February 1844.

Home Rule for the Hong Kong Chinese?

After signing the 1842 Treaty, Pottinger remained for a time in Nanking to continue the negotiation of outstanding questions, one of which was the place to be occupied in the Hong Kong constitution by the Chinese residents of the Island. This was the subject

of lively discussion between himself and the Chinese Plenipotentiaries, and also, in London, between the various government
departments principally concerned.

Charles Elliot's proclamation of 2 February 1841, on the occupation of the Island, had promised that 'the natives of the Island of
Hong Kong and all natives of China thereto resorting, shall be
governed according to the laws and customs of China, every description of torture excepted'. The same principle was laid down in the
commission of the chief magistrate on his appointment in April
1841, which required this official to 'exercise authority according
to the laws, customs and usages of China as near as may be . . .
over all the native inhabitants of the said island and the harbour
thereof . . .'.[1]

Elliot's proclamation of 2 February was disavowed by Palmerston[2] on the ground that no formal treaty existed by which Hong
Kong was ceded to Britain and that even if there had been a treaty,
no cession of territory could be formally recognized until ratifications had been exchanged. Elliot's promises were scarcely referred
to in the discussions; the problem of the treatment of the Chinese
in the new colony was debated in the context of normal British
colonial policy and not upon the necessity of honouring undertakings which Elliot had had no right to give at the time.

There were four main factors in favour of giving the Chinese a
special place in the constitution. It had been accepted in the
Canton days that Chinese and British communities lived apart,
each respecting the other's social customs and usages, and each
punishing its own criminals in accordance with its own law.[3]
Secondly, the Chinese negotiators in the discussions at Nanking
explicitly demanded that the Chinese in the ceded island should
remain subject to Chinese law and Chinese imperial officials.
Thirdly, the Evangelicals in England, who were influential in
Parliament and indeed in the Colonial Office itself, were instru-
mental in bringing to British colonial policy a humanitarian sense
of the duty to safeguard the interests of indigenous peoples. The
Slave Emancipation Act of 1833 and the Report of the 1837

---

[1] *The Canton Press*, 8 May 1841, Macao.

[2] Lord Palmerston to Capt. Charles Elliot, 14 May 1841, No. 9.

[3] The Chinese had never explicitly renounced the right to try British criminals,
and the demand for the surrender of the murderer of a Chinese Lin Wei-hsi in an
affray at Kowloon in July 1839 was one of the causes of hostilities.

Parliamentary Committee on the Treatment of Aborigines in British Settlements show ample evidence of awareness of the need to protect colonial peoples. There was no pressure therefore to force the new Chinese subjects of the Queen into a British mould, but rather the opposite; there was general agreement that they should be allowed to enjoy their own customs, laws and general way of life undisturbed.[1]

Lord Aberdeen expressed this clearly, as already mentioned, when he sought Pottinger's opinion on the courts and judicial offices that would be needed in Hong Kong.

The three main questions involved were, the introduction into the Colony of Chinese law, its administration by Chinese officials, and the general maintenance of Chinese social customs and usages in the mixed community of Hong Kong. The prolonged debate on these points show the seriousness with which the issues were regarded, and provide evidence of a genuine desire to respect the freedom of the Chinese to continue to live as Chinese.

Pottinger wrote to Aberdeen as early as October 1842 that the Chinese plenipotentiaries were very anxious about jurisdiction over the Chinese inhabitants of Hong Kong 'to a degree that I had not anticipated',[2] and he sent a translation of a letter from them dated 1 September 1842,[3] in which they claimed that on the precedent set by the English in Canton in insisting upon jurisdiction over their own people, the Chinese, wherever they lived, should similarly be subject only to Chinese jurisdiction. Pottinger's reply was to agree that all suspects who were subjects of China should be handed over to Chinese officers for investigation and punishment but, he added, the few hundred people residing in Hong Kong 'they will of course become subject to whatever laws

---

[1] It is of interest to see that even before the definitive cession of Hong Kong, an attempt was made to allow the Chinese to control themselves. In November 1841, A. R. Johnson, who was administering the Island, wrote to Pottinger that he had made 'regulations for persons in and resorting to the Bazaar'; one of them provided that each occupier was to have one vote for the election of three Commissioners or Headmen who were empowered to make minor regulations for the good conduct of the Bazaar; one of the three was to be responsible to the Government and receive a monthly salary. Nothing more was heard of this experiment. No doubt it was just a paper scheme, and was probably not unrelated to Elliot's promises, but it clearly reveals a willingness to allow the Chinese some freedom to pursue their own way of life.

A.R. Johnson to Sir Henry Pottinger, 12 November 1841, CO 129/10.

[2] Sir Henry Pottinger to Lord Aberdeen, 16 October 1842, No. 54, CO 129/3.

[3] *Ibid.*, Enclosure.

and regulations may be formed for the management of that settlement, but all temporary sojourners and casual traders will come
under the rule stated above'.

The Chinese opposed this distinction between permanent and
temporary Chinese residents in Hong Kong, and declared that
Keshen, the Chinese plenipotentiary who had ceded Hong Kong
in 1841, had been punished as a criminal because he had handed
over Chinese persons to British jurisdiction and not because he
had given up the Island. They pointed to the Chinese assistant
magistrate who resided at Macao to deal with the Chinese there
and suggested a similar arrangement for Hong Kong. In a subsequent letter,[1] the Imperial Commissioners argued that difficulties
in the administration of justice would be removed only by adopting
the principle that Chinese should be subject to Chinese and
English to English; they claimed that Hong Kong had been given
to the British 'as a place of residence', thereby implying that control
over the Chinese there had not been granted; they also quoted the
promise given in Elliot's proclamation of 2 February 1841.
Pottinger replied on 17 September 1842[2] that Chinese nationals
accused of serious crimes should certainly be handed over for trial
by Chinese officials, but for lighter offences there was not the
same need. He instanced large Chinese communities in the Straits
Settlements and in Mauritius who were all living happily under
British law. It was this correspondence that gave rise to the debate
among ministers and government officials in London.

Lord Stanley opposed Pottinger's concession that Chinese
accused of serious crimes should be handed over to the Chinese
authorities regardless of whether they were permanent Hong Kong
residents or casual visitors,[3] because of the difficulties it would
create. For example, the same crime might have to be defined
differently to satisfy British and Chinese legal usages, and there
might be discrimination where English and Chinese were jointly
accused of the same crime. He thought there was the danger that
if this concession were made, the Chinese government would
claim 'that Hong Kong was transferred in occupancy and not
sovereignty', and there was the further obstacle that parliamentary

---

[1] *Ibid.*, Enclosure.

[2] *Ibid.*, Enclosure.

[3] Colonial Office to Foreign Office (J. Stephen to H. N. Addington), 22
February 1843, CO 129/3.

authority was required before effect could be given to Pottinger's concession. Lord Aberdeen at the Foreign Office supported Pottinger and replied[1] that while the British might be embarrassed by agreeing to the Chinese demands, the Chinese would be equally embarrassed by a refusal to accept them; and he remarked that the 'Chinese government can hardly be expected to place greater reliance on British courts or on British law than the British government is willing to place on Chinese courts or on Chinese law'. He accepted Pottinger's distinction between Chinese who were domiciled in Hong Kong and those who were temporarily residing there for trade; for these latter, Aberdeen thought that a resident Chinese magistrate was preferable to Pottinger's suggested extradition procedure. Regarding permanent Chinese residents, he suggested they might be induced to renounce all claim to Chinese nationality, or alternatively, that Chinese law could be applied to them in the name of the Queen, and possibly administered by Chinese magistrates paid by the Hong Kong Government; such magistrates would correspond to the British consuls dispensing British law in the treaty ports.

Lord Stanley replied,[2] agreeing that it was impossible with any show of fairness to resist the Chinese claim to exclusive jurisdiction over persons of Chinese race corresponding to that claimed by the British over their own nationals; and he thought that Aberdeen's final suggestion of having Chinese judges acting in Hong Kong would be the best solution. Sir James Stephen, Permanent Under-Secretary at the Colonial Office, 1838–47, minuted 'as we do, so we must expect and submit to be done by', but he added that it would be preferable not to make any distinction between transient and domiciled Chinese in Hong Kong.

The Law Officers of the Crown were consulted and advised that Chinese residents in the Colony were British subjects, who 'should not look to a Chinese court for redress against wrongs, but should at once be considered and treated as subject to the English government and to the laws which the crown of this country may think right to declare . . .'. This legal opinion was disregarded and the decision was taken to allow the Chinese to be subject

[1] Foreign Office to Colonial Office (Addington to Stephen), 22 March 1843, CO 129/3.

[2] Colonial Office to Foreign Office (Stephen to Addington), 30 March 1843, CO 129/3.

to Chinese law and to restrict British law to the British and other foreigners. In April 1843 the correspondence on this subject was sent to Pottinger and he was instructed[1] to act on Lord Stanley's last suggestion of appointing Chinese magistrates in Hong Kong.

In the following June, Lord Stanley gave Pottinger additional guidance in carrying out his duties in a dispatch[2] in which the general principle that the Chinese were to be subject to their own law was clearly stated in these words: 'there will of course be in the island a large body of Chinese persons to whom the law of England would be a rule of action and a measure of right equally unintelligible and vexatious'; and it was necessary therefore that 'the laws and customs of China should supersede the law and customs of England' for the government of the Chinese residing there. But Stanley now admitted some exceptions to this principle, namely, that no law could be recognized which derogated from the Queen's sovereignty; and property and the succession to property must be regulated according to English law. He also added the further significant proviso that if any Chinese law were 'repugnant to those immutable principles of morality which Christians must regard as binding on themselves at all times and in all places . . .', then it should not be allowed within the Queen's dominions, even if pronounced by Chinese judges. This dispatch showed a manifest weakening by Stanley of his original position in that he now admitted a number of exceptions to the principle of Chinese law for the Chinese.

Meanwhile Pottinger and the Imperial Commissioners continued negotiations on this subject in the course of which Pottinger apparently shifted his ground and in doing so caused the whole question to be reconsidered.

In January 1843 Pottinger reported that he had agreed[3] with the Imperial Commissioners that the Chinese in Hong Kong should be governed by their own laws under mandarins appointed by the Chinese Imperial Government, to be stationed at Kowloon,[4] in Chinese territory, but that he had also insisted that the British

[1] Lord Aberdeen to Sir Henry Pottinger, 6 April 1843, No. 54, CO 129/3.

[2] Lord Stanley to Sir Henry Pottinger, 3 June 1843, No. 8, CO 129/2.

[3] Sir Henry Pottinger to Lord Aberdeen, 21 January 1843, No. 570, CO 129/3.

[4] A. W. Hope (Parliamentary Secretary at the Colonial Office under Lord Stanley), minuted on this 'it appears that Kowlung is not in Hong Kong itself, but on the mainland'.

must have police jurisdiction over all residents in the Colony. At the same time he admitted that the Imperial Commissioners were still very anxious that persons of Chinese race should not in any way be subject to British law or authority. Sir James Stephen was lukewarm about sending Chinese British subjects for trial out of the Queen's dominions and commented 'if it be right to establish such an innovation, I think the safest way of doing it will be to rely on the local legislature of Hong Kong'.

As the negotiations dragged on, Pottinger moved even further from his original position. In June 1843, he wrote to Lord Aberdeen[1] that his secretary, Malcolm, had just arrived from England with the ratification of the Treaty of Nanking and had reported opinion in Whitehall as against granting the Chinese the right to be subject to their own law officers on account of the difficulties involved. He decided therefore to make a stand for British jurisdiction over all the Chinese residents in Hong Kong, but without going to the length of making it a *sine qua non* in the negotiations. He enclosed a memorandum he had sent to the Imperial Commissioners stating the principle that Hong Kong must be subject to British jurisdiction, and all Chinese who objected would be allowed to leave the Island with full compensation for their houses and lands. Pottinger now claimed that without this jurisdiction over the Chinese, the cession of Hong Kong would be incomplete, and not in accord with Article III of the Nanking Treaty.

To this memorandum, Kiying, who had just assumed control of the negotiations on behalf of the Manchu Government, replied that the principle that the Chinese were to be subject to Chinese law and the British to British law, had already been agreed to in writing, and he justifiably accused Pottinger of changing his ground. He argued that the resident and visiting Chinese were the same people, and if it were right that the British should not be subject to the laws of China, 'it was a thing of the same nature' that the Chinese should be equally unwilling to obey the laws of England. As for Article III of the Treaty, Kiying contended that 'it was not therein provided that its inhabitants should become English people'.

Pottinger's dispatches and the communications between himself and Kiying were sent by Lord Aberdeen to the Colonial Office for

---

[1] Sir Henry Pottinger to Lord Aberdeen, 13 June 1843, No. 90, CO 129/3.

comment. Sir James Stephen minuted, 'on the question of the jurisdiction of British judges and courts over Chinese resident in Hong Kong, it seems to me that the Chinese High Commissioner has the best of the argument'. He said this was an international and not a colonial matter, and that the decision should rest with the Foreign Secretary, Lord Aberdeen; but he remarked that 'the exclusion of all Chinese authority from Hong Kong is highly desirable if it be attainable justly and peaceably'. Lord Stanley remarked cryptically 'I do not see that my interference would be productive of anything but confusion'.

The upshot was that the proposed appointment of Chinese judicial officials to administer Chinese law in Hong Kong was dropped, their residence in the Colony or in Kowloon for this purpose being equally unacceptable.

The British Government did not object in principle to the existence of extraterritorial rights by which the officials of one nation operated in the territory of another;[1] rather the fear was that the Chinese would claim a limited sovereignty over the island as they did over Macao. More important, the reports of prevailing lawlessness showed all too clearly that a strong hand was necessary in the suppression of crime. The Supplementary Treaty of the Bogue (8 October 1843) therefore contained no provision for the administration of Chinese law in Hong Kong by Chinese officials. Clause 9 merely provided for the mutual extradition of criminals, to prevent the mainland criminals from taking refuge in Hong Kong and vice versa.

It was of course possible to recognize Chinese law without necessarily appointing Chinese imperial magistrates to administer it. In the autumn of 1843, a case came before William Caine, the British Chief Magistrate, in which seven local Chinese were accused of murder by a Chinese who made his complaint to the Chinese magistrate at San On on the mainland. Caine thought that Chinese prisoners against whom a case had been made out should be sent to the San On magistrate for trial, but Pottinger disagreed. In a letter to Lord Aberdeen,[2] Pottinger claimed that 'the Chinese

---

[1] For example, in an earlier letter to Sir Henry Pottinger, 31 May 1841, on the subject of Elliot's proposal, in the 'Convention' of Chuenpi, that Chinese customs officials should continue to collect customs dues in Hong Kong exactly as if the trade were carried on at Whampoa, Palmerston accepted this in principle and gave examples where similar arrangements were operating.

[2] Sir Henry Pottinger to Lord Stanley, 9 December 1843, No. 27, CO 129/2.

Government have tacitly waived the right they first claimed of trying all persons (i.e. residing on the Island of Hong Kong) who might be charged with capital and other serious crimes'. He suggested that such cases ought to be committed for trial by the Supreme Court judge if, after enquiry by the British magistrate, sufficient evidence of guilt existed. In the event, the accused were set free for lack of evidence. Lord Aberdeen justifiably observed in reply[1] that it was not at all clear that the Chinese had renounced their claims and he asked for further information, but added that Pottinger should not provoke discussion on this matter.

The problem, still unresolved when Sir John Davis succeeded Pottinger as Governor in the early summer of 1844, was made all the more urgent because of the prevalence of crime. Davis attributed this to the triad societies, which he described as patriotic societies directed against foreign Manchu rule.[2] He concluded that crime would diminish if the Chinese were placed under their own laws, dispensed by Chinese officials. He drew up an ordinance appointing Chinese unpaid officials called, *Paouchong* and *Paoucheng*, to assist in controlling the Chinese through regulations made by the chief magistrate. But he soon changed his mind on the main issue of having Chinese law for the Chinese.

The struggle to maintain law and order induced the Governor to introduce transportation for the worst offenders, and to suppress the triad societies. Kiying protested against the transportation of Chinese, and alleged that members of Triad Societies were really fugitive criminals who should be sent back to China in accordance with the Treaty of the Bogue. He again urged that Chinese subjects should be tried only by Chinese mandarins. Davis refused this demand and replied that he was quite willing to carry out the treaty, but he pointedly asserted that Chinese were not compelled to live in Hong Kong and if Chinese committed offences there against British law they must have the same treatment as British subjects and that it would be impossible to govern Hong Kong otherwise.[3]

---

[1] Lord Aberdeen to Sir Henry Pottinger, 26 March 1844, No. 30, CO 129/8.

[2] Sir John Davis to Lord Stanley, 1 June 1844, No. 10, CO 129/6. Triad Society (Sam Hop Wui) 三合會 from the three principles, Heaven, Earth and Man, began as a secret anti-Manchu political society, but at this time its activities were directed more to assisting and protecting its members.

[3] Sir John Davis to Lord Aberdeen, 11 January 1845, No. 6, CO 129/11, and enclosures.

The question of the introduction of Chinese law into the Colony was posed as a definite concrete issue when the Supreme Court was set up by local ordinance[1] in 1844. The principle was that the law of England as at 5 April 1843 was to prevail in Hong Kong except where inapplicable, but on the side of criminal jurisdiction, the ordinance gave power to punish Chinese criminals according to the laws of China.[2] Sir James Stephen criticized these arrangements, in a long minute,[3] as showing 'little skill or perspicuity'. He regretted that Sir John Davis had not adhered more closely to the New Zealand Act which had been sent to him as a guide, and feared that to punish the Chinese according to Chinese law gave 'a hazardous discretion'. Lord Stanley agreed that amendments and explanations should be called for, particularly in the use of Chinese punishments.

Replying to these criticisms, Davis pointed out[4] that Chinese punishments, such as caning with the rattan, wearing the cangue,[5] and cutting the queue, had been used in the Colony because the more lenient English penalties were ridiculed by the Chinese, who were poor and so could not be fined and whose standard of living was so low that a spell in prison was a boon rather than a punishment. Stephen minuted that this was 'one of those insoluble problems that flow out of the anomalous position of Hong Kong'; British law had no terrors for the Chinese, 'yet there is no possibility of enforcing their laws by British courts and officers without a compromise of principles which we are bound to maintain inviolate. I do not know how these conflicting obligations are to be reconciled . . . no sagacity can discover a path to which plausible and well-founded objections may not be raised'. He argued that 'effective restraint and a government not to be trifled with are objects of such primary importance that it is worth while to secure it even at the expense of adopting a policy the most opposed to our feelings and prepossessions'. So, 'not knowing how to suggest anything better', he advised that Davis' proposals should be upheld. In extenuation of the principle of having the power to inflict Chinese punishments,

[1] No. 10 of 1844.

[2] Sir John Davis to Lord Stanley, 21 October 1844 (Ordinance enclosed), CO 129/7.

[3] *Ibid.*

[4] Sir John Davis to Lord Stanley, 8 March 1845, No. 24, CO 129/11.

[5] The cangue, from Portuguese *canga* meaning a yoke, was a large square wooden frame fastened around the neck to prevent the wearer from resting.

Davis explained[1] that 'it is however never likely to be exercised by the court and therefore better expunged', but the power remained.

That the interests of the Chinese needed safeguarding is shown by an ordinance passed in 1846 greatly extending the scope of summary jurisdiction of the courts and restricting the right of appeal to the Supreme Court to Europeans. It also adopted much more of Chinese criminal law.[2] Earl Grey objected to the confining of appeals to Europeans and opposed 'the indiscriminate adoption of the penal system of a people, who, however advanced in the arts of civilization, differ as widely as from ourselves'. Davis had to amend his proposals to give the Chinese the same right of appeal as others, and to curtail the maximum penalties to be inflicted by the Justices of the Peace and magistrates.[3]

The attempt to give the Chinese their own administrative officials was equally half-hearted. It has already been mentioned that Sir John Davis framed an ordinance in 1844 setting up local officials called *Paouchong* and *Paoucheng*.[4] Lord Stanley following Sir James Stephen's advice, gave a non-committal reply to this proposal saying that he had no means of judging how far it was possible to enforce their decisions and he demanded more detail. Davis explained they were unpaid Chinese officers, with the function of assisting the police in such matters as rioting, thefts, robberies, smuggling, illegal assemblies and registration. They clearly had very little power and little incentive to perform their honorary but onerous duties; Eitel says[5] the ordinances were never put into operation, and the records of the Colonial Office are silent on the working of this experiment. It is probable therefore that these offices soon became defunct. An attempt was made to revive them in 1853, when a new ordinance was passed[6] by Bonham giving the peace officers appointed under the 1844 act, and now referred to as *ti-paos*, power to settle civil disputes among themselves since the Chinese found the Supreme Court procedure expensive and difficult to understand. The ordinance was to operate only

---

[1] Sir John Davis to Lord Stanley, 16 July 1845, No. 100, CO 129/12.
[2] Sir John Davis to Gladstone, 12 September 1846, No. 108, CO 129/17.
[3] Sir John Davis to Earl Grey, 11 September 1847, No. 98, CO 129/21.
[4] Ordinance No. 13 of 1844.
[5] E. J. Eitel, *Europe in China*, Kelly & Walsh, Hong Kong 1895, p. 435.
[6] No. 3 of 1853.

where the Chinese ratepayers petitioned for it, and the ti-paos were to be paid from a fund derived from the assessment of the ratepayers. The ti-paos were given power to settle all civil disputes if the disputants declared before a Justice of the Peace their willingness to abide by his decision, or they could if preferred, bring the case before the courts in the usual way. The scheme did not work well and, in 1861, was dropped by Sir Hercules Robinson and the protection of the Chinese became a matter of concern to the Colonial Office and to the local colonial administration.

Sir John Bowring, Governor 1854–1859, initiated the policy which ultimately was adopted in regard to the protection of the Chinese, when in 1858, he recreated the office of Registrar-General with the additional title of Protector of the Chinese.

To sum up, the Home Government was ready to allow the Chinese to live under their own law administered by their own judicial officers; but this liberal policy was opposed by both Pottinger and Davis, the men on the spot, mainly because each felt he could not make headway against crime unless British courts were in full control. Chinese social customs presented less difficulty and were respected except where they conflicted with local ordinance.

The whole problem was ultimately solved in a typically British empirical manner along lines suggested by Sir James Stephen, who thought it better to leave such problems to the Legislative Council proceeding by way of local ordinance with the safeguard of review by the Colonial Office.

CHAPTER III

THE QUESTION OF REPRESENTATION
1843–59

First Unofficial Members of the Legislative Council, 1850

POTTINGER resigned in the summer of 1843 and remained in the Colony until his successor, Sir John Davis, arrived in May 1844. He felt that in bringing hostilities to a successful conclusion he had completed his mission and he now hoped to return to India with the prospect of preferment in the East India Company's service. His popularity vanished after the terms of the Treaty to the Bogue became known because its clauses restricting Hong Kong's trade with China to the open ports and imposing joint Anglo-Chinese controls over the junk trade were considered to be injurious to the Colony's economic well-being.

The circumstances which had forced the paring down of the Legislative Council in size to the minimum of two, did not have any corresponding effect upon its legislative output and Sir Henry Pottinger earned the soubriquet 'Sir Henry Notification'.[1] In the organization and work of the Legislative Council, Pottinger received from the Colonial Office a number of precedents for his guidance, including copies of ordinances passed by the Legislative Councils of the Cape of Good Hope and Western Australia, some imperial acts which dealt with police matters among others, and a copy of the standing orders of the Legislative Council of Ceylon. His main difficulty was that he had no competent officials to assist him in setting up the administration, particularly law officers, and thus the drafting of the early ordinances gave rise to much criticism at home. Sir James Stephen minuted on Pottinger's dispatch[2] sent with the first ordinances, that they 'must I presume, be judged leniently'.

The first ordinance passed by the Hong Kong Legislative Council was one to prohibit slavery in the Colony, but it had to be disallowed because this had already been effected by the British Parliament in the Slave Emancipation Act of 1833, which applied to all British possessions. The other ordinances were also severely

---

[1] J. W. Norton Kyshe, *The History of the Laws and Courts of Hong Kong*, Hong Kong 1898. Vol. 1, p. 50.
[2] Sir Henry Pottinger to Lord Stanley, 20 April 1844, No. 29, CO 129/5

criticized. Pottinger was not entirely without assistance for in June 1843, R. Burgass, a barrister practising in Bombay, 'happening to come to China'[1] as Pottinger naïvely phrased it, was given the temporary appointment of legal adviser to the government and Clerk of the Councils. Burgass came from the same part of Ireland as Pottinger, and his arrival in the colony may not have been so fortuitous as the Governor made out.

On 7 May 1844, Sir John Davis arrived in Hong Kong, as Governor, Superintendent of Trade and Plenipotentiary in succession to Pottinger. He was accompanied by a number of officials recruited in England for senior posts in the Colony's administration. Thus almost twelve months after the proclamation establishing the Colony, there was an adequate staff of officials from which to select suitable members of the two Councils. In this matter Davis exceeded his instructions. He criticized the existing Legislative and Executive Councils on the ground that they were composed of the same two people and were too few in number. He interpreted his instructions regarding the composition of the councils, which laid down that they 'shall always consist of three members', as meaning a minimum of three,[2] and he therefore increased the Legislative Council to five, consisting of the Major General in Command, the Chief Justice, the Colonial Secretary, the Colonial Treasurer and the Chief Magistrate, besides himself as chairman. He also nominated four members to the Executive Council, namely, the Major General, Colonial Secretary, Attorney-General and Chief Magistrate. In the same dispatch he said that it was not possible to nominate to seats on the Councils any one except officials because 'almost every person possessed of capital who is not connected with government is employed in the opium trade . . .'.[3] By this chance remark it appears he had considered the possibility of making nominations from among those who did not hold any official appointment, if only he had found candidates not in the contraband trade. There was nothing in the Hong Kong Charter or in his Instructions to prevent him making such an appointment, although he must have known that the Home Government's policy was to restrict membership of the Councils to officials.

[1] Sir Henry Pottinger to Lord Stanley, 13 November 1843, No. 23, CO 129/2.
[2] Sir John Davis to Lord Stanley, 13 May 1844, No. 4, CO 129/6.
[3] Ibid.

Sir James Stephen in a minute on Davis's dispatch said that he could not see how the Governor's Instructions could bear the interpretation Davis had given them, and repeated that the government's policy had been to keep the Councils deliberately small, namely three with a quorum of two, plus the Governor, to give the latter greater authority and allow him all the more easily to choose his co-adjutors. Lord Stanley agreed, and Davis was therefore told to reconstitute the Councils in accordance with his original instructions.[1] Davis in reply admitted his error, and in May 1845, on the receipt of Stanley's ruling, he re-organized the Councils so as to have three each in number additional to himself as chairman. The Executive Council now consisted of the Major General Commanding (as Lieutenant-Governor), the Colonial Secretary and the Chief Magistrate, and the Legislative Council comprised the Major General, the Chief Justice and the Attorney-General.[2] A. W. Hope, the Parliamentary Under-Secretary to Lord Stanley, minuting on this dispatch, questioned if a Legislative Council of three were adequate.[3] Sir James Stephen again argued that it was barely possible to err on the side of reducing the size of the Council, and thought that the Governor could bring all the local experience 'at and to its deliberations', and contended that a large Council was useless as weakening responsibility without adding any free or popular element, 'for which kind of principle there is no scope'. The arguments of Stephen prevailed and the reconstituted councils were accepted by Lord Stanley[4] in September 1845. It had taken just over two years to get the membership of the two Councils settled.

Davis also reported that he had separated the Executive and Legislative Councils, which 'had been blended under Pottinger'.[5] Evidently Pottinger had conducted the councils as one body, as a single undifferentiated council such as had existed at one time in Ceylon and Mauritius, and indeed the early minutes[6] do not show them as separate bodies. Under Davis, the two Councils became clearly differentiated as the Executive and Legislative Councils.

---

[1] Lord Stanley to Sir John Davis, 3 February 1845, CO 129/6.
[2] Sir John Davis to Lord Stanley, 20 May 1845, No. 62, CO 129/12.
[3] *Ibid.*
[4] Lord Stanley to Sir John Davis, 21 September 1845, No. 142, CO 129/12.
[5] Sir John Davis to Lord Stanley, 24 July 1844, No. 42, CO 129/6.
[6] CO 131/1 for the minutes of the Councils for the year 1844.

The restriction in the size of the Legislative Council to three had been defended on the ground that it strengthened the position of the Governor; and his power of initiation and of overriding decision made it clear that though the members of the legislature voted legislation, their real function was to advise the governor, who was himself the legislative authority, since he had both the first word and the final say.

It might be assumed that the Legislative Council was just a rubber stamp, but an incident in 1846 proved that this was not so. To Sir John Davis fell the unpopular task of organizing the Colony's public finances; the measures he took to secure a public revenue aroused great opposition among the inhabitants who believed that the Governor was hurrying towards premature financial self-sufficiency in the Colony at the bidding of the Colonial Office at home. One of his proposals, made in May 1846, to tax imported wines and spirits, met with the unanimous opposition of the Legislative Council on the ground that the revenue expected would not be worth collecting, and that such a tax would be contrary to the proclamation which had declared Hong Kong a free port. Davis maintained his ground and sent the proposed ordinance to the Secretary of State for approval, together with the dissentient opinion of the three members of the Council. Sir James Stephen thought it was quite impracticable to accept the proposal if all the Legislative Council were against it; Benjamin Hawes, the Parliamentary Under-Secretary (1846-51), advised that the Governor should be supported against the Council, but Gladstone, then Secretary of State (1845-46), ruled that it was impossible to go against the unanimous wish of the Legislative Council. The power of the Governor to override the council was not therefore upheld, and there is no instance in the records of the Council of its use.

Davis' successor, Sir George Bonham[1] arrived in the Colony in March 1848 and made an immediate change in the Legislative Council by replacing the Major General by the Colonial Treasurer, retaining the Chief Justice and Attorney-General.[2] Comment was made in the Colonial Office that since the General was also Lieutenant-Governor he ought to be on the Council and that it was hardly

---

[1] Sir Samuel George Bonham (1803-1863), Governor of the Straits Settlements 1837-1847, Governor of Hong Kong 1848-1854.

[2] Sir George Bonham to Earl Grey, 28 August 1848, No. 67, CO 129/25.

necessary for both the Judge and the Attorney-General to have seats there, but Bonham's change was accepted.

The most important event in Bonham's administration was the addition in 1850 of two unofficial members to the Legislative Council. The origin of this important constitutional change lay in the recommendations of the 1847 Select Committee of the House of Commons on the China Trade.

The proclamation of Hong Kong as a British Colony in the summer of 1843 was followed by a period of unrestrained optimism over the economic prospects, which was encouraged by Pottinger's frequent references to the Colony as destined to become the great emporium of the East. When the Colony's trade failed to develop as anticipated the mood changed to one of despondency. This ripened into open hostility when Sir John Davis began to raise a revenue by creating monopolies and farms, and levying rates on property for police and other local services regarded as municipal in character. Robert Montgomery Martin[1] the Colonial Treasurer, wrote a bitter report in which Governor and Colony were both thoroughly castigated. Land values fell and many holders, particularly the speculators, renounced their allotments of land.

The merchants presented a memorial to the Secretary of State, dated 13 August 1845;[2] *inter alia*, they complained of Davis's revenue measures, roundly condemned as unconstitutional an ordinance to impose rates, and called for some form of municipal self-government. They made this demand for a measure of self-government largely on financial grounds, to enable them the better to resist Davis' financial impositions. They asked the Home Government to contribute more generously towards the expenses of a colony which they claimed was held for imperial interests connected with the whole of the China trade, and not those of the Colony alone. These complaints and signs of dissatisfaction led in part to the official enquiry of 1847.

The 1847 Select Committee showed decided sympathy with the views of the merchants. After reviewing the whole China trade, it made the following observations on Hong Kong:

---

[1] Robert Montgomery Martin, published a *History of the British Colonies*, and *Statistics of the Colonies*, 1838; founded the *Colonial Magazine*, 1840. He was Colonial Treasurer of Hong Kong, May 1844 and resigned, July 1845.

[2] Enclosed in Sir John Davis to Lord Stanley, 20 August 1845, No. 114, CO 129/13.

Inconvenience appears to arise also from the dependence of the Governor on two Departments of administration at home. As Governor of a Colony, he is responsible to the Colonial Office; as in a manner representative of the Crown to a Foreign Court and Superintendent of Trade, to the Foreign Office. It would be well if this relation could be simplified.

We would also recommend that some short Code should be drawn up for the more convenient administration of justice, as a substitute for that general reference to the Laws of England, 'as far as they are applicable to the case', which in this, as in some other Colonies, is the sole rule of guidance, and creates much confusion and embarrassment. That drafts of all new laws and regulations of an urgent nature, should, as in India, be published for three or six months before they are finally enacted. That a share in the administration of the ordinary and local affairs of the Island should be given, by some system of municipal government, to the British residents.

The Select Committee's recommendations were gradually implemented over the next few years and will be referred to again. Their immediate effect was to encourage the merchant community in Hong Kong to renew their demands for relief from financial burdens and for constitutional reform. The first concession was gained in 1849 when an extension of the period of the land leases from 75 years to 999, virtual perpetuity, was conceded. The constitutional concessions did not come without some further pressure being applied. In January 1849, the leading inhabitants of the Colony sent a petition to Parliament alleging that despite repeated representations to H.M. Government, nothing had been done to implement the 1847 Select Committee's Report, except in the matter of leases; they particularly pointed out that no share in legislation had yet been given by either elected or nominated representatives of the inhabitants in the Council.

Progress in implementing the findings of the report had been slow because of the change of governor in 1848, and because Bonham during his first year of office had been preoccupied with a detailed investigation into the colonial establishment which he had been instructed to make with the object of effecting a thoroughgoing retrenchment. This had left him little opportunity to tackle constitutional reform.

Bonham sent home a copy of the petition,[1] of which, he acidly observed, he was aware only through seeing a copy in the local

---

[1] Sir George Bonham to Earl Grey, 26 February 1849, No. 22, CO 129/28.

press. With regard to the demand for a share in the local administration 'by some form of municipal government', he pointed out the vagueness of this phrase and referred to the financial difficulties regarding the institution of municipal government. His arguments are summarized in the next chapter.

With regard to the petitioners' complaint that they were excluded from any share in legislation, Bonham said that he saw no objection to the nomination of two principal local inhabitants to seats in the Legislative and Executive Councils. He thought such members would be advantageous because they would provide information which would be useful to government, the residents could make their wishes known through them, and they would assist the government to explain its policy to the community. Bonham then definitely proposed that two unofficial members should be nominated to each of the two Councils. Earl Grey, Colonial Secretary (1846-52) accepted the principle of nominating two unofficial members to the Legislative Council,[1] 'when you consider the time has arrived for making this change', but would not approve similar appointments to the Executive Council; for this differentiation, he gave no reasons.

The friendly and easy-going Bonham proceeded to make the nominations in a characteristic way. In December of this same year, 1849, Bonham wrote[2] that he found it difficult to decide on the two nominees and 'judged it more satisfactory to the public' to allow the Justices of the Peace to suggest 'the names of two gentlemen whom they thought most eligible'. So, 'after a considerable interval', the 'assembled justices, 16 in number, suggested the names of David Jardine and J. F. Edger', which Bonham then forwarded as his own nominations. There was no question of setting up an electoral body. The unofficial members were appointed by the Crown on the nomination of the Governor, and holding their seats on the Council at the royal pleasure. This informal procedure sprang from the close personal relations between Bonham and the leading merchants, for he was the first Governor to have easy social relations, and under him local society frequented Government House for the first time. Besides he had just revived the practice begun by Pottinger, but which had lapsed under the unpopular Davis, of appointing unofficial Justices of the Peace,

[1] Earl Grey to Sir George Bonham, 11 July 1849, No. 128, CO 129/28.
[2] Sir George Bonham to Earl Grey, 15 December 1849, No. 115, CO 129/30.

and they were his own nominees. His method of proceeding was capable of being misunderstood, and Bowring, the next Governor, thought election by the Justices a matter of right. Earl Grey raised no objection, and Jardine and Edger took their seats for the first time, the first unofficial nominated members, on 14 June 1850.

Sir John Bowring and the Legislative Council, 1854–59

Sir John Bowring arrived in the Colony in April 1854, as Plenipotentiary, Superintendent of Trade and Governor of Hong Kong, the latter post being held in name only. His standing was therefore at first very different from that of his predecessors because of this drastic change in the status of the governorship, of which Bowring was, temporarily as it proved, the first and only victim. The novel arrangement had been made abundantly clear to him and he had accepted it; but naturally he was dissatisfied with only half the authority, and incidentally half the salary, of his predecessor; and he began to interfere with the way in which William Caine, the Lieutenant-Governor conducted the government of the Colony. This led to a dispute between the two men which was referred to the Secretary of State, and although Bowring was unquestionably in the wrong, Palmerston upheld him, and condemned the compromise of a purely nominal governorship as 'an administrative solecism'.[1] On 25 June 1855, Bowring assumed full control of the colonial administration and Caine became nominal Lieutenant-Governor, with the additional title of 'Senior Member of the Legislative Council' as some compensation.

Bowring was full of reforming zeal. He had spent a year in the Colony, 1852, deputizing as Superintendent of Trade for Bonham who was on leave, but without any official position in the colonial government. His observations led him to believe that there were many local abuses which demanded a strong reforming hand, and it was therefore particularly frustrating when he returned in 1854, to find himself still a comparative spectator, this time as titular governor. In a series of private letters to Sir George Grey, first holder of the recently revived post of Secretary of State for the Colonies, with whom he was personally acquainted, he outlined his criticisms and proposals for reform. A friend of Bentham and

---

[1] Palmerston's minute of 15 April 1855, on dispatch of Caine to Sir George Grey, 14 February 1855, No. 19, CO 129/49.

a philosophical radical, Bowring wanted to make the local legislature the instrument of reform, for which purpose he wanted it to be increased in membership, and made at least partly elective so as to be representative of the community, and less the tool of the Governor, as he thought it had been. To Bowring, reform of the existing Legislative Council was the essential condition for the success of his other projected reforms.

In his first private letter to Sir George Grey, dated 24 January 1855,[1] he wrote that he was gradually 'giving importance to the Legislative Council as an instrument of great value. I found it an absolute nullity and that it had never been consulted by my predecessors on the all-important questions of income and disbursement', with the result, he said, that David Jardine, 'the only non-official of any weight, had ceased to attend'. This observation of Bowring was not surprising, since, though specific taxes were imposed in the form of an ordinance, there was as yet no provision for passing the annual financial budget in this form; further, the Council's standing orders did not permit the members to initiate any resolution.

That the Legislative Council was 'an absolute nullity' is highly unlikely. The Council minutes[2] which were sent to the Secretary of State every six months, naturally give no more than the bare record of what was resolved. Of debate they show no sign, but this does not prove there was none. Bonham was on good terms with his subordinates as well as with the merchant community, and since he consulted the Justices of the Peace on the nomination of the unofficial members of the Council, it is unlikely that consultation was halted in the council chamber, though the real discussions may well have taken place in a more informal atmosphere outside. In the same letter, Bowring said he hoped to reform abuses and make salutary changes by using the small amount of popular principle already introduced, and by strengthening and extending it to satisfy public opinion. He was referring to the nomination of the two unofficial members of the Legislative Council by the Justices of the Peace without realizing that that was an informal arrangement by Bonham, and did not denote any 'popular principle'.

Bowring thus, early in his administration, announced his intention to change the character of the Legislative Council, and to the

[1] CO 129/49.
[2] CO 131 series.

legitimate annoyance of Caine, he claimed the right of presiding over its deliberations. In a later private letter to Grey he suggested that its membership should be increased, that there should be greater publicity over the disposal of public funds, and that the Chinese section of the population should have 'special consideration as the source of the present and future prosperity of the island'. Since Grey left the Colonial Office in February 1855, these private letters ceased to carry much weight, and the reaction of the Colonial Office was to wait for Bowring to make specific proposals.

It was not kept waiting long, for soon after his assumption of the full governorship, Bowring brought forward his plan for 'a safe and satisfactory scheme' of legislative reform.[1] In a brief introductory note, he emphasized that the Colony was now financially self-supporting and explained that he wanted the Legislative Council enlarged so as to be more representative of the community whose interest and support he was anxious to enlist in meeting the cost of his projected expansion of education, public works and public amenities.

He proposed that the Legislative Council should consist of eight officials, the Governor, Lieutenant-Governor, Chief Justice, Colonial Secretary, Attorney-General, Colonial Treasurer, Surveyor-General, and Chief Magistrate plus five unofficial members. The latter were to be elected for a term of three years by the registered holders of Crown leases and all five were to be *bona fide* British subjects. He observed that as H.M. Government had decided that the two existing unofficial members should be selected from the bench of Justices of the Peace—a statement which showed a complete misunderstanding of Bonham's arrangement—he felt bound by this decision. He therefore proposed that at least three of the five unofficial members should be chosen from among the Justices of the Peace, leaving only two to be freely elected. The essential condition was that all five should not be holders of official positions in the administration. All registered holders, of an undivided lot of land leased from the Crown, regardless of race, who paid a minimum annual rental of £10 were to be entitled to a place on the electoral roll. For this the Sheriff was to be responsible, having to deal with all applications and objections, and to prepare a voters' list three months before an

---

[1] Sir John Bowring to Lord Russell, 2 August 1855, No. 110, CO 129/51.

election. The list was then to be placed before the Executive Council for final decision, and the revised list of electors published ten days before the election. Each elector had to take the oath of allegiance, and, if demanded by any elector, an oath against the use of bribery. Successful candidates were to hold their seats for three years, and in the event of a vacancy, the Governor was to have discretionary power to decide on a new election or to allow the seat to remain vacant. The rules of the Legislative Council were to be revised and brought more into line with those of public councils in England. A British consular representative was to have the right to attend the meetings of the Council when legislation affecting British subjects in China was being debated. The Governor was to preside and have a casting vote. In his covering letter Bowring suggested that publicity for the council debates would be beneficial, but he did not incorporate this suggestion in his scheme.

Herman Merivale, the Permanent Under-Secretary (1848-59) pointed out in a minute on Sir John's dispatch that there was only one Legislative Council which combined elected members with an official majority, that of Malta; he favoured Bowring's plan but thought that the electoral arrangements were not clear, particularly in regard to the Chinese and non-British foreigners. The Secretary of State, Lord John Russell, asked for more information about the proposed electoral body, regarding its number, the proportion it bore to the whole population, the number of European voters compared to the number of Chinese, and length of residence as a voting qualification. He also asked for details of the method by which the election of the three Justices of the Peace was to be ensured. He criticized the proposed decision of electoral claims by the Executive Council and thought these should go before an impartial judicial committee. In fact Russell was lukewarm and declared that he was 'not prepared to assent to the opinion that such a change such as you have suggested would at the present time conduce to the better government of the Island . . .'.[1]

In reply to the demand for a more detailed explanation of his proposals, Bowring answered[2] that his object was to get a popular element in the Legislative Council 'which should represent public opinion with its contribution of local information, its demands for

---

[1] Lord John Russell to Sir John Bowring, 23 November 1855, No. 2, CO 129/51.

[2] Sir John Bowring to H. Labouchere, 26 March 1856, No. 49, CO 129/55,

improvement, its interest in social reform . . .'. He said he did not want the infusion of a large elected element, but objected to 'its utter exclusion', and he was willing to purchase it by having more official members, and argued that action should not be delayed until the need of reform produced a popular clamour. He criticized the existing Legislative Council because it was not acquainted with the concerns of the Colony, it did not debate the Blue Book (annual statistical report), it could not initiate legislation, and the annual estimates were not placed before it. He thought the Legislative Council should have some control over finance, particularly since parliamentary aid was no longer needed, and the revenue expended was raised entirely by local taxation. He said he had put his last budget on the table and invited observations of the Council members, without submitting it to a vote.

Bowring was propounding the constitutional doctrine that where a Crown Colony was financially self-supporting, it should be allowed free discretion in the allocation and control of its own funds; that is, that the basis of the control by the Secretary of State was the existence of a parliamentary grant for the administration of which he was responsible. This was a novel colonial doctrine, though a logical extension of the traditional English constitutional maxim that redress precedes supply.

But Hong Kong was in fact only beginning to be financially self-sufficient. In 1854 it had been decided that the parliamentary vote to Hong Kong 'should be limited to the provision of the salaries of three of four of the principal officers of the Colonial Government',[1] and that 'it will be for the local government to defray out of colonial resources the whole remaining expenditure of the Colony'. In 1855 Bowring announced that no imperial subvention would be needed, and that the Colony was self-supporting; yet when the war against China came in 1857, the Governor had once more to go cap in hand to the Home Government for financial assistance.

Bowring admitted that official opinion in the Colony was against his scheme, and that Mercer, the Colonial Secretary, had said that the policy of adding two unofficials to the Legislative Council had failed, 'as had been predicted'. The Governor disagreed, pointing out that Edger attended regularly, and Jardine attended 'when

---

[1] Duke of Newcastle to Sir John Bowring, 10 March 1854, No. 7, CO 129/43.

important matters were being discussed', as his time was 'too valuable for trivialities'! Bowring thought the members of the Council should be responsible to the community and that the exclusion of non-British persons from the list of voters would be unpopular and unwise. British interests were amply secured by the provision that all candidates for seats on the Council must be British by birth or naturalization; and that if there were eight officials and three Justices of the Peace, that would in any case leave only two to be freely elected. He said he would be glad to associate the Chinese more closely with the work of the government, and suggested the possibility of bringing them in on an educational test. It was one of Bowring's weaknesses to throw out his suggestions for reform in this tentative way, avoiding definite clear-cut proposals. Regarding the electorate, he estimated 'the whole number of electors should be only 75 or practically only 45'. Those who leased land at an annual rent of £10 or more comprised 69 British, 42 Chinese, and 30 other foreigners. As a matter of interest and for comparison he gave the numbers of those paying police rates of £10 a year; they totalled 1,999, of whom 1,637 were Chinese, 186 British and 176 other foreigners. He proposed to secure the election of three Justices of the Peace by the simple expedient that each elector, handing in his list of names, should be disqualified if there were not the names of at least three Justices of the Peace upon it.[1]

All the Colonial Office officials minuted against Bowring's proposals, on the ground that the non-British element was too numerous to be left out and that an elected council would soon usurp financial control. Labouchere, who succeeded Russell as Secretary of State for the Colonies, noted briefly, 'I have no wish to try the experiment', because, 'a small change was not worth making and the proportion of Chinese and Foreign to British was conclusive against any big change'. He replied in a long dispatch[2] fully outlining the views of the Government on the question of electorates in the colonies and particularly in Hong Kong. He wrote of the Chinese, that the 'testimony of those best acquainted with them represent the Chinese race as endowed with much intelligence but as very deficient in the elements of morality', and

---

[1] A pencilled minute against this in the margin reads, 'How in the world would this do it unless you forced them to vote for all five'.

[2] Labouchere to Sir John Bowring, 29 July 1856, No. 82, CO 129/55.

thought that education had not made such progress in the Colony as to encourage him to think that the next generation would do any better. 'The Chinese have not yet acquired a respect for the main principles on which social order rests', he averred. The British were few and not permanently resident, and if they alone had the vote, the effect would be to give power over the permanent population to a small number of temporary residents. Labouchere argued that if the aim of the proposals was to assist the Governor in eliciting public opinion, that could be done without electoral reform; he thought elections could be defended only if they were intended to be a transitional step to give the Legislative Council full powers.

Labouchere further argued that 'the peculiar position of Hong Kong' was another obstacle. The island was held not because of its own advantages but 'simply as subsidiary to the intercourse between the Chinese and British Empires', and 'great commercial interests and the future progress of civilization throughout the East are to a great extent involved in the maintenance of British rule and of orderly government in Hong Kong'. There were also the complicating factors of internal insecurity and lawlessness, and of proximity to China. He considered that there was no reason why the Island's affairs should not be conducted with the greatest regard to the feelings and interests of the Chinese population, and suggested that competent Chinese should be considered for administrative posts in the Hong Kong Government and for membership of the Legislative Council; but he added that if the experiment of making such appointments were tried, great caution would be necessary. Finally he agreed to sanction a moderate increase in the number of the Legislative Council if Bowring wished to make such a proposal. The main plan for the infusion of an elected element into the Council was rejected.

Bowring had suggested a radical reform of the Council introducing elections; this seemed to be a liberal proposal but in fact he was not as liberal in his outlook as the government at home; moreover he was guilty of some confusion of thought. His arguments were all directed at giving the legislature more power, by making it more responsible, but his actual proposals retained the official majority, restricted the elected element and limited the candidates to British nationals; this destroyed the principle of responsibility. Bowring's scheme was inconsistent, and he never made it quite clear whether he wanted better advice from, or more power for, his Council. He put up a scheme in which his own principles were whittled down to what he thought would be accepted by the Colonial Office instead of one consistent with his own premises. The Governor was using the arguments of Bentham and Mill without taking sufficient account of Hong Kong conditions, and in particular, of the need to protect Chinese interests. Bowring was willing to give Chinese nationals the vote but unwilling to allow them to have seats in the Legislative Council. His proposals therefore would not in practice have associated them with the government as much as he claimed. Labouchere clearly brought out the objection to putting the Chinese majority under the control of a British minority. The British Government would not entrust the Chinese to the British merchants by any system of responsible government which excluded the vast majority of the population, and it was Labouchere, not Bowring, who made the liberal proposal that the Chinese should be considered for membership of the Council, and for administrative posts.

Bowring dropped his scheme of elections and, in November 1856, suggested[1] adding three official members, namely the Colonial Treasurer, the Surveyor-General and Chief Magistrate, and three unofficial members to the Legislative Council, the latter to be nominated by himself from a list of six names selected by the Justices of the Peace. He also suggested that the meetings of the Legislative Council should be open to the public. Labouchere regarded six new members as excessive and suggested four, two official and two unofficial, all to be nominated by Bowring; as for the opening of the Council meetings to the public, he thought this question should be taken up when the constitution of the Council had been settled.

After all this argument Bowring, in March 1857, at last took some positive action to increase the size of the Legislative Council. He now produced a different plan,[2] his third which departed even further from his own original scheme and from that just sanctioned by Labouchere. He decided to increase the Council by three additional members, of whom only one was to be an unofficial member. Another unofficial member was also needed to replace David Jardine who had just died in England. Bowring decided to

---

[1] Sir John Bowring to Labouchere, 11 November 1856, No. 177, CO 129/59.
[2] Sir John Bowring to Labouchere, 3 March 1857, No. 44, CO 129/62.

allow the Justices of the Peace to put forward three names, from which he selected one to be appointed a provisional member in place of Jardine and one of the remaining two to be the additional unofficial member. Fourteen Justices of the Peace attended an election meeting and Bowring accepted the result of their voting. Joseph Jardine, who headed the poll, was nominated a provisional member in place of his brother; and George Lyall, who came next, was nominated to the extra unofficial seat. At the same time, Bowring departed from precedent and also from his Instructions, by limiting the tenure to three years, instead of at the pleasure of the Crown. He nominated the Chief Magistrate and Surveyor-General as official members.

Merivale complained that Bowring had departed from his own plan without warning; he criticized the election by the Justices of the Peace, saying that the 'Crown ought not to hand over legislation in Hong Kong to a small aristocracy of white merchants, and cannot safely hand it over to a general constituency . . .'. Labouchere was also critical, being doubtful if the Justices of the Peace represented the community, and refused his assent to this method of election. He declared that Hong Kong was not adapted for representative institutions in the ordinary sense, and that it was best to have nomination by the officer administering the government. He accepted the names, but disapproved of the mode of selection and of the three years' limitation, and ruled that neither was to be regarded as a precedent.

The end was not yet reached, for two months later in May 1857, Bowring made another adjustment, this time of a minor nature, he proposed Forth, the Colonial Treasurer, Tudor Davies, the Chief Magistrate, and Lyall as the three additional members of the Legislative Council.[1] Labouchere reproached him with the remark, 'You appear to have forgotten that you have already recommended Jardine, Cleverly (Surveyor-General), Davies and Lyall'; but he agreed to the apparent substitution of Forth for Cleverly.

Bowring also in this same dispatch returned to the subject of publicity for the debates of the Council with the proposal that the second reading of a bill should be in public, and the other readings in private. Labouchere regarded this proposal as very 'singular'

[1] Sir John Bowring to Labouchere, 21 May 1857, No. 86, CO 129/63.

and thought that the Legislative Council should open or close its doors as it decided. This question of publicity had come up in an acute form because the clerk to the Chief Justice happened also to be editor of a newspaper, the *Hong Kong Register*, and used his official position to get inside information of the Council proceedings which he then published. Curiously the chief complaint against him was that his reports were garbled and not that they were printed. Bowring's initiative did bear fruit when, in January 1858, the Legislative Council took the first decisive step in opening its meetings to the public; it ruled that each member could introduce one stranger and the Governor any number of strangers, to attend the Council's sessions.[1] The Secretary of State sanctioned this procedure and the result was that in effect the proceedings of the Legislative Council were opened to the public.

Bowring's design for a reformed Legislative Council with a partly elected unofficial element as its central feature was not adopted, and to this extent he may therefore be said to have failed. All he achieved up to this point, after eighteen months of a strange combination of strenuous and yet wavering advocacy, was the enlargement of the Legislative Council by three members, of whom only one was an unofficial member. The proportion of unofficial to official members was thus slightly weakened instead of being strengthened as he had intended. He adopted on his own responsibility the principle of election of unofficial members by the Justices of the Peace, begun by Bonham as an informal arrangement having no constitutional sanction; but such election bore little or no relation to the kind of elections he had originally advocated, and earned the Secretary of State's disapproval. After the election of Jardine and Lyall in 1857, the principle of election by the Justices of the Peace was dropped, and was not revived until 1884, nearly thirty years later.

Bowring's scheme failed because the initiative came from him alone, and his seeming advocacy of the representation of Chinese interests lost him the support of the foreign community. Election by the Justices of the Peace who were all leading British merchants, meant the continued dominance of the British mercantile element only slightly disguised. Jardine and Dent were the respective heads of the two largest merchant houses in the Colony, and Lyall was

[1] Sir John Bowring to Labouchere, 20 January 1858, No. 11, CO 129/67.

a partner of the important house of Lyall, Still & Co. Besides, the 1857 election by the Justices was apparently held in private, since there is no reference to it in the press, and no election result was announced. In effect Bowring was handing over the nomination of the unofficial members to the British merchants, a proceeding against which Labouchere properly protested.

If the reform scheme was mainly a product of Bowring's own individual character and outlook, it did also partly reflect the changing conditions in the Colony. Trade had begun to improve, and the despondency which had been so evident under Bonham declined. For example, shipping using the port, entering and clearing, from 293,465 tons in 1849 increased to 1,164,640 tons in 1859. The outbreak of the T'ai P'ing Rebellion in 1851 created very unsettled conditions in the Kwangsi and Kwangtung provinces and led many Chinese to seek the greater security of the Colony, and to bring their families.[1] There was thus some substance behind Bowring's advocacy of Chinese interests.

The Governor's failure was partly due to the war against China following the *Arrow* dispute in 1856. If Bowring was liberal towards the Chinese, he was not so towards the Chinese Government, against whom he provoked hostilities by magnifying a comparatively trivial incident, in which, it was alleged, Chinese seamen were forcibly seized by the Chinese on the lorcha *Arrow*, a vessel owned by a Hong Kong Chinese but which was under the protection of the British flag. The war made any large scheme of constitutional reform inopportune. In January 1857, bread from a Chinese bakery in the Wanchai district was found to contain arsenic, fortunately in such large quantities as to render detection easy. This poisoned bread affair created strong racial antagonism in the Colony, and almost ruled out any measure of constitutional reform which offered the Chinese electoral rights; it possibly explains why the Governor did not press his original scheme. The bitterness against the Chinese was understandable; and when the employees of the bakery were tried in the Supreme Court, the press referred to the case as the

---

[1] Population growth is shown by the following figures:

1849	1,210 non-Chinese	28,297 Chinese	Total: 29,507
1853	1,481 non-Chinese	37,536 Chinese	Total: 39,017
		of whom 9,010 were females	
1859	1,661 non-Chinese	85,280 Chinese	Total: 86,941
		of whom 24,747 were females	

Queen *vs* the Poisoners.[1] Bowring refused the demand that the accused should be hanged without a trial, and when the men were found not guilty from lack of evidence, indignation was quite unrestrained, but British justice gained in reputation.

Another reason for Bowring's failure was that he gradually lost control of his administration. A new Attorney-General, Thomas Anstey, arrived in 1856 and proved to be a most peculiar character; his self-appointed task of rooting out injustice led him to bring charges against almost every colleague in the Government, and so to inaugurate a series of libel actions, counter-actions, public enquiries into charges of corruption and departmental conflicts which made Hong Kong 'the land of libel and the haunt of fever'. The aging Governor was at his wits' end and weakly referred the sordid mass of papers to the Secretary of State, Sir E. Bulwer-Lytton (1858–59) who remarked in the House of Commons that he discovered in them 'hatred, malice and all uncharitableness in every possible variety of aspect, and consequently what might be considered a description of official life in the Colony'. These quarrels are not given here because they mostly concerned personalities. If there was any constitutional issue involved, it was that officials holding high positions in the government were not on that account shielded from the rule of law which applied to governors and governed alike. Anstey was suspended in August 1858 after an official enquiry had found him guilty of unjustified allegations against a colleague.

The Home Government decided to allow Bowring to retire prematurely in March 1859 so as to permit the sending of a new governor to conduct an enquiry into the public service in Hong Kong. Sir John had already lost his diplomatic functions when Lord Elgin was sent to China as plenipotentiary after hostilities had commenced. He had lost the confidence of the imperial authorities and this robbed his reform proposals of their importance.

In 1858, because two officials were absent from the Colony on leave, Bowring suggested[2] the addition of one official member to the Legislative Council in order the better to conduct its business. This was a further sad falling away from his earlier principles and in making it he ran into fresh trouble. The proposal resulted in a

---

[1] See *The Friend of China* for 31 January 1857 and subsequent issues.
[2] Sir John Bowring to Sir E. Bulwer-Lytton, 27 November 1858, No. 154, CO 129/69.

protest by the unofficial members, who alleged that the Governor was upsetting the agreed proportion of official to unofficial members which had been three to two in 1850, and was now to be six to three. They complained that their influence was correspondingly diminished and pointedly asked that 'the extent to which the Governor can increase the numbers of the Legislative Council be distinctly made known'; they suggested that if the discrepancy were further increased it would be preferable to have no unofficial members at all. Bulwer-Lytton, sympathized with them[1] and thought a reduction in the disparity in numbers between the officials and unofficials should be considered; he therefore declined to agree to the change until the whole question had been weighed. This reply indicated the enhanced status of the unofficial members, and the importance attached by the Colonial Office to their presence in the Council.

The position of the unofficial members was also strengthened by an important reform in the arrangements for dealing with the annual estimates of income and expenditure. When in May 1857, the Justices of the Peace complained of the inadequacy of the building in which the magistrates' courts were held, Bowring wrote home asking for alterations to be sanctioned, entirely disregarding the awkward fact that such a contingency had not been provided for in the current budget. Labouchere took the opportunity to lay down[2] the orthodox mode of dealing with colonial expenditure, which he said must be decided according to the revenues, and must be put in the annual estimates and passed through the Council. That all expenditure had to be placed in the estimates and passed by the Legislative Council was suggested almost casually by Labouchere as if it were the accepted practice. Bowring pointed out in reply[3] that such had never been the practice in Hong Kong, but that he had always held the view that there was no good reason why the budget should not be submitted to the vote of the Council; and he had himself initiated the practice of submitting the estimates to the Council but solely for the purpose of eliciting suggestions, without allowing the Council to vote on them or modify them in any way. Merivale commented that Bowring was quite right and that the Colonial Office had not

[1] Sir E. Bulwer-Lytton to Caine, 12 March 1859, No. 18, CO 129/69.
[2] Labouchere to Sir John Bowring, 3 September 1857, No. 111, CO 129/63.
[3] Sir John Bowring to Labouchere, 18 November 1857, No. 167, CO 129/65.

observed the clause in the Colonial Regulations that all estimates
were to be submitted to the Legislative Council in the form of an
ordinance. As a result of Labouchere's ruling the Hong Kong
Government estimates were submitted to the vote of the Council
for the first time in December 1858. There was much criticism and
discussion particularly over public works which the unofficials
wanted to be extended; but Caine, deputizing for Bowring, ruled
that he could not accept any amendment of the Estimates Ordinance
unless it were clearly necessary. He pointed out that the colonial
regulations exempted from Council control expenditure already
fixed and agreed to by the Secretary of State, and he asked for a
ruling on the matter.[1] Lord Carnarvon, on behalf of the Secretary
of State, answered[2] that there ought to be a 'fixed establishment' or
'Civil List', consisting of expenses of a permanent nature, fixed by
law, and only the remainder should then be placed in the annual
estimates; he added he would instruct Bowring's successor to do
this; in the meantime, all expenditure without exception should be
voted by the Council.

The Legislative Council had now become an important body
which the Governor could no longer override in the way which had
been provided for in the original Instructions of 1843. As further
evidence of this, in September 1858, a proposal by Bowring[3] to
amend the rules of the Legislative Council to make members
responsible in the courts for libel was rejected by the Council.
Its action was upheld by Bulwer-Lytton who refused to limit freedom of speech in the Council, and very significantly added that in
any case he was unwilling to sanction an amendment contrary to
the Council's wishes.

There was as yet no ruling that the official members were
required to support the policy of the Governor. In February 1859,
for example, when a Praya Bill was[4] thrown out by a combination
of the three unofficials and three officials.[5] Bowring did not complain that the official members voted against him, only that they

---

[1] Caine to Sir E. Bulwer-Lytton, 13 December 1858, No. 166, CO 129/69.

[2] Lord Carnarvon to Sir John Bowring, 9 April 1859, No. 39, CO 129/69.

[3] Sir John Bowring to Sir E. Bulwer-Lytton, 4 October, No. 136, CO 129/59.

[4] This was a bill to compel holders of land facing the sea to join a scheme to
reclaim land and build a praya or road along the shore.

[5] Sir John Bowring to Sir E. Bulwer-Lytton, 12 February 1859, No. 35,
CO 129/73.

should have informed him beforehand. This freedom of the officials to vote as they pleased was soon to be curtailed.

Bowring's governorship (1854–59) marked an important stage in the development of the Legislative Council, despite his failure to bring about electoral reform. The increase in the number of the unofficial members, the opening of the Council meetings to the public, and greater control over finances combined to invest the Council with greater importance, and give the unofficial members greater influence. If the Imperial Government had rejected elections, it was not because it objected to governing in accordance with the wishes of the community, but for the very opposite reason, that elections would have given power to a privileged minority which might not have reflected the views of the inhabitants as a whole. The unofficials, by being freed from responsibility to a narrow electorate, were able to take a broader view of the common interest, and their support was sought particularly on questions on which they had special knowledge and their opposition was taken seriously.

CHAPTER IV

TWO ADDITIONAL EARLY PROBLEMS

The Link with the Treaty Ports and its Severance, 1843–59

THERE were two complicating factors in setting up the Hong Kong Government in 1843. One was the decision to extend the area of its control beyond the Colony itself to the treaty ports on the China coast, where British subjects were protected not by the flag but by treaty rights so far as they could be implemented. The other was the intention to grant some form of municipal self-government in Hong Kong.

That British subjects needed control more than protection is fairly clear from comments on their behaviour. Elliot complained that the coming of free trade had 'filled Canton with a class of people who can never be left to their own devices . . . without the utmost risk to the safety of this trade and to the respectability of the national character'.[1] The contraband trade in opium attracted a forceful adventurous type predisposed to act without much regard to ethics when the financial rewards were sufficiently alluring.

Elliot had censured these reckless dealers in opium who were blatantly defying the Chinese edict against opium and who were 'founding their conduct upon the belief that they were exempt from the operation of all law, British or Chinese'. He feared that strong action by the Chinese against the armed opium traders would result in violence. It was partly to control the British that he had urged the securing of an island station; 'there can be neither safety nor honour for either government until Her Majesty's flag flies on these coasts . . .' he wrote in 1839. This phrase 'for either government' was not bare-faced hypocrisy, but a reflection of the genuine concern he felt over this danger.

The Legislative Council was given its authority within the Colony by Order in Council in the exercise of the royal prerogative; but an Act of Parliament was necessary to give it jurisdiction over the British communities in China. The Treaty of Nanking had granted the right of residence to British subjects at five treaty

[1] Elliot to Lennox Conyngham (Private), 12 June 1837, quoted in W. C. Costin, *Great Britain and China*, Oxford 1937, p. 41.

ports, and though it did not expressly concede extraterritoriality, this privilege had been exercised in the past and its continuance was assumed, and so Parliament was asked to set up the necessary legislative and administrative machinery. An Act of August 1843[1] empowered the Crown to authorize 'the Superintendent of the trade of Her Majesty's subjects in China (so long as such Superintendent shall also be the Governor of the said Island of Hong Kong) to enact, with the advice of the Legislative Council of the said Island of Hong Kong all such Laws and Ordinances as may from time to time be required for the Peace Order and good Government of Her Majesty's subjects being within the Dominions of the Emperor of China'. At the same time it reserved to the Crown the right of concurrent legislation by Order in Council.

A second Act[2] passed in the same month allowed the Crown 'to hold and exercise any power or jurisdiction now or hereafter outside H.M. dominions, in as ample a manner as within her dominions', and provided for the establishment of law courts in China, with power to remit cases to a British colony, subject to certain safeguards in case of inability to produce witnesses. The court was empowered to apply the laws of the place in which the act which occasioned the suit was committed, and to send convicts to a British colony for execution or imprisonment. Since Hong Kong was thus to be the administrative centre from which British subjects in China should be protected and controlled, it was clearly desirable that the offices of Superintendent of Trade and Governor of the Island of Hong Kong should be held by the same person.[3]

In recognition of the strategic importance of the Colony, the military commander of its garrison was appointed Lieutenant-Governor and deputy for the Governor in case of death, absence or other cause of inability to act;[4] he was also given a dormant commission to act similarly for the Superintendent of Trade. Sir James Stephen was opposed to this divided authority in virtue of which the chief British official in China was to be subject to the Foreign Office as Superintendent of Trade, and to the Colonial Office as Governor of Hong Kong. 'It is an assumption indeed which I could not justify by what would appear to myself good

[1] 6 & 7 Victoria c. 80.
[2] 6 & 7 Victoria c. 94.
[3] Lord Aberdeen to Sir Henry Pottinger, 4 January 1843, No. 9, CO 129/3.
[4] Lord Stanley to Sir Henry Pottinger, 2 August 1843, No. 11, CO 129/2.

reasons, but I have no doubt there are very good reasons for it', was his comment on the earliest instructions sent by the Foreign Office to Pottinger in January 1843.[1] Stephen thought it preferable that all correspondence should pass through one Secretary of State, similarly to that concerning convicts in the Australian Colonies, in which the Home Secretary sent instructions through the Secretary of State for War and the Colonies.

He added a warning against the inconvenience of divided responsibility as giving rise to jealousies: ' . . . our experience in this office shows that such jealousies are the curse of all petty colonial societies and that governors are scarcely more above them than the humblest of their officers. From one end of our Colonial Empire to the other there is a constant exhibition of the mischievous effects of the local authorities having different official superiors in England. Nothing will convince them that the public officers here will not squabble with one another on behalf of their respective dependants and we are constantly witnessing all manner of foolish things done and written in the confidence of the support from the Lords of the Treasury, the Board of Ordinance and so on'. Lord Stanley incorporated nearly the whole of this minute in his reply to the Foreign Office,[2] but the division of authority was adhered to.

In pursuance of these two Acts of August 1843, Pottinger was given a series of Commissions,[3] and with them a long dispatch[4] in which Lord Aberdeen reviewed the whole constitutional position regarding the arrangements for controlling British subjects resident in China.

The Foreign Secretary pointed out that until the new arrangements under the recently passed Acts could come into force, the

[1] Stephen's minute on 12 documents sent to Pottinger, 3 January 1843, CO 129/3.

[2] Colonial Office to Foreign Office (Stephen to Addington) 8 Feburary 1843, CO 129/3.

[3] These were prepared by the officials of the Foreign Office and sent to the Colonial Department for approval. Stephen minuted that 'they were altogether wrong, the reason being that on subjects of this kind the Foreign Office was unavoidably destitute both of precedents and our experience. I therefore prepared drafts of them anew . . . in place of the original enclosures. They were accordingly adopted'. It was found that they had to be sent off immediately before Lord Stanley could see them. To this explanation, Stanley replied: 'In such a matter and indeed on most others, I rest entire confidence in your arrangements' (7 September 1843, CO 129/3).

[4] Lord Aberdeen to Sir Henry Pottinger, 2 September 1843, No. 81.

1833 Act[1] was the source of all authority currently being exercised. This latter Act had allowed the King in Council to appoint a Chief Superintendent of Trade, to create a law court and to regulate the British trade with China; under it, Aberdeen continued, three Orders in Council had been issued: one regulating trade, the second authorizing a law court and the third permitting the imposition of duties on British ships and cargoes entering Canton. All three had been ineffectual, and indeed, the third had been repealed within a few months, on 3 March 1834.

Aberdeen went on to say that an Order in Council of 4 January 1843 had transferred the court to Hong Kong; and another of 24 February of the same year, had restricted British trade to the five ports opened by the Treaty of Nanking. The Crown had no inherent prerogative of legislative authority over British subjects living in a foreign state or on the high seas; and that was why new legislation had been necessary, giving the Crown power to make laws for such subjects either by Order in Council or by setting up a local legislative authority. He said it had been decided to adopt the latter alternative, and the main feature of the new arrangements was that the Crown delegated to Pottinger and the Hong Kong Legislative Council the power to make laws for British subjects in China, and a commission under the Great Seal would be sent to him. The right of the Queen in Council to legislate for British subjects in China was preserved but Lord Aberdeen said that it was not expected that this power would be used.

The Foreign Secretary pointed out the difficulty that it might appear to be futile to enact laws governing British subjects in China where there were no police officers of the Crown specifically charged to see that the laws were carried out, but he thought that there would be a normal respect for law which would make it partly effective. This respect would derive additional strength from the fact that any breach of the law might be followed by a civil action in the courts; there was also the power to control shipping which would enable the clearance of a ship to be withheld if it were known that an offender were taking passage by her. On the definition of crimes, Pottinger was advised to pass a general ordinance to the effect that actions which would be interpreted as crimes in Hong Kong, would, if committed by British subjects in China, be similarly interpreted there. Though difficulties might arise over

[1] 3 & 4 William IV c. 93.

laws with penal clauses, Aberdeen thought other ordinances such as those dealing with shipping might be welcomed and command a willing compliance.

The whole problem was recognized to be difficult by Lord Aberdeen in the following guarded language: 'I am well aware that the trust is of a very peculiar and critical nature, and that nothing but the extreme hazard of exempting our fellow subjects in China from an effective local control would justify such an innovation on the general principles by which the exercise of the legislative authority of independent states is limited'. He told Pottinger to use moderation and solve the problems in a practical and empirical way. 'The anomaly such as it is in theory will, I am persuaded, be deprived in practice of the risks which might otherwise attend it by the care which you will constantly employ to promulgate no law which could give any just or plausible ground of offence to the Chinese authorities. Exercising your powers with constant moderation and with a vigilant regard to the prejudices no less than to the reasonable jealousy of the people and government of China, you will I trust be enabled to derive from them the advantage of an effective control over H.M. subjects.' Pottinger was to be guided by the laws he made for the Colony of Hong Kong, as far as analogous; but the two series of laws were to be kept separate, that for the Colony being promulgated by him as Governor of Hong Kong, and the other, respecting British subjects in China, by him as Superintendent of Trade; and they had to be separately reported to the respective Secretaries of State.

On the appointment in 1844 of Sir John Davis as Governor and Superintendent of Trade, Lord Aberdeen took the opportunity, in giving him his instructions,[1] of referring again to this problem of controlling British subjects in China. He observed that Davis was given 'a degree of authority more comprehensive in extent and more unusual in character than is normally imparted to any servant of the Crown'; he was Superintendent of Trade, Governor of Hong Kong, and Plenipotentiary, having authority to treat with the representatives of China, power to enact laws, control over the consular officials, and also having some control over the naval and military forces in China. It was to be 'his constant endeavour' to impress upon the Chinese that the British Government desired harmonious relations and he was to conciliate the good will of the

---

[1] Lord Aberdeen to Sir John Davis, 28 February 1844, No. 4, CO 129/8.

Chinese Government and people which 'may be unpalatable to some British subjects whose irregularities they may find it necessary to check'. Lord Aberdeen remarked that British subjects were by education and social habits most opposed to arbitrary power, 'and its exercise can only be justified by extreme necessity'; much firmness towards the Chinese and British subjects was required and in considering how far he could 'deal with civil disputes and punish or repress criminal offences', Davies was advised that the Levant consular practice might help.

The Legislative Council was thus constituted the legislative authority over British subjects in China. No provision was made for nominating additional members, or for this part of its work being performed by a separate committee; the same few officials were thought competent to make the two series of enactments. Membership of the Hong Kong Legislative Council was not therefore restricted to colonial officials, and of the three members first selected by Pottinger in August 1843, only one was an official of the Island's colonial administration, the other two were attached to the office of Superintendent of Trade under the Foreign Office.

Elaborate arrangements were made to ensure the smooth transition from the old arrangements to the new and the observance of the proper constitutional forms. The 1843 Act repealed Section 6 of the 1833 Act, but all action taken under that section was to be valid and the old Orders in Council made under the 1833 Act were to remain in being until those under the new act operated. A 'blanket' Order in Council dated 2 October 1843 enabled Pottinger to suspend the operation of any Orders already issued to meet the contingency that his legislative measures may have conflicted with the new Orders in Council then being issued.

The related problem of setting up a British law court in China might be briefly noted here. A British court had been provided for under the authority of the 1833 Act by an Order in Council of 9 December 1833, but Lord Napier had been told not to set up this court without the most serious consideration, and in fact it was never formally created, though the power to do so remained. After the Treaty of Nanking, an Order in Council of 4 January 1843 arranged that this court should be set up in Hong Kong.[1] In June 1843 Pottinger issued proclamations, acting as Superintendent

Enclosed with Dispatches and other Instruments in Lord Aberdeen to Sir Henry Pottinger, 4 January 1843, No. 4, CO 129/3.

of Trade and not as Governor of Hong Kong (for the Colony did not exist in 1833 and he was acting under the authority of the act of that year), establishing this court in Hong Kong with himself, as Superintendent, acting as judge.

This seemingly straightforward step proved to be extremely complicated. The Law Officers at home ruled that Pottinger's action was unconstitutional because the 1833 Act gave the Superintendent jurisdiction over British subjects within the Chinese dominions, whereas Hong Kong had by 1843 ceased to be part of the Chinese dominions. In addition, Pottinger had promulgated rules of the court, and though the 1833 Act permitted the Crown to delegate to the Superintendent of Trade the power to create the court, it did not empower the Crown to depute him to make any rules. The result was that Pottinger was instructed[1] to set up a court for the Colony, acting as Governor, and a second court for the British in the treaty ports, acting as Superintendent. The Hong Kong court was to be set up by the Legislative Council in pursuance of powers delegated by the Crown, and the Superintendent's court was to be created under the authority of the 1843 Act. In the event this Superintendent's court was not brought into being.[2] An Order in Council of 17 April 1844 gave the Hong Kong Supreme Court concurrent jurisdiction over British subjects in the treaty ports to which the Chief Justice would travel on circuit, and the same Order in Council gave the British consuls power to hear cases in which British subjects were involved in accordance with the ordinances passed by the Superintendent of Trade in the Hong Kong Legislative Council; and, where Chinese were also involved, in accordance with Article XIII of the General Regulations governing British trade in China (and incorporated into the Supplementary Treaty of the Bogue of October 1843) which laid down a procedure for the settlement of disputes between British and Chinese.

Maintenance of law and order amongst the British resident in China was sought in two other ways. Justices of the Peace were appointed by Pottinger in July 1843, and their commissions were phrased to give them authority over British subjects not only in the Colony but also in China.[3] This was apparently *ultra vires* and

[1] Lord Aberdeen to Sir Henry Pottinger, 10 December 1843, No. 104, CO 129/3.

[2] Lord Aberdeen to Sir John Davis, 4 May 1844, No. 35, CO 129/8.

[3] Indeed, curiously enough, their first commissions omitted all reference to Hong Kong, giving them authority only in China, and they all had to be sworn in again.

Lord Aberdeen ordered their commissions to be revoked[1] on the ground that no person, not employed by the Crown, could exercise judicial authority or act as a magistrate in China. The second method was by stationing at Pottinger's direct request one British warship in each treaty port principally in order that 'evil disposed subjects of Her Majesty shall be effectually restrained from riotous and disorderly conduct',[2] a policy which was unsuccessfully opposed by the Admiralty on the old principle that 'ships and men rot in port'. These ships came to be used more as a convenient means of exercising pressure on the Chinese local authorities than for the purpose for which they had originally been intended.

The Hong Kong Legislative Council's control over the British communities in the treaty ports of China lasted less than ten years, from 1844 to 1853. Its legislative output in this connection totalled only twenty-one ordinances: seven in 1844, one in 1845, five in 1847, four in 1849, two in 1850 and two in 1852.

The usual heading of the ordinances was 'An Ordinance for Her Majesty's subjects within the Dominions of the Emperor of China or within any ship or vessel of a distance of not more than one hundred miles from the coast of China'. The formula, 'Be it therefore enacted by His Excellency the Governor of Hong Kong and Superintendent of the Trade of Her Majesty's subjects in China, with the advice of the Legislative Council of Hong Kong', gave no clear indication that he was promulgating the ordinance in virtue of his powers as Superintendent of Trade and not as Governor of Hong Kong. Perhaps the distinction was unnecessary inasmuch as it had been arranged that one man should hold both offices. These ordinances prescribed the framework within which the privilege of extraterritoriality in China was exercised during these ten years.

The first ordinances of 1844 declared Her Majesty's subjects in China to be subject to English law and to the jurisdiction of the courts of justice at Hong Kong as if they were residents of the Colony; they established consular courts and gave the consuls power to inflict fines to a maximum of 200 dollars and imprisonment up to two months, to remit more serious cases to the Supreme

---

[1] Lord Aberdeen to Sir John Davis, 5 March 1844, No. 24, CO 129/8.
[2] Lord Aberdeen to Pottinger, 24 August 1843, No. 77, CO 129/3. See also General Regulations of Trade, published 22 July 1843, Article XIII.

Court at Hong Kong, and to deal with civil suits involving sums up to a maximum of 500 dollars. They obliged masters of merchant vessels to enter into a bond regarding the expense incurred in leaving members of their crews behind, and forbade them to trade at any Chinese port northward of latitude 32°N.[1] The fifth ordinance of 1844 provided that treaties between Britain and China should have the force of an ordinance, and gave the Superintendent and consuls power to enforce treaty provisions to the limit of the consuls' jurisdiction as already laid down, except that the Superintendent was given power to double the normal penalties in the case of flagrant offenders. The seventh ordinance of 1844 reduced the maximum fine which a consul could impose when acting alone to 100 dollars, but gave him authority to increase the fine or term of imprisonment by calling two, or not more than four, British residents of good repute, to sit with him in trying a case, and to deport British subjects under a second conviction. It also demanded that the proceedings of the consular courts were to conform to English practice, and arranged for the registration of British subjects. This power of deportation was re-defined by the one ordinance enacted in 1845.

The 1847 ordinances again dealt with the consular courts and proceedings; the necessity for these amendments followed from charges of irregularity brought by the Chief Justice of the Hong Kong Supreme Court against the consular courts as a result of the Compton case of 1846 (see page 70). They provided that the rules of the consular courts were to be sanctioned by the Hong Kong Legislative Council, their records were to be carefully kept, and the consuls had to obey such directions as were given to them by the Chief Superintendent of Trade at the instance of the Chief Justice.

The ordinances of 1849 returned to the subject of improving the consular court procedure by permitting two justices of the peace to issue a commission for the examination of witnesses. One ordinance of that year appointed consular agents to assist the consul but this provision was repealed later in the year, due to 'certain inaccuracies'; the agents were retained but appeals to the consul against their decisions were allowed.

---

[1] This being the approximate latitude of Shanghai, the most northerly of the treaty ports. An Order in Council of 24 February 1843 had this same prohibition. See p. 64.

In 1850 the jurisdiction of the official magistrates' courts of Hong Kong was extended to British subjects in China and Hong Kong police had similar powers regarding offences committed by British subjects in the treaty ports as if they had been committed in Hong Kong.

In 1852, proceedings for breach of the treaties were not to be made subject to appeal to the Supreme Court, but a copy of the proceedings had instead to be sent to the Superintendent of Trade who had the power to remit or abate the penalties.

All these ordinances, thus briefly summarized, were promulgated in Hong Kong and the treaty ports, and were printed for presentation to Parliament.

In 1853, the power of the Superintendent of Trade to legislate with the advice of the Legislative Council of Hong Kong for British subjects in China was abrogated. In that year, an Order in Council of 13 June resuming the power of direct legislation by Order in Council which had been retained under the 1843 Act, decreed that future legislative control over British subjects in China should be exercised by the Superintendent of Trade who was to issue regulations under the authority of Orders in Council. The Hong Kong Legislative Council thus ceased to act for British subjects in China. There is no reason to suppose that it proved itself incapable of carrying out this part of its task or that it had failed to provide for law and order in the British settlements at the treaty ports. The causes of the change were many.

The 1847 Select Committee on the China Trade had noted that the placing of the two offices of Governor and Superintendent of Trade in the hands of one man had the disadvantage of making him serve two separate ministers at home, resulting in divided responsibility. This was probably the decisive factor in separating the colonial and diplomatic functions, and in ending the dual role of the Legislative Council.

The Compton case brought up this question of separation more acutely. Compton, a British merchant in Canton, was accused of causing riots in June 1846 by assaulting a hawker and overturning his stall. The British consul at Canton found him guilty and fined him 200 dollars, the maximum that a consul could impose, and Sir John Davis approved the fine. Compton appealed to the Supreme Court at Hong Kong, where his conviction was quashed and the fine remitted by order of the Chief Justice, who found that the proceedings in the consular court had been irregular in that Compton had been charged under one ordinance and found guilty under another. This technical error was largely due to the lack of legal training on the part of the consular staffs, but the judge's strictures brought the existing machinery of British justice in the treaty ports under suspicion.

The Compton case was to embitter the relations between the Governor and the Chief Justice, who were already at loggerheads on other grounds. Their quarrel brought into prominence two diametrically opposed principles underlying the control of British subjects in the treaty ports. Davis considered that this control should rest with him as Superintendent of Trade since such questions as the preservation of order, the respect for treaty obligations, and the maintenance of good relations with China, were administrative matters for which he, and not the judge, was responsible. Hulme, the Chief Justice, regarded the issues as primarily legal and judicial, involving the interpretation of the law, the right of fair trial and the preservation of the freedom of the subject by the protection of the courts. There was much to be said for each of these views but they were irreconcilable.

In a private letter[1] to Lord Palmerston, Davis accused Hulme of habitual drunkenness. His object was to bolster various other official complaints which he had made against the judge and which he hoped would result in his dismissal. Palmerston and Earl Grey refused to regard this as a private accusation and insisted on withdrawal or a public enquiry. Thus the charges against Hulme's private character were made the subject of official enquiry before the Executive Council, to the scandal of public life in the Colony. Hulme was found guilty and suspended, but was exonerated on appeal to Earl Grey. Davis' other complaints were not supported at home, and he resigned.

Again, Hong Kong had not developed into the great centre of commerce that had been expected, and the 1847 Select Committee, doubting whether it would ever do so, recommended sweeping reductions in the Island's establishment. When Bonham went on leave in 1852, a division of his duties was decided upon; Major General Jervois, the Lieutenant-Governor, deputized for him as Governor of the Colony and Dr John Bowring was brought from

[1] Sir John Davis to Lord Palmerston (Private), 28 November 1846, CO 129/20.

his consulship at Canton to act as the Superintendent of Trade. This was the first significant step in the separation of the administration of the Colony from that of the British communities in the treaty ports, and seems to indicate that the division of the offices of Governor and Superintendent of Trade was already envisaged. While Bonham was in England on leave, the decision was finally taken that the status of the Colony did not warrant the appointment of his successor to a full governorship, and that on his retirement it should be placed under a lieutenant-governor and the post separated from that of Superintendent of Trade. The change was found to be impossible without amending the 1843 Act which had conferred legislative powers on the Superintendent of Trade conditional upon his being concurrently Governor of Hong Kong. To avoid legislation, Herman Merivale[1] suggested a *de facto* separation of the two offices by the device of promoting Caine, then Colonial Secretary, to be Lieutenant-Governor, with full executive power over the local Hong Kong government, while Bowring, who was to succeed Bonham, retained the nominal title of Governor to satisfy the letter of the act, with only half the pay of his predecessor since his active duties were confined to the superintendency of trade. It is not surprising that this awkward scheme broke down after a short trial, and that Bowring assumed full control of the Colony in 1855.

The growth of Shanghai was another factor in bringing about the legislative separation of 1853. The first Shanghai Land Regulations of November 1845, agreed upon between the British Consul and the Taotai, or the local Shanghai Chinese official, laid down regulations regarding disputes over land and recognized a committee of land renters. As Shanghai grew, it became more international in character. The next Land Regulations, those of 1854, which were jointly agreed upon by the British, American and French consuls, allowed the merchants to levy rates, elect representatives to a council and control the police, roads and wharves. This need for some municipal authority on the spot was clearly incompatible with control from Hong Kong.

Davis's contention that the control of British subjects in the treaty ports was an administrative and not a legislative question

---

[1] Herman Merivale, Permanent Under-Secretary of State for the Colonies, 1848–59.

was sound. After a period of experiment it was found easier to promulgate the general arrangements for control as was done in the Order in Council of 1853, following which the problem became the relatively simple one of administrative adjustment in the interest of smooth relations between British and Chinese. During the whole discussion, there was no suggestion that the Foreign Office was dissatisfied with the way in which the Hong Kong Legislative Council had exercised its powers during the years 1843 to 1853.

It must be remembered that in 1843 when the arrangements were made, no one knew how the treaty ports would develop, and the growth of teeming Anglo-Chinese cities in Hong Kong and Shanghai was quite unforeseen.

An Abortive Scheme of Municipal Self-Government

The successful infusion of an unofficial element into the Legislative Council in 1850, by which the community secured a degree of recognition, was partly offset by the failure of the plan to set up some form of municipal self-government. The first instructions from Lord Stanley to Sir Henry Pottinger, those of 3 June 1843, show that from the start it was the Home Government's intention to give the inhabitants a measure of control over their own affairs by means of a municipal organization. In them Pottinger was told that he should levy a rate on all town buildings for municipal and police purposes 'confiding to the house-holders, as far as possible, the power and the obligation to assess themselves and each other'.[1] Pottinger was not able to implement this instruction because negotiations over the many issues left unsettled by the Nanking Treaty occupied most of his time and he frequently and justifiably complained of overwork and lack of assistance.

His successor, Sir John Davis, reported[2] in July 1844 that he had divided the settlement into three districts, eastern, central and western, and that it was his intention to appoint commissioners to be responsible for police, lighting, roads and sewerage with power to levy rates. The phrasing shows how closely English administrative institutions and experience were followed in the colonies.

[1] Lord Stanley to Sir Henry Pottinger, 3 June 1843, No. 8, CO 129/2.
[2] Sir John Davis to Lord Stanley, 24 July 1844, No. 52, CO 129/6.

Local government at home was at that time undergoing great change. Until well into the 19th century, the Justices of the Peace were the local agents of the central government, having in addition to their judicial work a host of administrative duties.[1] The idea of municipalities doing administrative work was relatively new; borough corporations had been privileged bodies with little duty except to administer their property; such work as street paving, lighting, and scavenging was often done by Improvement Commissioners. The elected corporations, set up under The Municipal Corporations Act of 1835 did not for some years take over much administrative work.

Again, police forces were quite new in England. Peel had established the Metropolitan police force in 1829, directly controlled by the government; but when police forces were organized for the rest of the country, local control was insisted upon and they were placed under the Justices of the Peace in the counties.

Davis's references to commissioners to undertake municipal duties, and the proposal to place the Hong Kong police under municipal control, exercised by the Justices of Peace as local commissioners was therefore very much in accord with English practice at the time.

In a dispatch to Lord Stanley of January 1845[2] Davis again referred to the intended appointment of commissioners who would be responsible for police and roads, saying that they were to be appointed 'from among the principal inhabitants' and empowered by ordinance to levy the necessary rates. It is to be presumed that the commissioners were to be nominated, for he would certainly have mentioned elections if any had been intended, and from the subsequent correspondence it appears that the Justices of the Peace were to act as commissioners. The language was vague, perhaps deliberately so, for in the Annual Report for 1844, dated 3 May 1845, the Governor wrote that he had deferred the Police Rates and Assessors Ordinance 'until more property had been built'. Yet in that same month he took the intensely unpopular step of announcing his intention to introduce an ordinance imposing a rate for

[1] William Caine, the first Hong Kong magistrate, assumed that he had administrative as well as his judicial duties, and claimed the right to allocate land to the earliest applicants. This led to a dispute with the land officer who properly contested this right and the traditional view of the wide powers of the local magistrate. Memorandum by Pottinger, 22 March 1842, CO 129/10.

[2] Sir John Davis to Lord Stanley, 21 January 1845, No. 6, CO 129/11.

police purposes, to be levied by government direct and not by local commissioners or by any other representatives of the inhabitants.[1] This was contrary to his instructions and to his own declared intentions.

In June 1845 Davis informed Lord Stanley[2] that, regarding the police, 'it seemed less easy or expedient to vest the charge of defraying the cost in the public community'; and that widespread lawlessness and the difficulty of recruiting a reliable police force led him to take the police directly under government control. At the same time he stated that roads and sewers would continue to be under local commissioners. The police rates ordinance was delayed until August, and though the assessments were low, it aroused the greatest opposition amongst the merchants, who regarded the new rates as exorbitant and unconstitutional. They sent home the strongly worded memorial of 13 August 1845 which has already been referred to (see p. 43). They protested not only against the imposition of rates, but against the whole revenue system of licences and farms which Davis had established as sources of public revenue, which they referred to as 'harrassing taxation'. The merchants vaguely demanded some form of local self-government but instead of concentrating on the municipal issue and insisting on machinery by which they could assess themselves, they ranged over the whole field of action of a Governor who had made himself detested largely because he was doing his duty to raise public revenue. They were much more interested in opposing taxation than in the municipal issue since this would have shifted to them the burden of finding the money.

Sir James Stephen, at the Colonial Office, defended the Governor and criticized the memorial sent by the merchants.[3] On the general ground as to whether the Governor's action in levying rates directly and not through the commissioners were unconstitutional or not, he said the objections to municipal government in Hong Kong were: (i) 'The English minority can hardly be trusted with the powers which it would give them over Chinese and other alien and ignorant ratepayers'; (ii) Its existence would probably be incompatible with that 'decisiveness and energy of proceeding which are almost necessary for the very existence of a European government

[1] Sir John Davis to Lord Stanley, 9 May 1845, No. 57, CO 129/12.
[2] Sir John Davis to Lord Stanley, 7 June 1845, No. 74, CO 129/12.
[3] Sir John Davis to Lord Stanley, 20 August 1845, No. 114, CO 129/13.

surrounded by millions of Asiatics'. Thus very early in Hong Kong's history the doctrine that the fate of the native inhabitants must not be entrusted to a comparatively few British residents was recognized; but there was for long to be an incompatibility between this paternalist attitude and the growth of self-governing institutions.

The task of answering the merchants fell on a new colonial secretary, W. E. Gladstone.[1] He did not uphold the contention that rates could be levied only by a municipal body, saying that the circumstances of Hong Kong were different from those of Britain or of any other British colony, and that it was impracticable to introduce into Hong Kong institutions which had been successfully tried elsewhere. He therefore accepted the ordinance. Davis in fact aroused so much opposition on this question of rates and indeed upon other issues, that no progress could be made under his governorship towards any form of municipal institutions.

The merchants had also in their memorial put forward the general claim that since Hong Kong had been founded as a naval and military station for the furtherance of imperial interests, the inhabitants should not be called upon to pay the entire cost of the administration, or even of any large portion of it. Gladstone refused to accept this thesis and replied, 'the mercantile body have altogether mistaken the object of Great Britain in the occupation of Hong Kong. That occupation was decided on solely and exclusively with a view to commercial interests'. Opinion in the Colony seemed to be thwarted all round.

The municipal issue was revived by the report of the 1847 Select Committee of Enquiry into the China Trade. A merchants' memorial in January 1849 (see p. 44) alleged that nothing had been done to implement its recommendations that 'a share in the administration of the ordinary and local affairs of the island should be given, by some system of municipal government, to the British residents'. Bonham was popular and more in touch with local opinion than his predecessor had been, and on this question of municipal government, he took a commonsense practical line. Overlooking the discourtesy of the merchants in not sending him a copy of the memorial, Bonham wrote to Earl Grey in February 1849[2] that he had no objection to a municipal scheme, and agreed that if the inhabitants wished, and if competent persons could be

[1] Gladstone to Sir John Davis, 7 March 1846, No. 32, CO 129/13.
[2] Sir George Bonham to Earl Grey, 26 February 1849, No. 22, CO 129/28.

found to serve, the collection and expenditure of the police rates should be entrusted to them. He pointed out that the police cost £4282-1-0 and the police rate brought in £2500 per annum, and remarked that this made him wonder what the merchants had to gain in demanding municipal control.

The Secretary of State replied giving permission to proceed with the plan of municipal government, and Bonham consulted the bench of fifteen unofficial Justices of the Peace, whom he had recently appointed, on the question. He met them on 3 November 1849[1] and offered them control of the police if they would meet the deficit between the amount collected in police rates and the actual cost of the police; he suggested this should be done by a tax on carriages. The Justices refused to agree to any proposal that involved additional taxation. There is no record of any discussion of the elective principle, nor is it clear who were to form the municipal body, though it was in accordance with English precedent the Justices of the Peace should control the police, and carry out the proposed municipal functions.

On 10 January 1851, after a curiously long interval of fourteen months, Bonham wrote to the Justices and renewed his offer in greater detail. He offered them control of the police, with the exception of the superintendent and assistant superintendent of police, since these two officers had been appointed by the Secretary of State. For the year 1850, the deficit between police expenditure and the amount collected in rates was £1051-19-2½; to get the scheme started he offered to make good for the next two years any such annual deficit not exceeding that amount. He then pointed out that the general revenue had been insufficient for the proper repair and maintenance of the roads and sewers, and referred to the fact that before he left Davis had proposed an ordinance for levying additional rates on property to meet their full cost. Bonham said he had not proceeded with this as he had been 'excessively unwilling' to impose further taxation, and suggested the Justices might draft one combined ordinance dealing with police, roads and sewers, and might consider raising additional funds by taxes on horses, carriages and sedan chairs.

To this the Justices of the Peace replied on 31 January 1851. They asserted that the police force had been reduced in strength recently to make the deficit look smaller, that the force was ineffi-

1 Sir George Bonham to Earl Grey, 22 April 1851, No. 29, CO 129/36.

cient in any case, and that if they had control of it, they would find it necessary to raise its efficiency, at a cost which would involve a greater deficit than that which Bonham had offered to meet. The rates would probably fall in yield as memorials had already been sent home against the heavy taxation. They said the community had expressed a wish to have control over municipal matters, and they affirmed their willingness to assume control over police, roads and sewers, if the Governor would place sufficient funds at their disposal from the general revenues; they argued that provision for police protection and for streets should be the first charge on the revenues, since they were the most vital services in any community.

Bonham replied on 14 February 1851 denying that the produce of the rates would fall, rather the contrary since more houses were being built. He thought that in any case there would be less objection to taxation if it were imposed by a popular body. The present assessment was quite inadequate, and he proposed once more new taxes on horses, carriages and sedan chairs. He considered the police force adequate since there had been no increase in crime, and refused to increase it. He then renewed the offer he had previously made. The Justices of the Peace in their reply of 1 March 1851 still criticized the police as inefficient, attracting only bad characters who could not get a living elsewhere; they again refused the Governor's offer to make up any deficiency for only two years. The municipal body would, if it assumed control, have to decide what additional numbers and pay would be necessary, but they assured the Governor that this would be kept as low as possible. They brought up once more the familiar argument against increased taxation on the ground that Hong Kong was really founded to support the whole China trade. Their final argument was that horses, carriages and chairs were necessaries in Hong Kong and not luxuries, and should not be taxed.

On the 15 March the correspondence came to a close when Bonham replied that further taxation or an additional grant from home was essential if he were to meet the wishes of the Justices of the Peace. He ended by saying that if he could secure additional means he would be ready to consider further proposals.

Earl Grey's only comment on all this argument was to approve the course Bonham had taken. So ended this early attempt to set up a municipal organization in Hong Kong.

Bonham in April 1851[1] made a general report on this correspondence and gave his opinion that he was 'beginning to think that the majority of Justices had neither the time nor the inclination for the duties they were asking to assume'. This may have been more than a shrewd guess. He was friendly with them and he must have been well acquainted with their views. The correspondence between Bonham and the Justices of the Peace gives the impression that between the meeting with the Justices of the Peace on 3 November 1849 and the first of the series of letters, that of 10 January 1851, the negotiations for a municipal government had broken down. The correspondence of January to April 1851 which has just been summarized conveys a feeling of unreality, and that the Governor and the Justices were stating their irreconcilable views solely for the record.

Having secured representation on the Legislative Council in June 1850, that is, during the interval between the meeting of Bonham and the Justices on 3 November 1849 and Bonham's first letter to them 10 January 1851, the Justices may well have thought that they had secured a more valuable concession than the municipality for which they would have been called upon to pay. This would explain their lack of enthusiasm in the correspondence with Bonham, and why the central issue of municipal government, its form and function, was allowed to remain in the background.

Two points emerge from this episode. The initiative in suggesting some form of local municipal autonomy for Hong Kong was taken by the Home Government as a matter of principle, but when Davis and Bonham ran into difficulty over it, the principle was readily abandoned. Secondly, there is little evidence of any clear wish, on the part of the influential residents at least, for representative municipal institutions as a matter of constitutional conviction, or that the Chinese were to be included in any municipal scheme. The merchants were demanding municipal government mainly as a stick with which to beat the unfortunate Davis. The maximum freedom at the minimum administrative cost was the dominant note.

[1] *Ibid.*

CHAPTER V

CONSTITUTIONAL DEVELOPMENTS 1859-82

Adjustment and Consolidation, 1859-77

THE twenty years that followed the retirement of Sir John Bowring in 1859 were years of adjustment and consolidation. Without departing from the main principle of Crown Colony government, changes were gradually introduced, chiefly of an administrative nature in the working of the Legislative Council, to make it an effective law-making body.

It was a period of expansion and development in the Colony's history. The Arrow War was brought to an end in 1858 by the Treaties of Tientsin, and renewed hostilities, caused by the refusal of the Chinese to accept a British envoy at Peking, were ended in 1860 by the Convention of Peking. By these agreements, nine additional Chinese ports were opened to foreign trade, including three on the River Yangtze, that great highway into the interior. British subjects were allowed to travel in China and there was toleration for the Christian missions. The treaties with Siam in 1855 and Japan in 1859 moreover opened up those countries to British trade. These extended opportunities of trade benefited the Colony, for the 'outports' brought more banking, insurance, and shipping business and a demand for professional services, for example in law and accountancy. By the 1860 agreement with China, Kowloon Peninsula, on the mainland opposite the Island, was ceded, but without immediate advantage to the Colony because the naval and military authorities tried to monopolize the area, though it ultimately provided invaluable and much-needed living space.

The total sea-going tonnage entering and leaving which in 1859 was 1,164,640 tons, had increased by 1878 to 5,209,437 tons; the population rose from 86,941, including 85,280 Chinese, in 1859 to an estimated 139,144 in 1876 of which 130,168 were Chinese.[1] The Hong Kong Chamber of Commerce was founded in 1861, and The Hongkong and Shanghai Banking Corporation in 1865. Modern amenities were introduced; the city was first lit by gas in

[1] The figures are taken from the *Historical and Statistical Abstract of the Colony of Hong Kong 1841-1930*, Noronha & Co. Government Printers 1932. The number of resident whites excluding the armed forces was given in 1876 as 2,767.

1864, the first large dock company, which became the Hong Kong and Whampoa Dock Company was founded in 1864, and telegraphic communication with Europe was completed by the laying of the cable between Hong Kong and Shanghai in 1871. A greater civic spirit evinced itself in the erection, by public subscription of the City Hall in 1869. A public clock tower in 1862, a drinking fountain in 1863, and a Sailors' Home in 1870 were built by private gifts. The Botanical Gardens were laid out in 1860, and the first postage stamps were issued in 1862. The opening of the Suez Canal in 1869 expedited ships and mail; this with the introduction of the telegraph in 1871, revolutionized trading conditions. No longer was it necessary to keep on hand large stocks of goods since specific orders could now be placed quickly, and the great agency houses were no longer given the same discretion in the conduct of business as was formerly necessary, since the manufacturer in Britain was better posted regarding market conditions.

Sir John Bowring was the last who held the combined offices of Governor and Superintendent of Trade. His successors were able to devote the whole of their attention to the colonial administration. He was also the last of the political appointees; succeeding governors were normally colonial officials, schooled in the colonies and looking to the colonial service for their career. They had the assistance of cadet officers, selected by competitive examination and competent in the local Cantonese language, of which the first appointments were made in 1862.

The three governors during these eighteen years, 1859–77, were Sir Hercules Robinson[1] (1859–65), Sir Richard Graves MacDonnell[2] (1866–72) and Sir Arthur Kennedy[3] (1872–77).

[1] Sir Hercules George Robert Robinson (1824–1897). Left the army in 1846 for a post in the Irish Government. In 1854 became President of Montserrat in the West Indies; Lieutenant-Governor of St. Christopher in 1855, and Governor of Hong Kong 1859–65. Afterwards was successively Governor of Ceylon 1865–72, New South Wales 1872–79, New Zealand 1879–80 and the Cape 1880–86 and 1887–89 and 1895. Raised to the peerage as Lord Rosmead, 1896.

[2] Sir Richard Graves MacDonnell (1814–81). Called to the Bar at Lincoln's Inn 1838; Chief Justice of the Gambia, 1843; Governor of British Settlements on the Gambia, 1847; Governor of St. Lucia, 1852; of South Australia, 1855; Lieutenant-Governor of Nova Scotia, 1864 and Governor of Hong Kong, 1866–72.

[3] Sir Arthur Edward Kennedy (1810–1883). Army career, then served the Irish Government. Governor of the Gambia, 1851; Sierra Leone, 1852; Western Australia, 1854; Vancouver Island, 1863; West African Settlements, 1867. Governor of Hong Kong, 1872–1877. Then Governor of Queensland, 1878. Died in the Red Sea on his way home.

It has been shown that already the Legislative Council had strengthened its position in relation to the Governor and that the unofficial members had gained an enhanced status as the responsible voice of public opinion in the Colony. On the appointment of Sir Richard MacDonnell as governor in 1865 opportunity was taken to revise his Instructions to give these new developments more formal recognition and to lay down principles of some constitutional significance.

In the Instructions to MacDonnell dated 16 October 1865[1] the distinction between official members and unofficial members of the Legislative Council was redefined. It was laid down that the Legislative Council was to consist of the Chief Justice, Colonial Secretary, Attorney-General, Colonial Treasurer and Auditor-General, *ex officio*, to be known as official members, and of certain other persons mentioned by name, and not exceeding four in number, who were to be known as unofficial members. These four were: H. J. Ball,[2] Francis Chomley,[3] James Whittall[4] and Thomas Sutherland.[5]

In the event of any of the four unofficials being for any reason unable to act, the Governor was empowered to appoint a person to the vacancy provisionally pending the signification of Her Majesty's pleasure. All members were to hold their seats at the pleasure of the Crown. The official members were to have precedence over the unofficials and, amongst themselves, in accordance with the office held, each office ranking in the order given in the Instructions. The Governor or senior official present was to preside and be entitled to vote and to have in addition a casting vote.

[1] CO 381/35.

[2] Henry John Ball (1819–74) of London and Oxford Universities, Attorney-General of British Honduras 1855. Judge of the Hong Kong Court of Summary Jurisdiction 1862–74. Member of the Legislative Council 1863 and 1869–73. An epileptic.

[3] Francis Chomley. Admitted a partner of Dent & Co. 1 July 1857. First Chairman of the Hongkong and Shanghai Banking Corporation 1864. Member of the Legislative Council November 1861–1866.

[4] James Whittall (1827–93). Joined Jardine, Matheson & Co. 1856, became partner in 1861 at Shanghai. Member of the Hong Kong Legislative Council April 1864 to September 1867 and July 1872 to August 1875 when he returned to England.

[5] Sir Thomas Sutherland (1834–1922). Superintendent of the P. & O. Steam Navigation Co. at Hong Kong, and one of the founders of The Hongkong and Shanghai Banking Corporation. Member of the Hong Kong Legislative Council 1864–65. Chairman of the P. & O. Steam Navigation Co. and M.P. for Greenock 1884–90. Knighted (K.C.M.G.) 1891.

Five members constituted a quorum. The Governor, with the advice of the Legislative Council, could make, renew, or amend the standing orders of the Council. All ordinances were to be enacted by the Governor with the advice of the Legislative Council, and due notice was to be given where the interests of private person were affected. The doctrine of repugnancy which had always been assumed was expressly stated, and no ordinance and no proceedings of the Council were to be repugnant to the Charter or to the Governor's Instructions or to any Act of Parliament.

There followed in the Instructions a list of subjects upon which ordinances were not to be passed without express permission; these included divorce, the granting of land to the governor himself, the number and salary of public officers, paper currency, differential duties and taxes and any ordinance inconsistent with treaty obligations. The most important addition here was the clause which forbade the passing without previous sanction, of 'any ordinance whereby persons of African or Asiatic birth may be subjected . . . to any disabilities or restrictions to which persons of European birth or descent are not also subjected'.

The Instructions made a corresponding change in the composition of the Executive Council, which was to consist of three *ex officio* members, the Senior Military Officer, Colonial Secretary and Attorney-General, two of whom formed a quorum, and over whom the Governor, or if absent, a member appointed by him, presided. The Governor alone proposed the business, but members were now given the power to make a written application to the Governor for a particular subject to be discussed and to have such an application recorded on the minutes. The Governor had to consult with the Executive Council in all cases, but he was empowered to act contrary to their advice, in which case he had to report his action fully, and the members had the right to have their advice recorded on the minutes.

These Instructions of 1865 brought significant changes in the structure and balance of the Legislative Council. The personal influence of the Governor was reduced; in the past he had been empowered to choose his official and unofficial colleagues on the Council at his absolute discretion subject only to the assent of the Secretary of State, who confirmed the appointments in the name of the Queen. Now this discretionary power was much curtailed. It was Bowring who had initiated the proposal that certain officials

ought to be members of the Council in virtue of their office, and
not on account of their personal standing with the Governor, and
this principle was now conceded. Of the four unofficial members,
H. J. Ball, held office as judge of the Summary Court which had
been created in 1862, since his legal experience was thought to be
valuable. He was therefore an unofficial member in name only and
according to the definition given in the 1865 Instructions. In fact
he was an official member. The arrangement by which the unofficial
members of the Legislative Council were those individually
nominated by the Governor, regardless of whether they held office
in the Government or not, remained the rule until 1884 when
Council was reorganized. For nearly twenty years, the four
unofficial members consisted of one Government official and three
members of the community; only for a brief period in 1867, were
all four non-office holders. The Instructions appeared to disturb
the balance between official and unofficial members by laying down
that the latter should not exceed four, but in fact it was not
intended that all four should be non-office-holding. Sir Hercules
Robinson in December 1859,[1] strongly recommended that the
proportion of officials to non-officials should be two to one, excluding the Governor, and this ratio was maintained.

By the Instructions, all ordinances were to be made by the
Governor 'with the advice of the Legislative Council'; the overriding legislative power of the Governor which had not been used
in practice, thus disappeared. The Governor retained the right of
initiation and he alone could propose bills and subjects for debate,
but a member now had the right to have entered on the minutes
any statement he wished to make. When Kennedy was appointed
Governor in 1872, his Instructions[2] were further amended so
as to strengthen the right of the individual member and limit the
Governor's monopoly of initiation of legislative business. From
that date any subject except that of finance, duly proposed and
seconded by any two members of the Legislative Council had to be
debated by the Council. Financial resolutions still could be
proposed only by the Governor or with his express sanction, and
in this way, the Colony's finances remained firmly under his
control. This did not mean that financial questions could not be

[1] Sir Hercules Robinson to the Duke of Newcastle, 25 October 1859, No.
23, CO 129/74.
[2] CO 381/91.

discussed. In 1872, a Finance Committee of the Council was set up consisting of all the members of the Legislative Council under the chairmanship of the senior member present, with a quorum of three, to meet as required, and consider all financial questions submitted to it by the Governor. This Finance Committee followed the precedent set by the Colony of Mauritius, proposed two years earlier in 1870 by Earl Granville, Secretary of State for the Colonies (1868-70). The Governor's control of the Council was further weakened by a Colonial Office ruling that for each unofficial vacancy, three names had to be submitted to allow the Secretary of State more latitude in considering the Governor's recommendations. This rule was first applied in Hong Kong in November 1861.

On the other hand, these reforms which assisted the Legislative Council to become an active debating body, were offset by a new ruling which deprived the officials of the freedom to vote as they pleased, and this bolstered the authority of the Governor. The ruling came about in the following way.

In 1864 the Home Government asked for the payment of $20,000 annually for defence. The demand created the liveliest opposition from all sections of the community led by the unofficial members of the Legislative Council. When the Council met in September 1864 to vote the demanded sum, the Colonial Treasurer, F. H. Forth, joined the three unofficial members in voting against the provision, which was carried by a bare majority of one. A year later, in September 1865, Forth carried his opposition to the length of seconding a resolution proposed by Thomas Sutherland deleting the amount of the military contribution from the estimates.[1] Cardwell, the Secretary of State (1864-66), expressed his strong disapproval of Forth's conduct and warned that if Forth had been suspended by the Governor his suspension would have been upheld. Arising out of this reprimand, Sutherland asked the new Governor, Sir Richard MacDonnell, if there were any difference in the matter of privileges between official and unofficial members. MacDonnell answered that all members could speak and vote freely, but he thought that if an official directly opposed the policy of the Secretary of State, an explanation might be demanded.

Cardwell was not satisfied with this statement of the position and laid down a ruling on the subject in these terms.[2] 'Her Majesty's

[1] Mercer to Cardwell, 23 September 1865, No. 140, CO 129/106.
[2] Cardwell to Sir Richard MacDonnell, 31 May 1866, No. 92, CO 129/112.

Government have the right to consider opposition by the official members of the Legislative Council to its settled policy as incompatible with retention of office, and I am equally of opinion that they are bound if required to do so, to support by their votes, and not to oppose by any public act, a policy which may originate with the governor.' He said that the Governor would be expected to use his discretion in the enforcement of this obligation, but hoped that unanimity amongst the officials would make its enforcement unnecessary 'except for carrying out the instructions of the home government'. He also warned the officials that it must not be inferred from MacDonnell's reply to Sutherland 'that a Governor is precluded from requiring the support of official members of the Council in respect of a policy originated by himself, even before the policy has been submitted for the approval of the home government'. Cardwell's ruling followed normal British constitutional practice by which the members of a government are expected to support its measures by their votes in the Legislature or else resign. A career official has little choice, and the principle means that he has to voice his opposition in private and not in public. From this time the official majority has always voted as a body in support of, and if necessary to carry, the measures of the colonial administration. Forth, the man who occasioned this statement of principle was a man of peculiar temperament who had opposed his colleagues on other occasions. William Mercer, acting Governor after Sir Hercules Robinson left, referred to him once, as 'a worse than useless public officer';[1] but in this matter his very defects served a useful public purpose.

The intense opposition to the imposition of the military contribution led to the formation of a Reform Association which was set up in 1867 with a local editor called Sinnett as its secretary and guiding influence. Its object was to appeal directly to Parliament to bring pressure to bear on the imperial authorities not to impose decisions contrary to the wishes of the local community, and its immediate object was to present a petition to Parliament against the military contribution. Sinnett had taken a strong line against this impost in his paper, *The Daily Press*, and against the Stamp Ordinance which had been passed to raise the amount required. He claimed that the Stamp Ordinance was frightening

---

[1] Mercer to Duke of Newcastle (Confidential), 18 November 1862, CO 129/88.

the Chinese and would drive Chinese traders away from the Colony. These arguments were reproduced in the petition which was sent direct to London without reference to the Hong Kong Government.

The Reform Association, which also partly owed its origin to the 1867 Reform Act in England, did not last long. In the following year, MacDonnell stated[1] that, though articles in the local press expressed much criticism of the administration and demanded a more representative form of government, yet, he said, 'I believe the community at large is profoundly indifferent on the latter subject', and that the best informed opinion in the Colony did not believe that such a reform was either practicable or desirable. He reported that the Reform Association which had been founded to urge such changes 'had died out through sheer inanition', and that having regard to 'the singular constituent portions of its (i.e. the Colony's) population and the influence directly exercised over that population by a foreign government in the immediate vicinity of the Colony, it would be difficult to devise a more practically useful constitution for it than that which is established here at present'.

The advocates of greater representation of the community in the Legislative Council pointed to the successful functioning of the Shanghai Municipal Council. In Shanghai the land-renters not only elected all the members of the Council but themselves retained some control of taxation at their annual meeting. Since the majority were British, the implication was that a similar system might justifiably be applied in Hong Kong. It was argued too that Shanghai was exempt from the payment of a military contribution though it gained equally from the presence of British forces in Hong Kong. These arguments had little result. The demand for representative government soon faded out because it rested not on abstract principles, but on popular opposition to a military contribution and attendant taxation.

The views of the unofficial members of the Legislative Council during these years received greater attention particularly in financial matters. They strongly criticized a new Companies' Ordinance and a new Bankruptcy Ordinance, though there was a suspicion that they were representing the interests of the old agency houses

---

[1] Sir Richard MacDonnell to Earl of Granville, 15 September 1869, No. 793, CO 120/139.

which were partnerships and were making it difficult for new
joint-stock firms to come into existence.

The unofficials were consulted about repairing the praya after
the 1874 typhoon and on a large scheme to extend the praya to
the east to take in the naval and military areas. In 1872 they
resisted a considerable increase in the numbers and cost of the
police and secured some reduction in the police estimates.

A change was made in 1860 in voting the annual estimates by
the Legislative Council, by which certain fixed annual charges
such as salaries of the government officers were placed in a civil
list and not submitted to an annual vote. In this way no action
could be taken against an unpopular official by threatening to
reduce his salary.

In 1873 Phineas Ryrie[1] complained about the short time allowed
to examine the annual estimates, there being only seven days
between the first and second readings. His motion found no
seconder, but the Earl of Kimberley, Secretary of State for the
Colonies (1870-74), thought Ryrie's protest was reasonable. In
1874 the Colony was struck by a severe typhoon, and the Captain
Superintendent of Police was severely criticized because he kept
the police in barracks while it was raging. Ryrie protested against
his action in the Legislative Council, but J. Gardiner Austin, the
Colonial Secretary who was temporarily administering the government, refused to enter the protest on the minutes, on the ground
that a member could protest only against a decision of the Council
and not against a decision of the head of a government department.
In the next annual estimates, the unofficial members made an
unavailing attempt to strike out provision for the police chief's
salary.

The unofficials were not always unheld; for example in 1871
there was trouble between Ryrie and the Colonial Secretary, C. C.
Smith.[2] Ryrie acting on information from Chinese sources, strongly
complained of a proposal alleged to have been made by Wade,
the British Minister in Peking, to allow the Chinese Government

---

[1] Phineas Ryrie, of Turner & Co., arrived in the Colony 1854 and resided
until his death in 1892 and was a member of the Legislative Council some 25
years (1867-1892). Chairman of the Chamber of Commerce, 1867-68, 1871-76,
and 1886-89.

[2] Sir Cecil Clementi Smith (1840-1916). One of the first Cadet officers
appointed by examination in 1862. Went to Singapore as Colonial Secretary
1878; Colonial Secretary, Ceylon, 1885; and became Governor of the Straits
Settlements (1887-93).

to set up a customs station in the Colony. The Governor's offer to give the information confidentially to the unofficial members was refused and a debate in the Legislative Council on the subject was rejected on the ground that Wade's dispatch was confidential. Ryrie accused Smith of supporting Wade and demanded the production of the relevant documents to the members of the Council as a matter of privilege. This was refused and the Secretary of State in London ruled that Ryrie's contention could not be upheld. The rulings meant that the unofficial members of the Legislative Council could not claim to debate general matters of policy and could not claim to control the Executive.

During this period, the unofficial members were invariably selected from among the leading British merchants. Looking through the list of unofficial members of the Legislative Council in the years 1859–77, as given in Appendix D, we find that the three unofficial members of the Council were chosen from a limited number of commercial houses.

Jardine, Matheson & Co., 'The Princely Hong', are continuously represented over the period, and Dent & Co. until their bankruptcy in 1867, when their place was taken by Gibb, Livingston & Co. The third member is shared by seven firms.[1]

This virtual monopoly of the British mercantile interests to the non-official seats on the Legislative Council was shortly to come to end.

Sir John Pope Hennessy and the First Chinese Member of the Legislative Council, 1877–82

The appointment of the first Chinese member of the Legislative Council was made in 1880, on the initiative of Sir John Pope Hennessy,[2] Governor 1878–82, as part of his policy of assisting and

---

[1] A petition of 9 February 1865 by the Chamber of Commerce to the Governor against the rejection by the Legislative Council of a Limited Liability Ordinance, shows the membership of the Chamber as 49, made up of 42 firms, 5 banks and 2 shipping companies, of which 30 were British, 8 Indian and the remainder of various nationalities.

[2] Sir John Pope Hennessy (1834–91). Born in County Kerry, Ireland, Member of Parliament 1859, the first Roman Catholic Conservative who sat in Parliament. Called to the Bar, Inner Temple, 1861. Governor of Labuan, 1867; the Gold Coast, 1872; Bahamas, 1875 and of Hong Kong, 1877–82. Governor of Mauritius, 1883–1889.

conciliating the Chinese section of the population. Hennessy has been described as 'an able and typical Irishman, quick of wit and repartee, of human and sympathetic but impulsive temperament'. His failure as a Colonial Governor was due to his want of tact and judgment, and his faculty of 'irritating where he might conciliate'. Unhappily too, his mind worked tortuously and he never acquired the habit of making definite and accurate statements'.[1]

The time for giving the Chinese community greater influence in the Colony's administration was becoming ripe, for the Chinese were contributing to the commercial prosperity and revenue of the Colony by expanded business undertakings and taking over more Crown leases. Victoria was virtually becoming a Chinese city. The growth of the Chinese section of the population which has already been noticed, accelerated under the beneficent rule of Hennessy. In 1877 the population was estimated to be 139,144 of whom 130,168 were Chinese including 36,168 women; in the 1881 census the population was 160,402, of whom 150,690 were Chinese including 43,029 women. The growing Chinese population brought about the expansion of secondary industries and minor trades.

In the all-round expansion of the Colony's fortunes which followed the treaty settlements with China of 1858 and 1860, the Chinese played a notable part. The numerous and growing Chinese overseas communities, in the United States, Australia, Malaya, the Indian Ocean, the Pacific Islands, South America and the West Indies which clung tenaciously to the Chinese way of life, created a demand for Chinese products which was generally supplied through Chinese merchants in Hong Kong; the Island also became the centre of an important Chinese passenger—carrying trade. The distribution of British and foreign goods to ports on the China coast other than the treaty ports, and to the interior was largely handled by the Chinese and this applied equally to the purchases of Chinese goods for the British and foreign market. This was happening not only in Hong Kong but in all the treaty ports. In reply to a circular letter from Sir Rutherford Alcock, the British Minister at Peking, in 1869, all the British consuls agreed that the distribution of British and foreign

---

[1] From the *Dictionary of National Biography*, quoting *The Times*, 8 October 1891.

goods was passing into the hands of the Chinese.[1] Chinese-owned shipping received a great fillip by the protection it received from the local ordinance which allowed Chinese holders of Crown lands in the Colony to register their ships on the Colony register of shipping and so secure the protection of the British flag. They benefited from the stability of the Colony's economic life and of its currency, and from the absence of irritating restrictions.

One result of the expansion of Chinese business was pressure on the accommodation for the Chinese available in the Colony. In Hong Kong there was a tradition inherited from the old Canton period that the Chinese and foreign communities lived apart, and since their social habits and customs stood in such marked contrast, this arrangement was mutually convenient. The custom grew up of reserving certain areas for houses of European and Chinese types respectively; its only sanction was a clause in the land leases which had been interpreted in practice as giving this power, and though the restriction technically applied to houses and not to persons, in effect it resulted in racial segregation. In 1877 Hennessy in a long dispatch[2] pointed to the growth of Chinese-owned business and suggested that the Chinese should be allowed to hold property in Queen's Road, hitherto the main European thoroughfare. The Colonial Office comment on this dispatch was a laconic observation that they already knew that Hong Kong was becoming a Chinese city. In July 1880, Hennessy wrote again saying that the Chinese were growing in wealth and importance, and showing great industry and probity; he explained that they could place British goods on the eastern markets cheaper than the British merchant houses with corresponding advantage to British manufacturers; that they were the largest owners of real property and held 90% of the note issue and contributed over 90% of the Colony's revenue. Commenting on the census held in 1881, Hennessy noted that since 1876, the year before his arrival, the Chinese population had increased in number by 20,000, while the Europeans had increased by only 276, and European males had shown an actual decrease, that the Chinese Nam Pak Hongs[3] had increased

---

[1] See N. A. Pelcovits, *Old China Hands and the Foreign Office*, p. 35 and references on pp. 306–07. Institute of Pacific Relations, New York 1948.

[2] Sir John Hennessy to the Earl of Carnarvon, 27 September 1877, No. 123, CO 129–179.

[3] *Nam Pak Hongs* 南北行 (literally, South North Hongs) were trading associations or guilds of those engaged in trade with China and S.E. Asia.

from 215 to 395, and the number of Chinese traders from 287 to 2,377 and Chinese bullion dealers who first appeared in this period by 1881 numbered 34. In August 1881 Hennessy sent home a list of the largest ratepayers in the Colony, these paying $1,000 or more per quarter, which showed that there were 17 Chinese names and only one British (Jardine, Matheson & Co.) in this category.[1] During the period January 1880 to May 1881, the Chinese had bought land from European owners to the value of $1,710,000. Hennessy said he had encouraged the Chinese to buy land in Queen's Road because it was impossible 'to keep back the free current of commercial life', and permitted it because there was 'no legal impediment'.

Hennessy from the first pursued a policy of encouraging the Chinese in Hong Kong and of acting in defence of their interests and so giving them greater self respect. Besides allowing them to buy land in the European quarter, he gave them more educational facilities, protected their cemeteries, checked the practice of deportation, abolished the branding and the public flogging of Chinese criminals, and proposed the first typhoon anchorage to protect their boat population. Under him, junior posts in the government service were further opened to the Chinese by competitive examination, and he began the practice whereby local Chinese and other aliens, were given British nationality by private ordinance, which, however, was valid only in the Colony. That Hennessy should attempt to extend his liberal Chinese policy to the constitutional field was not surprising.

Until then the Legislative Council was regarded as a British preserve, and local demands for a more effective representation of the community upon it had been discussed in the context of British commercial interests. The economic and social progress of the Chinese was such that their admission to a share in the constitution could not in any case have not been long delayed; Hennessy acted therefore in anticipation of a natural development of events.

In 1879 the Chinese sent a memorial to the Governor saying that since they were ten times the number of the foreigners 'henceforth it would be but fair to allow the Chinese community a share in the management of public affairs of the Colony'. This request

---

[1] Sir John Pope Hennessy to Earl of Kimberley, 31 August 1881, No. 140, CO 129/194.

2. NG CHOY (Wu Ting-fan) 伍才（廷芳）
First Chinese member of the Legislative Council, 1880.
From J. Norton-Kyshe, *History of the Laws and Courts
of Hong Kong*. T. Fisher Unwin and Noronha & Co.,
Hong Kong 1898.

Facing page 93

was acted upon by Hennessy with an alacrity which suggests that it might have originated with him. In 1879 when Henry Lowcock, an unofficial member of the Legislative Council, left the Colony on leave, the Governor suggested that he should be replaced by a Chinese. Hicks Beach, the Secretary of State (1878–80), decided that such a proposal should be allowed to wait and H. B. Gibb, a former member of the Council and Lowcock's colleague in Gibb, Livingston & Co., was appointed.

In January 1880 in the temporary absence of Gibb, Hennessy again proposed[1] a Chinese, this time a barrister, Ng Choy,[2] as a temporary member of the Legislative Council and provisionally appointed him. He argued that the time had come to place on the Council a man who fairly represented the interests of the Chinese community and reported that the 'wealthy and better Chinese' whom he had consulted had agreed that Ng Choy was well able to represent them. Hennessy pointed to the precedent of Singapore where a Chinese, Hoo Ah Kay Whampoa, had been appointed to the Legislative Council in 1869, and to his own earlier action as Governor of Labuan in which Colony he had appointed a Chinese, Chou Massoo, to its Legislative Council.

Hennessy followed up his action in nominating a Chinese as a temporary member, by a proposal to reorganize the Council to provide for permanent Chinese representation. He proposed to increase the Legislative Council to eleven members, six official and five unofficial, plus the Governor. He suggested that as the posts of Colonial Secretary and Auditor-General, the holders of which were both *ex officio* members, were held by the same man, Price, the Surveyor-General should be an official member in place of the Auditor-General, and as the sixth official member he suggested the Harbour Master, on the ground that the port was the biggest in the Colonial Empire and a centre of Chinese emigration.[3] To

---

[1] Sir John Hennessy to Sir Michael Hicks Beach, 19 January 1880, No. 4, CO 129/187.

[2] Ng Choy 伍才 (1842–1922), a British subject by birth, born in Singapore. Educated in England. Called to the Bar at Lincoln's Inn 1877, the first Chinese to be called. Appointed temporary stipendiary magistrate 1880, the first Chinese to hold a senior appointment, and member of the Legislative Council 1880–82. Joined the Chinese Imperial Service, under the name Wu T'ing-fang, became secretary to Li Hung-chang and rose to be Chinese Ambassador to the United States in 1896, 1897. He held high cabinet posts under the Republic.

[3] Sir John Hennessy to Sir Michael Hicks Beach, 20 January 1880, No. 9, CO 129/187.

the existing four unofficials, he suggested the addition of one, who was to be a Chinese. His proposal amounted to the addition of a Chinese unofficial member and a compensating increase of one in the official side. Since this proposal was made only nine days after the appointment of Ng Choy, clearly its object was to provide him with a permanent seat. Hennessy proposed that if Price, the Surveyor-General, who was sitting temporarily as an unofficial member became a full *ex officio* official member, the vacancy among the unofficials thus created should be given to E. R. Belilios,[1] described by Hennessy as 'born in India but a leading member of the English community'.

The Secretary of State was unimpressed by Hennessy's arguments and replied that he saw no reason to make any changes. He allowed the appointment of Price not as an *ex officio* member but as an unofficial member, using the argument that though Price himself was excellent, if he were absent his deputy might not be equally acceptable. He rejected the nomination of Belilios and preferred instead that the Governor should nominate an Englishman, 'a representative of one of the great English firms or banks would be preferable', he said. He accepted Ng Choy as a temporary member, since Gibb was absent on leave and had not resigned, but only for three years or until Gibb returned. In the Colonial Office minutes on Hennessy's dispatch, the arguments used against giving Ng Choy a permanent seat were, that if the Governor wanted to consult the Legislative Council secretly or if relations with China became strained, the presence of Ng Choy on the Council might be awkward; Hicks Beach also advanced the view that if a Chinese were appointed to the Legislative Council, it ought to be a Chinese merchant. The importance of the mercantile interest thus received explicit official recognition.

Ng Choy took his seat as the first Chinese member of the Legislative Council on 19 February 1880 and the occasion was marked by a deputation of the leading Chinese members of the Colony which called at Government House to congratulate the Governor and themselves on the appointment.

[1] Emanuel Raphael Belilios, appointed to the Legislative Council temporarily 1881, member of Legislative Council 1892–1900 when he resigned. Established scholarships at Queen's College, and at the Hong Kong Medical College for Chinese 1887, and helped to build Belilios School. Received the C.M.G. in 1893, the first local resident to be so honoured. He was one of the principal opium merchants.

H. B. Gibb did not return to the Colony and when he resigned from the Council in July 1880, Hennessy proposed that Ng Choy be given a permanent seat. The Liberals had just taken office under Gladstone, but the new Secretary of State, the Earl of Kimberley (1880–82), was no more encouraging than his predecessor Hicks Beach had been. He replied[1] that Lowcock was now back in the Colony and since he was a former member of the Council, he could not be overlooked, and should be provisionally appointed. If Lowcock were not remaining in the Colony then Ng Choy should continue to hold his seat on a temporary basis, but for not longer than the three years which had already been set as the limit. One Colonial Office official minuted on Hennessy's letter that Ng Choy was a cipher on the Legislative Council much as Whampoa had been on the Council at Singapore. Lord Kimberley's revealing comment reads 'Tell Hennessy's successor that it is desirable to have a Chinese on the Legislative Council'; this shows that in seeming to make difficulties, his distrust was of Hennessy rather than of the Chinese. In August 1881, Hennessy nominated Belilios to an unofficial seat on the Council in place of Price temporarily absent, but his suggestion that a paid official should not in future be nominated to one of the four unofficial seats was not accepted and Price on his return to the Colony in 1882 resumed his unofficial seat.

Hennessy had previously upset colonial opinion in the Bahamas and had had to be moved, and the Colonial Office in England distrusted him. Herbert[2] noted in 1877, 'We must watch all his proceedings very narrowly . . . and when we see any tendency to bolt to the right or to the left from the path of established procedure in Hong Kong (which is an intricate one surrounded with special dangers arising from the Chinese character which he does not understand) he should be firmly and as gently as possible led back to it'. R. Meade[3] noted in this same year, 'Mr. Hennessy is showing signs of mischievous activity which will bring us into trouble unless civilly but promptly suppressed'. Hennessy was an impetuous man who took up causes in a way that showed little balance. In

---

[1] Earl of Kimberley to Sir John Hennessy, 24 September 1880, No. 56, CO 129/189.

[2] Sir Robert George Wyndham Herbert (1831–1905), Permanent Under-Secretary of State for the Colonies (1871–1892).

[3] Richard James Meade, Parliamentary Under-Secretary.

addition be proved himself a bad administrator. He hindered educational development by refusing to vote money for the new Central School, he delayed the rebuilding of the praya and the Civil Hospital which had been damaged by a typhoon, and by supporting Chinese ideas of night-soil sanitation, held up the most essential schemes of increasing the water supply. He encouraged the Chinese but did not anticipate the great boom in land values that this created or the distress caused when a recession followed his departure.

It was something of a tragedy that advocacy of Chinese interests in Hong Kong should have been associated with him, because he attached his own unpopularity to this cause. Yet he performed a signal service in appointing the first Chinese member to the Legislative Council on his own initiative and responsibility.

CHAPTER VI

THE RECONSTRUCTION OF THE LEGISLATIVE COUNCIL 1884

SIR John Pope Hennessy made his unregretted departure in March 1882, and was succeeded by Sir George Bowen[1] who arrived in the Colony in April 1883. During the interval, the Colony was administered by the Colonial Secretary, William Marsh.[2]

A reorganization of the Legislative Council was needed for many reasons. The permanent appointment of a Chinese member could not be shelved indefinitely, the practice of appointing government officials to seats on the Council as so-called unofficial members was unpopular, and there was also the standing challenge to self-government provided by the Shanghai Municipal Council, which was not unsuccessfully controlling a population equal to that of the Colony.

Ng Choy's term as a member of the Legislative Council was due to expire on 21 January 1883, and as he proposed to go on leave then, a decision about his successor had to be taken. In fact Ng Choy resigned at the expiry of the tenure of his seat; he had got into financial difficulty in 1882 on the collapse of the boom caused by land speculation and Marsh wrote[3] that he had been saved from bankruptcy only by the intervention of a wealthy mother-in-law. He went to Tientsin, from which city he sent his resignation, and joined the Chinese Imperial Service as legal adviser and interpreter to Li Hung-chang;[4] in 1897 he was appointed Chinese

---

[1] Sir George Ferguson Bowen (1821–1899). Born in County Donegal. Fellow of Brasenose College, 1844. President of the University of Corfu, 1847. Chief Secretary of the Government in the Ionian Islands, 1854. Governor successively of Queensland 1859, New Zealand 1867, Victoria 1872, Mauritius 1879 and Hong Kong 1883–85.

[2] Sir William H. Marsh (1827–1906). Served in Mauritius, 1848–79 and became Auditor-General 1876. Colonial Secretary and Auditor-General of Hong Kong 1879–87. Administered the Government of Hong Kong 1882–83, September to October 1883 and 1885–87. Retired in 1887 after 39 years of service, and knighted K.C.M.G.

[3] Marsh to Earl of Kimberley (Confidential), 2 June 1882, CO 129/201.

[4] Li Hung-chang (1822–1901). Came to the front in the fighting against the T'ai P'ing rebels. 1867 Viceroy of the Hu-kuang. 1870 Viceroy of Chili. Negotiated the Peace of Shimonoseki 1895 and the agreement with Russia of 1896. Viceroy at Canton during the Boxer troubles and called to be Viceroy of Chihli 1900.

ambassador to the United States. He is better known in China under his official name Wu T'ing-fang. If he did not make any remarkable contribution as a member of the Legislative Council, at least he secured a first seat for the Chinese.

The Earl of Derby, Secretary of State for the Colonies (1882-85) had agreed that the Chinese community should be represented on the Council but he preferred to delay a decision on Ng Choy's successor until Bowen had arrived and had time to give his considered recommendation. So Ng Choy was not immediately succeeded by another Chinese.

Bowen after due enquiry, supported the principle of Chinese membership of the Legislative Council. 'For many obvious reasons, I am strongly of opinion that the overwhelming Chinese majority of the population of Hong Kong . . . should be represented by at least one member of the Colonial Legislature', he told Lord Derby,[1] but he thought the choosing of such a member 'a task of considerable difficulty and delicacy', because 'I am informed that most of the leading Chinese merchants resident here are not British subjects', and it 'will not be easy to find among those qualified as British subjects, a native gentleman combining in his own person the proper social position, independent means and education'. By independent means, Bowen presumably meant that a prospective member should be independent of the Government, and not independent of any gainful occupation.

Bowen did not treat the question of a permanent Chinese member in isolation, but as part of a wider scheme of reform of the Legislative Council which he thought needed a general overhaul.[2] The changes which he sought to introduce into Hong Kong were based on the practices then existing in the colonies of Mauritius and Ceylon. He considered that popular elections were impracticable in a heterogeneous community circumstanced as Hong Kong; instead he suggested a change in the system of nomination by which members of the Council should be more representative of public opinion and more responsible to it, by entrusting public bodies such as the Chamber of Commerce and the bench of Justices of the Peace, with the power to make nominations. He urged that the practice of having paid government officials serving on the Council as unofficial members should be ended, remarking

[1] Sir George Bowen to Earl of Derby, 4 April 1883, No. 4, CO 129/208.
[2] Sir George Bowen to Earl of Derby, 14 May 1883, No. 62, CO 129/209.

that at that time, May 1883, two of the four unofficial members were paid officials. As has already been explained, the distinction between official and unofficial members was a purely technical one, but the point is that it appeared to be an anomaly, and as Bowen pointed out, as such was a source of justifiable complaint. Sir George Bowen considered that the Senior Military Officer in Hong Kong should be a member of the Legislative Council, as was the case in Singapore, because his exclusion caused personal animosities.[1] The Governor also criticized the presence in the Legislative Council of the Chief Justice on the principle that the judiciary should be completely independent of the rest of the administration as the guarantee of its impartiality.

Bowen proposed the addition of three official members to the Council, namely the Senior Military Officer, the Registrar-General and the Surveyor-General, and two unofficial members, thus bringing the total Council to eight official and six unofficial members besides the Governor with his ordinary and casting votes. To increase its representative character he suggested that the Chamber of Commerce should nominate two members and the Justices of the Peace one member; for he said, these two bodies 'represented the intelligence, education and property of the Community'. In his view one, if not two, of the six unofficials should be a Chinese, following a corresponding rule in New Zealand, the Straits Settlements and Ceylon. The nominations would in all cases be made by the Governor subject to the approval of the Crown.

Bowen suggested other changes. He thought that the unofficial members should hold office for six years and not for life. He complained that the Legislative Council had been 'summoned at rare and uncertain intervals', and proposed a regular annual session in November at which a review of the Colony should be given together with the Government's legislative programme, so as to allow the unofficials to debate policy.

He also proposed that the Executive Council should be increased in number from five to seven by the addition of the Treasurer and Registrar-General, and indeed urged the desirability of all the officials in the Legislative Council being members of the Executive

[1] There had been a number of instances of quarrels between the Governor and the General, and a Colonial Office minute on one of Sir Arthur Kennedy's dispatches (6 September 1876, No. 173) reads 'There is always a row between the Governor and the General at Hong Kong . . . and I conclude it is one of the local occupations'.

Council since they had to support the Executive's policy by their votes. In any case, what with absences due to leave and illness, five was too few.

The Earl of Derby accepted the scheme broadly, but with changes of detail. He rejected the argument that the Senior Military Officer should be a member of the Legislative Council on the ground that he could not be compelled to support the government measures and his possible opposition might create a difficulty; he also said that the Senior Military Officer had not been a member of the Legislative Council since Major General D'Aguilar in 1843 and Colonel Caine in 1855.[1] He agreed that the Registrar-General and Surveyor-General should be additional official members, making the total six.[2] With regard to officials being nominated to unofficial seats, Derby ruled that the practice was to designate only a few important officials to hold seats *ex officio*, and to select other officials best fitted for membership of the Council either because of personal qualities or in virtue of the duties performed, and that this practice would continue. He suggested that since he had reduced the number of official members the number of un-official members should be five only, 'at least one of whom shall be a member of the Chinese community'. He agreed to allow some unofficials to represent public opinion as expressed by some of the leading business institutions, but since there were only five unofficials instead of six, the Chamber of Commerce should nominate only one member. Lord Derby also reduced the proposed increase in the Executive Council by one making it six instead of seven, the Registrar-General being added but not the Colonial Treasurer. Thus amended, the new constitutional arrangements came into force, and the newly constituted Legislative Council sat for the first time on 28 February 1884.

The Chamber of Commerce was fairly international in character; of its 34 members, 20 were British and one American, six Euro-peans and two Chinese, besides three Jews, one Parsee and one American. To qualify for membership the main requirements were a moderate fee and an election by its committee. At the meeting for the nomination of a member to the Legislative Council,

---

[1] Caine in fact was not Senior Military Officer but Lieutenant-Governor.

[2] The five *ex officio* members amounted only to four because the Auditor-General's office was held by the Colonial Secretary, and the two additional appointees therefore made only six.

F. Bulkeley Johnson urged the granting of a greater degree of self-government. Thomas Jackson,[1] chief manager of The Hongkong and Shanghai Banking Corporation was unanimously elected.

In the time of Hennessy a Chinese Chamber of Commerce had been mooted, but did not last long and failed to establish itself as the voice of Chinese business opinion.

There were 60 unofficial Justices of the Peace all of British nationality as a condition of their appointment, of whom 62 were of British extraction, seven Chinese, three Jewish and seven Parsees and Armenians. It was agreed that the 19 official Justices of the Peace should take no part in the election, so that the elected member should be more representative of opinion in the community. This was a private arrangement, the official Justices merely abstaining of their own free will, as a gesture to the community. The position was regularized in the following April (1884) when the Legislative Council resolved that the official Justices of the Peace should not be entitled to vote in future elections.

The election held by the unofficial Justices caused some excitement; three candidates were nominated and after some campaigning, their choice was Frederick Sassoon[2] a British subject of an Indian-Jewish family who had been educated in England. The Justices felt that the British were adequately represented on the Council, and so they deliberately avoided using their English majority to elect one of their own number.[3]

As the Chinese member of the Council, the Governor nominated Wong Shing.[4] Bowen complained[5] to Lord Derby of the difficulty

[1] Sir Thomas Jackson, BT. Appointed chief manager of The Hongkong and Shanghai Banking Corporation in 1876. Retired in 1902, and served on the London Committee of the Bank until his death in 1915. Knighted 1899 and became a baronet in 1902. Resigned from the Legislative Council in 1887.

[2] Frederick David Sassoon. A member of the Sassoon family originally from Bombay which occupied the leading place in the opium trade.

[3] Sir George Bowen to Earl of Derby, 7 January 1884, No. 1, CO 129/215.

[4] Wong Shing 黃勝 (Huang Shêng). 1825–. Bowen described Wong Shing as a man of property, 'much travelled, speaking good English and willing to be naturalised'. He had served with the great Li Hung-chang in China, and had been a member of the Chinese legation staff in Washington and was 'fully qualified to look at Chinese affairs with English and at English affairs with Chinese eyes'. He was one of the first directors of the Tung Wah. He was born in 1825 near Macao and had been educated at the Morrison Institution in Hong Kong, and later entered Monson Academy at Monson, Massachusetts, in the United States. He was associated with the London Missionary Society for whom he directed its printing establishment under Dr James Legge.

[5] Sir George Bowen to Earl of Derby, 28 December 1883, No. 355, CO 129/214.

that most of the Chinese in Hong Kong retained their Chinese nationality and in addition were only temporarily resident, and that his choice was very limited. Bowen said he consulted Frederick Stewart the Registrar-General, and prominent Chinese who agreed with this nomination, and he added that Wong Shing was satisfactory to the British too. The five unofficial members were therefore F. Bulkeley Johnson of Jardine, Matheson & Co., and Phineas Ryrie of Turner & Co. (the two existing unofficial members), Thomas Jackson, Frederick Sassoon and Wong Shing. They were all to hold office for a term of six years, and not for life.

In assembling the members of the Council for their first meeting in February 1884 there was an unfortunate hitch. Phineas Ryrie and F. Johnson being already unofficial members, were naturally re-appointed. Price the Surveyor-General and Stewart the Registrar-General, who had been sitting as unofficial members became official members. The Attorney-General, O'Malley, interpreted the wording of the Instructions of the Secretary of State to mean that the places of these two officials should be taken by the two members elected by the Chamber of Commerce and the Justices of the Peace respectively. This meant that Wong Shing therefore could not take his seat without the prior approval of the Colonial Office. The latter did not at first uphold this ruling, although later it admitted that O'Malley had been right. The awkward situation was met by Thomas Jackson who voluntarily stood down to allow Wong Shing to attend the first meeting of the reformed Council; his magnanimity spared the Chinese from what might have been a grievous loss of face.

With Bowen's reorganization, the Legislative Council assumed its modern shape and subsequent reforms have not radically altered its character. The principle of the representation of Chinese by Chinese was accepted, and since there had to be 'at least' one member of the Chinese community on the Council the way was automatically open to increasing their representation.

Indirect election was now definitely recognized as a permanent element in the Colony's constitutional machinery. Two public bodies were allowed to elect one nominee each, but the names had to be submitted to the Secretary of State by the Governor who could no doubt refuse to forward them if he had good reason; in any case the Home Government possessed a veto, but in practice, the nominations were always accepted and the system worked smoothly.

Election by the Justices was no new thing, Bonham had introduced it tentatively in 1850 as an informal arrangement, and Bowring in the 1857 election had tried to make it definitive. Now the Justices, like the Chamber of Commerce, made their nomination as a matter of right. The system gave great influence to the relatively small group of important merchants who controlled the Chamber of Commerce and who were also Justices of the Peace.

The representatives elected by the Chamber of Commerce to serve on the Legislative Council were, up to the turn of the century:

1884–86	Thomas Jackson	The Hongkong and Shanghai Banking Corporation.
1886–90	Alexander Palmer MacEwen	Holiday, Wise & Co.
1888–89	Bendyshe Layton (temporarily acting for MacEwen, absent)	Gibb, Livingston & Co.
1890–1902	Thomas Henderson Whitehead	Chartered Bank of India, Australia & China.
1894–95	Alexander MacConachie (temporarily acting for Whitehead, absent)	Gilman & Co.
1900	Herbert Smith (temporarily acting for Whitehead, absent)	Butterfield & Swire.

For more than half this period 1884–1900, the Chamber of Commerce chose a banker, able to speak with a knowledge of commercial and financial conditions as a whole; the two bankers chosen, Jackson and Whitehead, were both men of outstanding personality.

The Justices chose as their nominees on the Council:

Frederick David Sassoon	1884–87
Catchik Paul Chater[1]	1887–1906

Both were successful and wealthy business men of Asian origin yet were very westernized. Chater became an influential public figure

[1] Sir Catchik Paul Chater, C.M.G. (1846–1926). Of Armenian extraction from Calcutta, came to Hong Kong 1864 as assistant in the Bank of Hindustan, China and Japan. Resigned 1866 to be exchange and bullion broker, unanimously elected to the Legislative Council 1887, again 1893, and for a third term in 1899. Retired at the end of the third term in 1906. Member of the Executive Council 1896–1926. Initiated the Central Praya Reclamation, 1887. Founder of many enterprises, e.g. the Wharf Company, coal mines in Tonking, iron mines in New Territories. Knighted 1902.

in Hong Kong, associated with the Executive and Legislative Councils for nearly forty years. Though their nominees were well able to represent the foreign community, nevertheless the Justices must be given credit for taking this liberal attitude in the exercise of their electoral privilege.

The remaining nominated unofficial members, except the Chinese, were again chosen from a very limited number of important commercial houses. The chief exception was E. R. Belilios in 1881 and again in 1892–1900. By his own business ability, and his generosity in subscribing to public causes he had won public esteem. Sassoon, Chater and Belilios were all Asian in origin but accepted socially and supported by the European community to which the majority of the Justices belonged. The Bowen reforms did not therefore impair the influence of the leading commercial houses and helped to continue the representation of property and commercial interests but not of the people or communities as such.

The government was there to protect the individual; as Bowen put it, the 'governor as representative of the Queen, is bound to protect impartially the interests of all Her Majesty's subjects of every race'. The Chinese were protected not only by representation on the Council, but also by the Registrar-General, whose subsidiary title since 1858 had been 'Protector of the Chinese'. It was his function to deal directly with the Chinese on all matters concerning their relations with government, for example to receive all Chinese petitions and deputations, to see that Chinese interests received due consideration, that the government's views were made known to the local population, and that all government ordinances, notifications, etc. were accurately promulgated in the Chinese language. The importance of his office had grown with the growth of the Chinese community, and we have just seen that in 1884, he became an *ex officio* member of the Legislative Council. Hennessy had wanted to replaced this office by a Chinese secretaryship, with the same status in relation to the Chinese as the Colonial Secretary occupied in relation to government business transacted in English, and he temporarily abolished the Registrar-General's powers as 'Protector of the Chinese'. Hennessy handled the project badly, but his idea of attaching great importance to relations with the Chinese was adopted after he left by enhancing the prestige of the Registrar-General. His special responsibility was to see that Chinese customs and usages were respected and that the normal processes of law were mitigated in this respect. These arrangements to protect Chinese reflected that humanitarian liberalism which characterized British colonial policy and to which all parties in England subscribed. Some Chinese, educated in the West, began to object to any difference of treatment between Chinese and foreigners, and wished to abolish the office of Registrar-General on the ground that there should be no official entrusted with the duty of dealing specifically with the Chinese, and that all people of Hong Kong regardless of race should deal with the government through the same channels.

The Chinese had an alternative means of safeguarding their interests through the Directors of the Tung Wah 東華, signifying 'for *Chinese* of the Kwang-*tung* province'. This Chinese organization was founded in 1870 to tend the sick, care for the aged and homeless, and repatriate those wishing to return to China but unable to find the means. It was given recognition by ordinance and the most prominent and influential Chinese became its directors. In 1882 Marsh complained[1] to the Secretary of State, Lord Kimberley, that the Tung Wah Hospital committee did not limit themselves to hospital affairs, but seem 'to be recognised by the Chinese as a kind of tribunal to which petitions for redress of grievances should be addressed, and in fact to have exercised the duties of which the Registrar-General was relieved, of Protector of the Chinese'; it summoned witnesses and communicated directly with Chinese imperial officials. All these responsibilities were assumed quite openly with no attempt at concealment, and Kimberley advised great caution in bringing the committee back to its true charitable function, because it was a society of great benefit to the Chinese.

Bowen wished to increase the powers of the Legislative Council as well as strengthen its personnel. In December 1883 he wrote to Lord Derby[2] that the British in Hong Kong contrasted their position with that of the British merchants in Shanghai, who had self-governing powers by means of a council elected by the ratepayers. Both cities had approximately 2,000 Europeans and 150,000 Chinese, and many thought that Shanghai was better governed than Hong Kong where the Secretary of State controlled all administrative details. Bowen gave it as his opinion that the leading

[1] Marsh to Earl of Kimberley (Confidential), 20 March 1882, CO 129/199.
[2] Sir George Bowen to Earl of Derby, 10 December 1883, No. 334, CO 129/213.

residents of Hong Kong were much superior in personal character, property and essential qualifications of administrators to the average members of ministries in the self-governing Australian colonies. In December 1883, the Legislative Council resolved that it be allowed to exercise, under the Colonial Office, the same functions as the Shanghai Municipal Council, but Lord Derby rejected the plea 'having regard to the peculiar circumstances of the Colony and to the fact that a large proportion of local questions bear directly or indirectly on points of imperial interest'. Nevertheless Bowen strongly and repeatedly supported this demand. The Governor also thought that Hong Kong, as the 'Gibraltar of the East', should have the senior military officer as the governor: 'In fact neither Hong Kong nor Gibraltar is a colony in the proper sense of the term . . . the ordinary work of a civil governor at Hong Kong (with occasional exceptions when there arise grave questions concerning foreign relations and the resident Chinese Community) is not materially different from the ordinary work of the Mayor of Portsmouth or Plymouth or of any other large garrison town in England'[1] was his verdict.

Bowen was also able to effect some reform in the machinery of the Legislative Council. At the Council meeting held on 29 December 1883, F. Bulkeley Johnson, moved 'that all votes of public money should be laid before the Finance Committee before being forwarded to the Secretary of State'. Bowen accepted the suggestion, and replied that 'except in emergency, all votes of public money should for the future, be considered in the first instance by the reconstituted Legislative Council'. Lord Derby assented to the change. A substantial gain in the status of the unofficial members resulted because they could now make their views heard before decisions were finally approved by Whitehall. Also by his institution of an annual review outlining the Government's policy, corresponding to the Speech from the Throne in British parliamentary practice, to which the members had an opportunity to reply, Bowen provided them with 'a constitutional opportunity of expressing their opinion of the conduct and proposals of the Government'.[2]

Arising out of Bulkeley Johnson's question, Bowen added in his reply, that he considered that Legislative Council Standing

[1] Sir George Bowen to Earl of Derby, 23 May 1883, No. 82, CO 129/209.
[2] Sir George Bowen to Earl of Derby, 1 March 1884, No. 63, CO 129/215.

Orders 'as in other Colonies' should be introduced into Hong Kong. The result was the drawing up of new standing orders, dated 10 April 1884[1] by which the committee system was further developed. Section 43 provided that 'At the opening of every session the President shall appoint the following standing committees: *(a)* A Finance Committee consisting of the Colonial Secretary (chairman) and other Members of the Council except the Governor; *(b)* A Law Committee consisting of the Attorney-General (chairman) and four other members; *(c)* A Public Works Committee consisting of the Surveyor-General (chairman) and four other members'.

This brought into existence two more standing committees, besides the Finance Committee established earlier in 1872.[2] On 10 December 1884, it was moved by the Colonial Secretary that the Law Committee should consist of the Attorney-General, Colonial Treasurer and three unofficial members (Phineas Ryrie, F. D. Sassoon and Wong Shing), and the Public Works Committee of the Surveyor-General, Colonial Secretary, Registrar-General and two unofficial members (William Keswick and T. Jackson).

Bowen helped to give the reorganized Council additional status by printing its minutes together with annual *Departmental Reports* and other papers laid before the Council; thus began in 1884, the annual series of Hong Kong *Sessional Papers*.

Bowen was eager to set up an elective municipality, having set up many in Australia and New Zealand in the course of his long career as governor, but he concluded that it would be impossible in Hong Kong as the English ratepayers were so few in number that it was extremely unlikely that any would be elected;[3] he gave the number of ratepayers as 83 British, 647 Chinese and 98 others, chiefly Portuguese. He explained that though he admired the Chinese and had always shaped his course so as not to run counter to their national feelings, yet 'Chinese views, habits and customs respecting water-supply, sanitation, police, harbour regulations and most other political and social questions are widely different

---

[1] *Government Gazette*, 12 April 1884.

[2] At the Legislative Council meeting held on 27 August 1886, one of the Unofficials, A. P. MacEwen, asked how many times these committees had met, and referred to them as having been set up in 1883. But as the *Government Gazette* of that year make no reference to them, his memory was probably at fault.

[3] Sir George Bowen to Lord Stanley, 5 September 1885, No. 348, CO 129/222.

from those . . . in Europe' and this made it impossible to have
an elective municipality in charge of the health of a garrison town
and a harbour with $5\frac{1}{3}$ million tons of shipping, if the Chinese
predominated. He salved his conscience by saying that the
Legislative Council was really a municipal council and represented
the community, *now*, he emphasized, i.e. after his reforms.

He noted that the imposition of rates was vested in the Executive
Council and he altered this to secure that rating should come under
the control of Legislative Council, in the same way as ordinary
taxation. In the same letter Bowen enunciated the constitutional
doctrine that the official majority 'should not be used to control an
absolutely united unofficial minority especially in financial questions'. This issue was to come up in an acute form a few years later.

Bowen's advocacy of greater representation of the community
and greater power for the Legislative Council arose partly out of
his irritation at the amount of control which the Colonial Office
exercised over the colonial administration especially since the
coming of the telegraph. He particularly wanted a military adjutant
for the police and was annoyed when the proposal was rejected.
He had been a governor for twenty years and adopted the tone of
an elder statesman. His claim to have done more, in the short period
of less than three years that he had been in Hong Kong, than had
been done in any three years before, led an irreverent Downing
Street official to remark, 'Sir George Bowen blows his own trumpet
rather loudly'. Bowen in his dispatches used to criticize 'some
permanent gentlemen of the colonial department' and brought
upon himself a magisterial reproof from Lord Derby, who referred
to 'the very unusual language in which you have referred to the
Colonial Office . . . you are not justified in criticizing the conduct
of the Colonial Office as independent of the Secretary of State . . .
I am alone responsible for what is written to you'.[1]

Bowen became extraordinarily egotistical, and claimed an oracular
quality for his pronouncements; Hong Kong society enjoyed the
fun of this display of pretentiousness, but there was general relief
that he did not return in 1887 as had been intended. He was a keen
advocate of imperial federation and wanted all colonies represented
in the Parliament at Westminster. No one took him too seriously,
and yet perhaps despite himself, he made an important contribution
to the constitutional development of Hong Kong.

[1] Earl of Derby to Sir George Bowen, 8 September 1884, CO 129/216

CHAPTER VII

THE PETITION OF 1894
FOR REPRESENTATIVE GOVERNMENT

Financial Strains

SIR George Bowen left for England on leave in December 1885 and was allowed to retire without the formality of returning to his post. Nearly two years elapsed before his successor, Sir George William Des Vœux[1] arrived in Hong Kong. In the interval, W. H. Marsh again administered the government from December 1885 to April 1887, and Major General W. G. Cameron for the remaining few months before Des Vœux's arrival in the following October. Des Vœux was Governor 1887 to May 1891 and was followed, after an interval of six months, May-December 1891, during which time Major General Digby Barker administered the government, by Sir William Robinson,[2] who was Governor from 1891 to 1898.

After the reorganization of the Legislative Council by Sir George Bowen, the five unofficial members became extremely active in examining and criticizing government measures, particularly those concerning finance and public works, and some were debated with great acrimony. From these heated debates arose the demand for representative government, that is for a majority of elected members in the Legislative Council, which was made in a widely signed Petition by the ratepayers in 1894. Dissatisfaction was also partly financial; as in 1847, 1850 and 1864, the demand for a greater measure of self-government originated in resistance to increased taxation, actual or threatened. Before dealing with this Petition, a brief review of conditions in the Colony during the ten years 1884-94 will be helpful.

The Bowen reforms worked smoothly. Wong Shing was content to adopt a co-operative attitude which at least had the merit of

---

[1] Sir George William Des Vœux (1834-1909), of a Huguenot family. Balliol College; migrated to Canada, 1856; took law. Stipendiary Magistrate, British Guiana, 1863; Administrator of St. Lucia in 1869; Governor of Fiji, 1878-1885; Governor of Newfoundland, 1886; Governor of Hong Kong, 1887-91; then retired.

[2] Sir William Robinson (1836-1912). In 1854 joined the Colonial Office as a clerk. 1874 became Lieutenant-Governor of the Bahamas, and Governor, 1875; Governor of the Windward Islands, 1880; Governor of Trinidad, 1885; Governor of Hong Kong, 1891-98. Knighted, 1883.

demonstrating that no hazard was likely to result from having a Chinese representative permanently on the Legislative Council; when his six-year term was up in 1890, he asked not to be re-appointed.[1] His place was taken by Dr Ho Kai[2] who had been educated in England where he had been called to the Bar and also had qualified in medicine. He had been considered for a seat on the Council by Bowen in 1884, but had been rejected because he was young and too westernized.[3] He dressed as a European, was married to an English woman, and on that account was not at first acceptable to the Chinese as their representative on the Council. He proved himself a stronger character than his two Chinese predecessors and identified himself fully with the other unofficial members in a policy of opposition to the government. In August 1886, Marsh recommended John Bell-Irving of Jardine, Matheson & Co. for a seat on the Legislative Council in place of William Keswick of the same merchant house who went on leave, and in making it, he naïvely remarked to the Secretary of State, 'It seems to have been the custom since Hong Kong was a Colony for the senior partner in this, the largest mercantile firm in China, to have a seat in the Legislative Council and I have followed tradition';[4] the Jardine member used jokingly to be referred to outside the council chamber as 'the member for East Point', the latter being the site of the firm's wharves and godowns.

In August 1886, the unofficial members secured the publication of the proceedings of the Finance Committee of the Council. Alexander Palmer MacEwen, the Chamber of Commerce representative, moved 'that in future all matters of public interest, and more particularly the voting of public funds, be discussed openly in Council and not as heretofore at private meetings of the Finance Committee'.[5] The acting Attorney-General in reply proposed that

---

[1] F. Fleming to Lord Knutsford, 4 March 1890, No. 53, CO 129/244.

[2] Sir Kai Ho Kai 何啟 (1859–1914). Born in Hong Kong, son of Rev. Ho Tsun Shin of the London Missionary Society. Educated at the Government Central School and in England. Qualified as a doctor at Aberdeen University and St. Thomas Medical and Surgical College. Called to the Bar at Lincoln's Inn, 1881. Returned to Hong Kong, practised medicine, then in 1882 turned to the Bar. Founded the Alice Memorial Hospital in memory of his English wife and was one of the founders of the Hong Kong Medical College 1887. Served on many boards and committees. C.M.G., 1892. Member of Legislative Council, 1890–1914. Knighted, 1912.

[3] Sir George Bowen to Earl of Derby, 28 December 1883, No. 355, CO 129/213.

[4] W. H. Marsh to Secretary of State, 20 August 1886, No. 271, CO 129/228.

[5] Hong Kong Sessional Papers, 1886–87, p. 2.

it is unnecessary to interfere with existing practice which had been laid down as recently as 10 April 1884; this motion was carried by the official votes with assistance from Wong Shing, against the four remaining unofficials. However, it was decided to lay the minutes of that committee before the Council with any relevant minutes from the Governor, and from 7 January 1887, the minutes of the Finance Committee were printed with those of the Council. Though they contained little more than the bare record of decisions, this proceeding automatically ensured some publicity and indirectly strengthened the position of the unofficial members. In November 1887 Des Vœux went further and ruled that all meetings of the Finance Committee should be open to public unless a member moved that there be a closed session. The Public Works Committee and the Law Committee continued to meet in private until June 1891 and November 1897 respectively. By the Council's new standing orders which came into effect in July 1890, the Finance Committee was to consist of all the Council except the Governor, the Public Works Committee of the Surveyor-General, Colonial Secretary and three named unofficial members, and the Law Committee of the Attorney-General and four unofficials. Otherwise the revised standing orders of 1890 contained only minor changes, for example, the quorum was reduced to five, and, in voting resolutions, a bare majority instead of the former three-quarters was deemed sufficient. From 1890 the printed proceedings of the Finance Committee contained a fuller record of divisions and questions. An account of the proceedings of the Council and of its committees was also given in the Hong Kong *Hansard;* it is not known when this was first published but copies exist from 1890 onwards and are noted on the title page as being 'Reprinted from the *Hong Kong Daily Press*, revised by Members'; this continued until 1928 when it apparently became an official publication.

The annual session of the Council introduced and keenly supported by Bowen was dropped by Des Vœux. Bowen, now in retirement, wrote to Des Vœux privately in 1888[1] and induced Lord Knutsford the Secretary of State (1887–92) to raise the matter. Des Vœux explained[2] that there was no need for any annual session and recess, since all members lived in such close proximity, that

[1] Des Vœux, *My Colonial Service*, Vol. II, p. 275.
[2] Sir William Des Vœux to Lord Knutsford, 21 January 1889, No. 28, CO 129/241.

the formal opening and closing of the session tended to excite ridicule in such a small community, and that in presenting the annual estimates, the Governor had ample opportunity to make any review of government policy that might be necessary. Similarly, Des Vœux said he had given up the weekly meeting of the Executive Council and summoned it only when business warranted. The practice of having an annual session of the Legislative Council was revived by Sir William Robinson in 1893 and continued until 1901, each session opening in November with a speech by the Governor, and the introduction of the Appropriation Bill for the following year. The session usually closed in June but extra meetings were sometimes held later to transact urgent business. By 1902 these extra meetings had become so numerous that the idea of sessions was apparently dropped, and the Council met throughout the year.

In 1890 Des Vœux suggested that the Council should be increased by four members, two official and two unofficial. The proposal was made haphazardly and for no more compelling reason than his desire to promote to membership a young official, N. G. Mitchell-Innes, Registrar-General, and he naturally felt it was preferable to recommend an increase of two officials and a corresponding increase of two unofficials. For the second official he suggested the Police Magistrate. Lord Knutsford declined to entertain any increase, and Mitchell-Innes became a provisional member only, deputizing for a permanent member.

The financial stress which marked the years preceding the Petition of 1894 sprang from three sources, a particularly extensive programme of public works, the heavy demands upon the Colony for defence, and the fall in the value of silver causing a depreciation of the currency which was based on silver.

The need for and cost of, public works was quite exceptional. For nearly twenty years before Bowen, these had been much delayed. Sir Richard MacDonnell had to contend with a severe economic depression, a great financial set-back caused by the Hong Kong Mint fiasco,[1] and with trouble brought on himself by his legalization of gambling. Under his successor, the easy-going Kennedy, little was achieved, while Sir John Pope Hennessy caused

---

[1] A Hong Kong mint, proposed by Sir Hercules Robinson, began operations in May 1866 and closed in April 1868 having made a loss of almost $440,000.

further delay by his administrative ineptitude and unwillingness to take any action that might give offence to the Chinese.

By 1883 therefore, the provision of needed public works of all kinds was much in arrear and it was one of Bowen's first tasks to put in hand an exceptionally heavy programme of public works the most important of which were the Tai Tam waterworks estimated at $600,000, a new gaol at $400,000, a new Central School building at $100,000, five other schools at $24,000, the Observatory at $19,000, a lunatic asylum at $9,500, Police barracks and stations at $135,000, and a sea-wall and Water Police station at $35,000—in all $1,323,500. The water scheme though essential, was costly as it involved constructing a tunnel through the hills from reservoirs on the south side of the island. The Home Government, following the prison reform legislation in England of 1885, had pressed for some years for a new gaol to relieve the overcrowding that was reported each year. The unofficials all opposed the vote for a new gaol, and the Chinese member, Dr Ho Kai, particularly argued against the separate cell system as being unsuited to the Chinese temperament and, in 1893, influential members of the Chinese community signed a memorial against the gaol extension. The opposition was so strong that the most that Robinson could secure was $96,000 for extensions to the existing gaol and even this limited sum was not voted until the autumn of 1893. The prolonged dispute over the gaol and the Imperial Government's insistence on more humane standards of gaol accommodation did much to annoy the unofficials, who were less tender towards the Chinese criminal class and more familiar with the primitive conditions in which so many Chinese lived.

There was yet another serious difficulty. The increase in the Chinese population and their spilling over into the European areas brought problems of sanitation. As a result of complaints from the military, Osbert Chadwick, a civil engineer formerly in the army, was sent out in 1882, and produced Hong Kong's first report on public health.[1] He recommended an extensive public works programme to implement the sanitary measures which he considered urgent, without, as he put it, 'waiting for the necessity to be demonstrated by the irresistible logic of a fever epidemic'. Chad-

---

[1] 18 July 1882 Mr Chadwick's *Report on the sanitary condition of Hong Kong with appendices and plans*, Colonial Office, November 1882, Eastern No. 38.

wick's words were prophetic and little enough was done until the outbreak of bubonic plague in 1894. The chief sanitary works were, the Tai Tam waterworks which has already been referred to, and which had been shelved by Hennessy; a new central market for the more hygienic handling of food, estimated to cost $150,000, the Causeway Bay reclamation, $300,000, the reclamation 'of a pestilent and foetid swamp at Yaumati', provision of dust-bins, carts, latrines, $43,158, and a new and improved sewage scheme for the City of Victoria, $46,550. Additional expenses were incurred with the appointment of sanitary inspectors and other supervisory staff, and the compensation payments in rebuilding old insanitary properties. Opinions differed as to the need of all this expenditure on sanitary improvement. Osbert Chadwick had written in his report that the Government in Hong Kong ' . . . has allowed to grow up in a new city . . . a Chinese quarter, more overcrowded, more filthy, more deficient in all the primary elements of health and decency than any quarter of Canton . . .'. Yet Dr Ho Kai, the Chinese member of the Sanitary Board (see p. 148), declared in 1887 'Hong Kong as it now stands is a paradise, a model of cleanliness . . .', compared to Canton or Kowloon City. In 1890 a scheme for a complete reconstruction of the sewage arrangements in Victoria to cost $282,500 was voted, over the protests of the unofficial members of the Legislative Council, who did not think that the expenditure of this enormous sum was desirable. Chadwick returned to the Colony in 1889 to draw up plans and supervise their execution, and he was appointed a special member of the Executive Council for this purpose. In 1890, public works were voted in two sections, extraordinary and recurrent, and this division continued for some years because of the unprecedented programme of capital expenditure.

Another source of financial dissatisfaction were the heavy demands made upon the Colony for defence. The old *pax britannica* in the Far East which had been a concomitant of British mercantile, financial, and naval dominance was beginning to function less effectively, for other European powers now wished to play a more influential role. France, after her gains in Tonking following her hostilities with China of 1884–5, aimed at extending her influence in Yünnan and the southern provinces of China; Russia in alliance with France after 1893, had ambitions in Korea, Manchuria and Mongolia and in 1891 started to build the Trans-Siberian Railway.

Imperial Germany, born in the triumphs of the France-Prussian War of 1870 and, after 1890, free from the moderating influence of Bismarck, was expanding her trade and influence in the Far East. Japan's turn was to come after her victory over China in the war of 1894–95.

To strengthen imperial defence, Great Britain set up an Imperial Defence Committee to plan defence measures. Its leisurely enquiries extended over many years, and one of its demands was for greater contributions from the colonies. They were asked to undertake and pay for local defence works and to contribute to imperial defence as a whole. In the case of Hong Kong plans were drawn up for the construction of fortifications, ear-marking of defence sites and the raising of a locally recruited force, the Hong Kong Regiment, composed mainly of local Indians under regular British officers. In September 1884, the Colony was asked to pay £56,000 for defence works in addition to the normal annual military contribution of £20,000. The outbreak of Sino-French hostilities in 1884, with the fear that Russia might join, made defence preparations in that year a matter of urgency. Bowen panicked during the hostilities and made so many demands for improved defence, that he brought upon himself a rebuke from the Earl of Derby that the Home Government 'was thoroughly aware of what is necessary for the defence of the Colony'.

A special sum of £56,000 ($280,000) was voted by the Legislative Council in December 1884, but only on the understanding that the latest type weapons would be supplied.[1] Next year, 1885, more military works were proposed which would cost the Colony further £54,000. Bowen rightly complained that a fixed local defence plan determined by a local defence committee, was a necessity, since each Commander Royal Engineers had different ideas on the subject of fortifications. Even this sum was increased to £60,375 and after much protest was voted by the Legislative Council in March 1886 and only on condition that it was the final sum for defence; with the £56,000 previously voted, it made a total of £116,000 ($580,000). As these sums could not be met out of revenue, a loan was inevitable. This was a source of further trouble since the Home Government refused the proposal of the unofficial members to raise the loan locally through The Hongkong and

---

[1] Sir George Bowen to Earl of Derby, 2 May 1885, No. 206, CO 129/221 and reply.

Shanghai Banking Corporation at 6% when it could be floated in London at 4 or 4½%. On 12 March 1886 the Loan Ordinance was passed raising £200,000 in debentures at 4½% on the London market.

Then in 1889, the Home Government decided to double the annual military contribution from £20,000 to £40,000 on the ground that the increased defence works needed an increased garrison.[1] The defence burden was now regarded as excessive and there was an immediate protest, the reply to which made it clear that the increase was demanded because the Colony could afford it and not because of the increased garrison as local opinion had been led to suppose. The doubled military contribution was voted unanimously on 26 March 1890, but after the vote certain resolutions were passed by the Council that, *(i)* the vote had been passed in the belief that the increased garrison would comprise 3,018 men of whom 2,525 would be Europeans; *(ii)* no demand for payment should be made until the garrison had been in fact strengthened; and *(iii)* the military held 337 acres of land in the Colony, valued at 3 million dollars, which in itself was a valuable contribution to the cost of defence. European troops 'of the line' had been promised, but they turned out to be a Madras regiment and the Colony, by an oversight, had not been informed of the change. This led the Officer Administering the Government remark to Lord Knutsford that the Imperial Government should submit the necessary measures 'in a frank and open manner'.[2] On 1 December 1890, the unofficial members again protested against imposing the increased military contribution until the increased garrison had been sent. Knutsford[3] rejected the protest on the ground that the increased contribution had been fixed in January 1890 at 17% of the revenue of the year 1888, and that the sum now demanded was only 11½% of the current revenue; he observed that the original military contribution of £20,000 first imposed in 1863 constituted 16½% of the revenue of that year. There was a further sharp protest in May 1891 when a half of the military contribution which had been held over from 1890 was voted by the Legislative Council, though it transpired that in fact

[1] Lord Knutsford to Sir William Des Vœux, 21 October 1889, No. 207, CO 129/242.

[2] F. Fleming to Lord Knutsford, 10 September 1890, No. 327, CO 129/246.

[3] Lord Knutsford to Sir William Des Vœux, 7 March 1891, No. 47, CO 129/249.

it had already been paid by Des Vœux on his own authority. As late as March 1894, Sir William Robinson was still urging a reduction in the military contribution.

This greatly increased bill for defence came at a particularly inopportune time when the silver dollar was subject to serious depreciation following the fall in the world price of silver. It declined in value from 4/1¼ in 1876 to 2/1½ in 1896 and to 1/11½ in 1899, and Hong Kong, China and all countries with a currency based on silver, were the victims. The effects of this depreciation were serious. Payments and remittances overseas except to those countries with a similar silver standard, were made more onerous; imports from the West and from the United States cost more and raised the cost of living; and retirement pensions payable in dollars were reduced in value in Britain. To meet a demand for increased salaries for the government officials, a committee consisting of the unofficial members of the Legislative Council recommended in December 1889 that the salaries of the British officials should be placed on a sterling basis and that other officials should get a 20% rise, except coolies and labourers whose wages were considered to be already in excess of those they would receive in China. Lord Knutsford would not accept a sterling basis for the government salaries, but agreed to a 35% increase for staff recruited from Britain and a 20% increase for those locally recruited. These increases were duly voted by the Legislative Council in 1890 to take effect in 1891. In April 1891 Thomas Whitehead, the manager of The Chartered Bank, and the most active unofficial member of the Council,[1] proposed that the salary increases should be withdrawn because the Colony could no longer afford them. When Des Vœux refused on the ground that the increases had already been voted, Whitehead urged the Secretary of State to withhold his sanction. In November 1892 the appropriations embodying the salary increases were carried by the official majority against the unanimous votes of the unofficial members. At the next meeting of the Council in December the unofficial members protested that the vote was unconstitutional and that the Appropriations Ordinance for 1893 was illegal because

[1] Thomas Henderson Whitehead (1851–1933). Entered the service of The Chartered Bank; Manager of the Hong Kong Branch, 1883. Superintendent of its Far Eastern branches, 1893. London Manager, 1902. Member of the Hong Kong Legislative Council 1890–1902. Member of the Hong Kong Executive Council 1902.

the officials had a personal interest in voting their own salary increases. The Marquis of Ripon, Secretary of State for the Colonies, 1892–95, did not uphold this protest because it would have given the unofficials control of all business by refusing to vote salaries. Since the appropriations were being carried against the wishes of the unofficials, the latter in January 1893 embodied in a memorial to Lord Ripon their protest against the Appropriations Ordinance and asked for a commission of enquiry into the Colony's finances. Lord Ripon in rejecting these representations, replied[1] that the revenue had shown a rise of 76% between 1884 and 1892, whereas the cost of the salaries of the establishment had increased in that period by only 37%, and pointed out that the increase recommended in 1889 had been unanimously recommended by the unofficials themselves. He admitted that the unofficials 'may be regarded as in some degree the special guardians of the public purse', and to soften the blow of his refusal he suggested a Retrenchment Committee, consisting of the unofficial members 'and one or two other government officers'.

Robinson appointed in August 1893 a Retrenchment Committee of three officials and three unofficial members of the Legislative Council with the Chief Justice as chairman. Whitehead objected to its composition as contrary to the Secretary of State's instructions and demanded a majority of unofficials. The Governor reluctantly agreed, but then found that the Chief Justice refused to preside over such a committee. Robinson thought it essential to have Whitehead on the Committee, but Whitehead refused to serve except on his own terms. The Retrenchment Committee of three members, none of whom were officials and only two of whom were unofficial members of the Legislative Council, was eventually constituted in 1894 and suggested economies by amalgamating posts.

The demand for representative government must be seen and judged against this background of heavy expenditure, all of which came in a period of declining value of the silver dollar and much of which was controversial and imposed on the Colony from without. This situation drove the unofficial members more easily into the role of a constitutional opposition.

They had fallen foul of successive Secretaries of State on many important issues, for example, the doubling of the defence con-

[1] Lord Ripon to Sir William Robinson, 21 April 1893, No. 71, CO 129/258.

tribution in 1889, raising a public loan on the local money market, the increased government officials' salaries, the Retrenchment Committee and better gaol accommodation, with the result that liberation from control by the Secretary of State was sought by means of constitutional reform.

The Petition of 1894

Matters came to a head in 1892 over the officials' salaries and in December of that year, Sir William Robinson wrote home[1] giving his view that the real reason for the unofficials wanting to reduce the officials' salaries was not lack of finance but 'soreness over the increased military contribution', and resentment over the Secretary of State insisting on a new gaol with better accommodation. He said a small knot of English residents wanted constitutional change and hoped to secure it by persistent opposition. They did not want elections but hoped to have power through an unofficial majority of nominated members, and, led by T. H. Whitehead, tried to get their own way by threatening to resign as a body; for example, they all threatened to resign over the question of a new gaol. Robinson observed that Hong Kong could not cease to be Crown Colony as it was important to the British Empire from every point of view and there was 'the possibility, remote perhaps, of China attempting to regain it'. The non-Chinese were a mere handful, who did not settle in the Colony and with interests often antagonistic to the Chinese. He thought that the existing system of government 'governs in the interest of the whole community and especially safeguards the rights of the indigenous population', and that there could be no change without transferring power to the people. He alleged that Whitehead did not want representative government, but rather that 'a very small alien minority should rule the indigenous majority'; and to achieve this he was endeavouring to reduce the present form of government to an absurdity. Robinson ended by saying he proposed to let things take their course and if the unofficials resigned, to fill their places, or if he could not find suitable candidates, to leave them vacant.

On this dispatch appears an interesting minute from the Colonial Office, which noted that Jamaica, Honduras and Mauritius all had

[1] Sir William Robinson to Lord Ripon (Confidential), 6 December 1892, CO 129/256.

representative institutions in which voting rights were exercised irrespective of colour; this assumed that the negro was capable of participating in representative institutions 'whereas it is common ground between us and Mr Whitehead that an ordinary Chinaman is not'.

In June 1894 Whitehead, supported by Paul Chater and Ho Kai but not by J. J. Keswick or E. R. Belilios among the unofficial members of the Legislative Council, organized a petition widely signed by the Hong Kong ratepayers to the Secretary of State asking for constitutional reform. The petitioners pointed to the prosperity of Hong Kong, with its population of a quarter of a million, its public revenue of two million dollars and its annual trade estimated at £40 millions. They affirmed that though this thriving community had been created by British merchants, traders, and shipowners, these men had only a small share in the government of the Colony because the Legislative Council was controlled by the official majority and that despite the fact, as they pointed out, that the senior officials often were men with only a short period of residence in the Colony and so unable to judge its needs.

They pleaded that many Crown Colonies were given more liberal treatment by having unofficial members in the Executive Council and an unofficial majority in the Legislative Council and they asked for similar treatment in Hong Kong. They agreed that they must be subject to the Imperial Parliament and to the Queen in Council, but argued that it was the 'common right of Englishmen to manage their local affairs and control the expenditure of the Colony where imperial considerations were not involved'. The petitioners made two specific demands; they asked for 'free election of representatives of British nationality in the Legislative Council', and 'a majority of such representatives in the Legislative Council'. They asked also for freedom of debate for the official members.

Sir William Robinson sent a copy of the petition to Lord Ripon together with his comments.[1] He agreed there was much prosperity in Hong Kong but questioned the assumption that this had been achieved despite the system of Crown Colony government. He thought that the formation of a municipal council would improve the administration of local affairs, but doubted if enough gentlemen were available in Hong Kong to form such a Council. He advised

---

[1] Sir William Robinson to Lord Ripon, 5 June 1894, No. 133, CO 129/263.

as a concession that the unofficial element in the Legislative Council should be slightly increased and that unofficial members should be added to the Executive Council, and suggested J. J. Keswick or Thomas Jackson as the first unofficial member of the Executive Council 'in the absence of a suitable Chinese'; but he added that unofficial members on the Executive Council might be an anomaly because they could not be controlled.

Lord Ripon treated the Petition with respect in his lengthy and detailed reply, in which he made some important comments on the problem of government in Hong Kong at that time. He referred to the population figures of the 1891 census which showed 211,000 Chinese out of a total of 221,400 and observed that 'under the protection of the British Government, Hong Kong has become a Chinese rather than a British community', and that Chinese settlement 'has been one main element in its prosperity'. The Europeans and Americans numbered 8,500, but only 4,200 were civilians, and of these only 1,450 were British, of whom only 800 were male adults. The tendency was for the Colony's trade to pass more and more into Chinese hands and clearly the mass of the population, the Chinese, had prospered under the existing form of government and in any scheme of change, their interests had to be carefully watched. He argued Hong Kong had 'prospered as a British Colony, but in great measure because it has been British Colony', though it owed much to its geographical position and to British protection, and to its harbour. There was plenty of evidence that the Hong Kong government possessed strength and justice, but Hong Kong, he said, differed from other Crown Colonies like Cyprus, Malta and Mauritius, in that it possessed no traditions, no history, and no record of political usages or constitutional rights, and 'it has few life-long residents, whether British or Chinese'.

He criticized the petitioners' demands as lacking in clarity. They asked for the free election of representatives of British nationality, but made no reference to the qualifications of the voters. If the petitioners intended that only those from the British Islands should vote and be elegible for election, this would exclude nine-tenths of the entire population, and the military would in any case swamp the civilian portion. He dismissed the claim to have a majority of elected representatives as merely a corollary to elections. Free debate by officials was impossible because paid servants could not be allowed to oppose the government, but like all supporters of an administration, must support government measures or resign.

With regard to the demand for greater local control, Lord Ripon said this pointed to municipal government as in the Straits and Ceylon, but the difficulty in Hong Kong was to distinguish between colonial and municipal affairs, and he was not sure whether a municipality was what the petitioners wanted. He affirmed that the policy of the Colonial Office was always that 'the claims and interests and even the prejudices of each colony' should be 'clearly set out and fully considered'. He thought that Hong Kong was not suited to any form of self-government because it was an imperial station with imperial interests, on the borders of a foreign land. The petitioners wanted control by a small oligarchy of some 800 persons, but, he went on, 'I consider that the well-being of the large majority of the inhabitants is more likely to be safeguarded by the Crown Colony system under which as far as possible no distinction is made of rank or race, than by a representation which would leave the bulk of the population wholly unrepresented'.

Ripon outlined three possible courses. First, there could be additions to the Legislative Council, but if the unofficial element was increased, the official side must be proportionately increased. He thought that, on this point, a second Chinese representative appeared to be the most equitable course, but the petitioners did not want this, neither did J. J. Keswick who had suggested that one European unofficial member of the Executive Council might be appointed. He said he was willing to sanction this, but the petitioners must remember that a Chinese might be appointed since 'it would be invidious and inequitable to lay down that Chinese subjects of the Queen shall be debarred from appointment to the Executive Council'. None of the other eastern colonies had unofficial members of the Executive Council, and Ripon suggested, as a second possibility, that as the unofficial members of the Legislative Council were already consulted, they might be invited to take part in the Executive Council discussions, but not to have seats. Thirdly, he said 'with regard to the institution of a municipal council, I frankly say that I should like to see one established at Hong Kong', and he suggested that the Sanitary Board might develop into a satisfactory municipal council. In any case, he said, because of the present crisis in the Far East, there could be no constitutional change until the future was tolerably clear.

Lord Ripon had the better of this exchange largely because the petitioners were not arguing for representative government as such, for they certainly did not want Chinese representation; their main object was to prevent excessive taxation at the bidding of the Secretary of State and, to a less extent, of the local government. That was why their petition was carefully vague; they did not and could not argue for full representative government which would have handed the Colony over to the Chinese. They wanted an oligarchy of some 800 voters and defended this illiberal proposal by appealing to liberal arguments which lost their force by its racial exclusiveness. They still hankered after a Council similar to the Shanghai Municipal Council, which at that time denied the Chinese any representation.

The solution of a municipal council commended by Lord Ripon and the Governor did not find favour with the petitioners for the reason just given. Their object was self-government, not as a principle, but as a means of checking what were held to be inequitable financial demands. A municipal council would not have given them the substance of control. Whitehead went on leave in 1894 and saw Lord Ripon at the Colonial Office but failed to induce him to alter his view that Hong Kong must remain a Crown Colony. There was talk of replacing the Sanitary Board by a municipal council, but it came to nothing.

Lord Ripon in a confidential letter to Sir William Robinson[1] agreed that if the unofficial members of the Legislative Council would not accept a municipal council, then as an alternative, there should be two unofficial members nominated to the Executive Council and, considering the extent of the Chinese contribution to Hong Kong, and the undesirability of making any distinctions of race, and because, too, of the great importance of sanitary questions, that one of them ought to be a Chinese. He also thought there should be an addition to the Legislative Council of one official and two unofficial members, to make a total of eight officials and seven unofficials, exclusive of the Governor. The General should have the new official seat, and since the Chinese element was clearly under-represented, one of the two additional unofficial members should be a Chinese. The second unofficial seat should go to a class or interest unrepresented or inadequately represented,

[1] Lord Ripon to Sir William Robinson (Confidential), 28 June 1895, CO 129/266.

for example 'some European representative of retail trade or skilled labour'. The Governor in reply doubted[1] if the proposed increase in the Legislative Council would add to its efficiency. He also opposed having a Chinese on the Executive Council as he 'could not and would not be an independent member', and an Anglo-Chinese representative like Ho Kai, would not have the confidence of the Chinese. He thought the Chinese did not understand representative government. He considered everybody would be satisfied if the senior unofficial member of the Legislative Council became a member of the Executive Council—as long as it was not Whitehead or Francis,[2] he cautiously added, for they were his principal opponents. Robinson reported in the previous May that he could not find any real desire among the inhabitants of the Colony for any change in its constitution, and he said there was no interest in elections, and instanced the election for the unofficial members of the Sanitary Board held in June 1894, when only 25 people voted out of a total electorate of 500. This was a misleading deduction because that election was uncontested (see page 153).

Robinson was guilty of inconsistency because he himself held a plebiscite of the British community in June 1896 on the subject of whether the reconstituted Sanitary Board should have an official or an unofficial majority.

In 1895 the Unionist Party returned to power in Britain with Joseph Chamberlain as Secretary of State for the Colonies, so the final decision regarding the Hong Kong Ratepayers' Petition rested with him. On 29 May 1896 Chamberlain gave his views, which were very similar to those of Lord Ripon. He wrote

'As Hong Kong is to remain a Crown Colony, no useful purpose would be served but, on the contrary, a considerable amount of needless irritation would be caused, by balancing even the unofficial members and the officials. But, having regard to the fact that, in the absence of the Governor, the Officer Commanding the troops will in future administer the government, I consider that it would be of advantage that he should be a member of the Legislative Council; and, if he is added to it, I am willing to add one unofficial member to the unofficial bench. Who the latter should be, and what special

[1] Sir William Robinson to Joseph Chamberlain (Confidential), 16 August 1895, CO 129/268.

[2] J. J. Francis (?–1901). Acting Puisne Judge, 1879. Q.C., 1886. In 1894 was presented by the Hong Kong Government with a silver inkstand for his services on the special plague committee of the Sanitary Board, but he returned it to Sir William Robinson as 'ludicrously inadequate'.

interest, if any, he should represent, I leave to the Governor to de-
termine. I may observe, however, that the Chinese community is the
element which is least represented, while it is also by far the most
numerous, and that I should regard as valuable any step which tended to attach them more closely to the British connexion and to increase
their practical interest in public affairs'. On the question of appointing unofficial members to the Executive Council, his judgment was
' . . . in view of the fact that the Colonial Government was dis-
charging municipal duties, representatives of the citizens might fairly
be given a place on the Executive'. He proposed that ' . . . the
Executive Council shall in future include two unofficial members to
be selected at the discretion of the Governor. It is obviously desirable
that they should, as a rule, be chosen from among the unofficial
members of the Legislative Council, and the choice should, and no
doubt will be, inspired by consideration of personal merit, and have
no reference to the particular class or race to which the persons
chosen belong'.

The final upshot was that the Legislative Council was increased
by two members, one official member, the General Officer Commanding, and one unofficial member. The latter, appointed in July
1896, was Wei Yuk.[1] Two first unofficial members of the Executive
Council were J. Bell-Irving of Jardine, Matheson & Co., and C.
P. Chater, and they took their seats, on 22 October 1896. In spite
of all the trouble he had given, Whitehead was recommended by
Robinson in September 1896 for a further term of six years as
member of the Legislative Council, and this was confirmed by the
Colonial Office with the ironic comment 'H.M. opposition must
be confirmed'.

The demand for greater representation was possibly stimulated
by the activities of the China Association which was founded in
London in April 1889 by old China hands such as William
Keswick, Sir Alfred Dent and retired officials like Sir Thomas
Wade and Sir George Bowen. By 1895 it had a membership of 400.
Committees of the Association were set up in Shanghai and Hong
Kong in 1892 because the Chambers of Commerce at those two
centres were too cosmopolitan to be a satisfactory reflection of
purely British interests. For long the China Association had the
ear of the Foreign Office.[2]

---

[1] Wei Yuk 韋玉 (1849–1921). Born in Hong Kong, son of compradore of
the Chartered Mercantile Bank of India, London and China. First Chinese to
be educated in Britain (Dollar Academy). J.P., 1883. Member of Legislative
Council, 1896–1914. Married the daughter of Wong Shing. C.M.G., 1918.
Knighted, 1919.

[2] See N. A. Pelcovits, *Old China Hands and the Foreign Office*, passim.

CHAPTER VIII

CONSTITUTIONAL DEVELOPMENTS IN THE 20TH CENTURY TO THE OUTBREAK OF THE WAR IN THE PACIFIC, 1898–1941

The New Territories

IN 1898 an area of 365½ square miles, consisting of a portion of the Chinese mainland lying immediately to the north of the Colony, and some 235 adjacent islands to the east, south and west, was leased to Great Britain for 99 years; first referred to as the New Territory, it soon acquired and has since retained the designation *New Territories*.

Its acquisition was part of that scramble for concessions which characterized European relations with China following the Sino-Japanese War of 1894–95, which revealed China's military weakness. The threatened anarchy could be solved by restriction of claims by agreement or by carving out spheres of influence at the expense of China. Great Britain was faced with the dilemma of attempting to maintain her traditional open door policy or of joining in the scramble. The acquisition of the New Territories must therefore be seen in the light of these conditions, as part of what was essentially a European diplomatic struggle. Russia secured Port Arthur, and railway concessions in Manchuria; Germany, Kiaochow and concessions in Shantung; France, a rectification of the Tonking frontier and Kwangchowan; and Britain secured the lease of Weihaiwei as long as Russia remained in Port Arthur, the lease of the New Territories and the opening of the West River to navigation. The Powers also secured from China certain declarations of non-alienation regarding areas in which they were particularly interested.

The reason assigned for the extension of the Colony in the preamble of the 'Convention between Great Britain and China respecting an Extension of Hong Kong Territory signed at Peking, 9 June 1898' was: 'whereas it has for many years past been recognised that an extension of Hong Kong territory is necessary for the proper defence and protection of the Colony . . .'[1]. By the

---

[1] The Convention is printed in Hertslet's *China Treaties*, Vol. 1, p. 120; also *Parliamentary Papers*, Treaty Series, No. 16 (1898).

Convention the boundaries of the extension were only 'indicated generally' on an annexed map, and provision was made for their more exact determination after 'proper surveys had been made by officials appointed by the two governments'. It was agreed that within Kowloon City 'the Chinese officials now stationed there shall continue to exercise jurisdiction except so far as may be inconsistent with the military requirements for the defence of Hong Kong', and to assist this retention of Chinese jurisdiction in Kowloon City, Chinese officials and people were allowed to use the road from Kowloon to Hsinan,[1] and Chinese warships and merchant vessels were allowed to use the landing place near the city. There was to be no expulsion of the Chinese or expropriation of their land within the leased territory and land required for public use or military fortification was to be paid for, and Chinese warships had navigation rights in Deep Bay and Mirs Bay. Subject to these stipulations Britain had sole jurisdiction over the leased territory.

It is clear from these clauses which allowed a Chinese garrison to continue at Kowloon City, and Chinese warships to use the landing place there, and to use the two large bays the waters of which were included within the boundary of the leased territory, that defence of the Colony was envisaged not against China, but against attack by one or more European powers. This is further borne out by the instruction given to the Governor not to obstruct the passage of Chinese Imperial troops through the leased territory for the purpose of conducting operations against the revolutionary reformers at Canton.[2] The boundary commission, composed of J. H. S. Lockhart, the Colonial Secretary, and Wang Tsin-hsien[3] representing China, fixed the boundary along a line joining the heads of Deep Bay and Mirs Bay, following the Shum Chun river for much of its course, and to include the islands of Lantao, Cheung Chau, Lamma and many smaller ones. The local British authorities claimed Shum Chun, on the Chinese side of the river, and also Shataukok on Mirs Bay; these two disputed points were referred to the respective national authorities at Peking, where it was agreed that Shum Chun be excluded from the leased area and the boundary at Shataukok should run along the middle of its main street.

[1] San On 新安, in Cantonese.

[2] Telegram, Joseph Chamberlain to Sir Henry Blake, 17 October 1900, CO 129/301.

[3] Wong Tsin Shin in Cantonese.

The assumption of British authority in the New Territories met with opposition. The Chinese villagers with their traditional peasant life evinced a natural hostility to outsiders. Rumours that the British would seize all the land were spread by Hong Kong Chinese with the object of bringing down the price and enabling them to buy it up cheaply. The continued functioning of Chinese customs stations set up by agreement with the British in 1886[1] to combat opium smuggling also caused difficulties. The take-over was arranged for 17 April 1899 but the British advance parties were fired on and confronted with other evidence of preparations for resistance, with the result that troops were sent and the British flag was raised on the 16th. The sporadic opposition ceased ten days later.

Taking over the New Territories posed not a military but an administrative problem. An Order in Council of 20 October 1898[2] declared the Territories to be 'part and parcel of Her Majesty's Colony of Hong Kong in like manner and for all intents and purposes as if they had originally formed part of the said Colony', and the Governor and Legislative Council were to make laws for the peace, order, and good government there; all laws and ordinances in force in Hong Kong were also after a declared date to apply to the New Territories. The British Government soon decided that the defence requirements of the Colony were incompatible with maintenance of Chinese control of Kowloon City and the city was taken over in 1899. This was done by the Order in Council of 27 December 1899,[3] where it was stated that

> The exercise of jurisdiction by the Chinese officials in the city of Kowloon having been found to be inconsistent with the military requirements for the defence of Hong Kong . . . The city of Kowloon shall be . . . part and parcel of H.M.'s Colony of Hong Kong . . . as if it had originally formed part of the said Colony.

This unilateral declaration, though in accordance with the terms of the 1898 Convention, has never been accepted by the Cantonese.

The extension of British territory once more brought to the fore the problem of government in Hong Kong. The British tradition

---

[1] The Agreement of 1886. See the author's *A History of Hong Kong*, Oxford University Press, London 1958, p. 213.

[2] Hertslet, *China Treaties*, Vol. 2, p. 728.

[3] *Ibid*, p. 749.

was not to interfere with local custom and usage as far as these were compatible with peace, order and good government. The undertaking that had been held out in 1842 when the Island was taken over, and repeated in 1860 when part of Kowloon peninsula was ceded by the Convention of Peking, that Chinese law would continue to apply, was again given. Yet Chinese law was quite inadequate to deal with the mass of disputed claims to ownership of land, inaccurate or even spurious title deeds, and holdings with no recognizable boundaries.

These traditional problems of Chinese land tenure re-appeared on a larger scale in 1899 in connection with the administration of the New Territories. Major General Wilsone Black, the Officer Administering the Government, suggested in August 1898 that the new area should be administered separately from the Colony and placed under a Resident on the ground that the Chinese there needed a more personal form of government. The decision devolved on Sir Henry Blake[1] who assumed office as Governor of Hong Kong in November 1898. His first suggestion was to appoint F. H. May, the Captain Superintendent of Police, as the resident magistrate, but Chamberlain would not sanction the appointment without further examination of what was needed. Some decision had to be taken because of crime, insecurity, extortion, disease, fever especially malaria and clan fights which were frequently resorted to in the settlement of village disputes. Blake felt that it was impossible to govern the New Territories' Chinese on exactly the same lines as the more urbanized Chinese in the City of Victoria, especially as Chinese officials had in the past exercised little control beyond exacting annual payments.

Sir Henry Blake's policy was to interfere as little as possible, to recognize the traditional way of life in the New Territories and adopt the Chinese customary methods of administration for the maintenance of order and the collection of Crown revenue. He hoped to govern the leased area through the village elders and reduce the number of British officials to a minimum.

Blake divided the New Territories into districts and sub-districts each under a committee composed of village elders who were to regulate the affairs of the village and maintain order. He visited

[1] Sir Henry Arthur Blake, 1840-1918. Born in Limerick, Governor of Bahamas, 1884-87; Governor of Newfoundland, 1887-88; of Jamaica, 1889-97; Governor of Hong Kong, 1898-1903; Governor of Ceylon, 1903-07. Knighted, 1888.

each district, met the elders and explained at length his administrative plans and the function of the committees. He promised to work for economic improvement, and warned against the collection of money except the authorized rates and taxes. He promised that there would be no interference with Chinese custom, except that all punishment must be in accordance with the law as laid down, and the elders would be held responsible for all rioting. He admitted that there was much crime but promised that normally all residents would be protected. Land rent would continue as Crown rent, but all other customary and monopolistic dues were abolished. To implement his promises Blake was forced to spend much more on policing than he anticipated, and piratical attacks from the sea forced him to double the water police. The Committees were organized under a Local Communities Ordinance, No. 11 of 18 April 1899, and identified as closely as possible with the geographical divisions long recognized by the Chinese inhabitants themselves. A sub-district usually comprised a single valley with its self-contained group of villages and hamlets, or a single island; Lantao Island which is larger than Hong Kong Island was divided into three sub-districts. An exception was also made in respect of that part of the leased territory generally called New Kowloon, which was adjacent to British Kowloon ceded in 1860, and with it formed a well-defined peninsula lying to the south of a range of hills marking it off from the rest of the New Territories; it was thought best that New Kowloon should not be treated differently from the rest of the Colony 'especially as the inhabitants are well acquainted with the laws and customs of Hong Kong proper'.[1] The island of Lamma, on account of its proximity to Aberdeen was similarly excluded from the operations of the Local Communities Ordinance. In all, there were 8 districts and 48 sub-districts with 597 villages and an estimated population of 100,000.

The villagers were asked to recommend the names of those whom they wished to act as sub-district committee-men; these were allocated on the basis of one committee member for each hundred of the population, except that each village with a population of from 50 to 100 persons was allowed one committee-man, and similarly groups of smaller hamlets with a combined population of 50 to 100 persons were allowed one committee-man.

[1] Report on the New Territory by J. H. S. Lockhart, 7 February 1900, submitted to the Governor. Hong Kong *Sessional Papers* 1900, p. 252.

The committee-men as a rule are those who possess influence in their own immediate neighbourhood, whose advice is listened to, and whose lead is generally followed. The wisdom of affecting with responsibility those to whom the people have been accustomed to look for leadership and of using them to elucidate the objects of government, is evident.[1]

The appointment of chairmen of these committees was delayed pending more experience. The Local Communities Ordinance also provided for local tribunals composed of elders to deal with petty cases but they never functioned satisfactorily because of the reluctance of the elders to co-operate. In the annual report on the New Territories for 1902,[2] Blake had an illuminating comment on the working of the system of indirect rule. He said that though the village elders had been appointed district elders and had been given some judicial power to deal with petty cases in their own districts, he had to confess his surprise that the elders' courts were not appreciated or used by the people, and that

as a matter of fact the Elders displayed no anxiety to take the duties upon themselves, and from the beginning the community showed perfect confidence in Mr. Lockhart and subsequently in Mr. Hallifax who is now acting as police magistrate . . . but whose practical work is more often that of an arbitrator, whose decision is accepted without demur.

The fact that there was a European magistrate with concurrent jurisdiction and to whom appeal could be made may well have convinced the elders that to attempt any judicial work on their own was futile, especially in a voluntary capacity.

All occupiers of land had to register their holdings, but the settlement of land claims proved so thorny a task that it was placed in the hands of a specially created land court set up by Ordinance No. 8 of 28 March 1900. On this matter the Secretary of State ruled that the enquiry into land ownership should not be too technical and that due regard should be paid to long occupation and evidence of improvement. To assist in deciding claims, a new survey of the New Territories was carried out and the existing property boundaries were found to be hopelessly inaccurate. The western boundry of the New Territories too had to be slightly adjusted because the existing Admiralty chart was also found to be incorrect, and the 113° 59′ 29·7″ meridian which formed that boundary did

[1] *Ibid.*
[2] Hong Kong *Sessional Papers* 1902, p. 348.

not strike the Chinese and Lantao coasts as expected. A team of surveyors from India undertook the survey, which occupied them until May 1904. The Land Court which could hardly function without the survey also completed its work by the end of 1904. The magnitude of the task is shown by its demarcation of 354,277 lots[1] in addition to settling innumerable disputed claims. New rent rolls were prepared but the report says that many villagers protested against them, and the proclamation fixing the Crown rents was delayed until July 1906, and an undertaking was given that the rents would not be raised. Leases were fixed at 75 years from 1 July 1898, renewable for a further 24 years.

The district committees were unco-operative at first; they treated the government with suspicion and frequently ignored its request for information. The result was the Summoning of the Chinese Ordinance, No. 40 of 30 December 1899, by which the Chinese could be summoned to appear before the Registrar-General in Hong Kong to answer questions and give information. The main object was to gain information about land, but the Ordinance gave more far-reaching powers and drew a strong protest from Thomas Whitehead, addressed to the Colonial Secretary, which, however, was not supported by his two Chinese unofficial colleagues on the Council,[2] and though this protest was not upheld, Chamberlain accepted the Ordinance only if it were limited to two years. Sir Henry Blake also found it advisable to give an assurance that the Ordinance would not be used for the purpose of police enquiries.

Until the system of committees of elders was tried out, the administrative arrangements for governing the New Territories remained fluid, and much experiment was necessary before a solution of the problem of its administration could be found. Though the Secretary of State, Joseph Chamberlain, had ruled that there was to be no separate administration and that the leased area was to form part of the Colony, in fact it differed in character from the rest of the Colony and therefore required different treatment. That many Hong Kong Ordinances were not applicable there was realized, and an Ordinance for the Better Regulation of the New Territories, No. 10 of 18 April 1899, exempted the New Territories from the operation of certain ordinances, for example,

---

[1] Hong Kong *Sessional Papers* 1905. Report on the Blue Book, p. 441.
[2] Hong Kong *Sessional Papers* 1900, p. 107, and Hong Kong *Hansard* 1899–1900, p. 51 (15 February 1900).

those dealing with public health, slaughter-houses, markets, opium, licensing, and registration. The argument used was that British laws should be applied only gradually and that the Chinese customary system of taxation should be adhered to. The Ordinance in effect established the principle of a separate administration and though it was intended to be only temporary, the arrangements it made proved to be enduring. Blake wanted to use traditional methods of Chinese administration, just as Elliot had wanted to do for the whole colony in its early days, since the New Territories Chinese were living in their traditional way. G. N. Orme, the District Officer in his report on the New Territories of June 9, said,[1]

> life of the villager does not differ much from that of Chinese in other parts of China, nor has it altered much during the few years of British occupation, if anything, it falls rather behind the general standard of freedom and enlightenment in the Canton province.

He ascribed this to its remoteness from Canton so that it was, before its cession, little touched by external influence. He said

> A Chinese community like that of the New Territories is by its structure and its long habit of decentralised government very easy to administer. But its old-established customs and institutions must not be lightly changed or affronted, and necessary innovations have to be introduced with the greatest delicacy. The Chinese villager does not set great store by cleanliness or better housing; he finds himself entirely unable to understand our aims and ideas, and our dismal condition of unrest: he frankly dislikes our iconoclastic spirit, our want of imagination and our blindness to all the forces of nature . . . .

At first British officials were limited in principle to two, dealing with police and land. In 1899 a police magistrate was appointed and also an assistant land officer to deal with land cases, and the police were placed under the Captain Superintendent in Hong Kong. At the close of 1899 it was decided to make the police magistrate also an assistant superintendent of police. In 1907 the police magistrate had his various offices amalgamated under the title of District Officer, and in 1909, the Assistant Land Officer was made subordinate to him with the title Assistant District Officer. The latter post was abolished in 1913 and replaced by a police superintendent confined to purely police duties. The islands, and later, an outlying part of the mainland, were organized

---

[1] Hong Kong *Sessional Papers* for 1912, p. 43.

separately as the Southern District, with an assistant land officer appointed on 1 January 1905; he became an Assistant District Officer in 1910. The Northern and Southern Districts were administratively separated in 1909 each officer making his separate report.

By 1913, after much experiment an administrative pattern was evolved. The New Territories were divided into Northern and Southern Districts under a District Officer and Assistant District Officer respectively, acting as magistrates, but not as police officers, and having civil jurisdiction in debt cases for sums not exceeding $200. In addition, by a New Territories Land Ordinance, embodied in the New Territories Consolidation Ordinance of 1910, the District Officer Northern District, and Assistant District Officer Southern District, were given very wide powers in connection with land disputes, the appointment of trustees, and property holding, and in their courts no lawyer was allowed to appear in land cases without their permission. It was not until 1920 that the Assistant District Officer, Southern District, secured equality of status with his colleague in the Northern District, each being called District Officer.

In 1926 a number of *tsz-yi* or 'head-boroughs' were appointed to assist the District Officer in matters of local interest or dispute; the appointments were intended to be for one year and to give recognition to elders with long and faithful service.[1] They developed into a senior advisory council, known as the Heung Yee Kuk 鄉議局 and became something of a closed body, appointing other elders at their discretion to vacancies as they arose.

This division of the New Territories into two districts, northern and southern, each under a District Officer remained the pattern of the administration until after the World War of 1939-45. The principle of separate administration remained, though gradually some Hong Kong ordinances were applied, e.g. by a series of New Territories Regulation Amendment Ordinances of 1923, 1938 and 1940, power was given to apply certain clauses of Hong Kong Ordinances regarding sanitation and the abatement of nuisances.

[1] *Administration Reports* for 1926, Appendix J, p. 3. They are not mentioned in the report for that year for the Southern District.

3. Hong Kong Police in their uniform from about 1880 to the First World War

Facing page 134

4. The Governor, Sir Frederick Lugard (Lord Lugard), arriving on 28 July 1907. By courtesy of the Hong Kong Government Information Services.

Facing page 135

Constitutional Developments

Though the attempt in 1894 to pass beyond the stage of Crown Colony government by the introduction into the Legislative Council of an elected majority of unofficial members had miscarried, an undercurrent of desire for constitutional change remained. It was almost exclusively European and regarded the constitutional problem in Hong Kong from the European standpoint; it failed because it assumed that the modes of constitutional advance applicable to colonies of English settlers, were equally appropriate in Hong Kong. Lord Ripon's reply to the 1894 petitioners was conclusive, and its subsequent support by Joseph Chamberlain in 1896 proved that the two main British political parties agreed that the conferring of greater political autonomy on the British residents was incompatible with the moral obligation to protect the interests of the Chinese inhabitants. The principles of Crown Colony government were therefore even more firmly entrenched in Hong Kong as a result of the 1894 Petition.

The main argument was that the interests of the Chinese were likely to be better safeguarded by the Colonial Office than by a small local European oligarchy, however democratically elected amongst themselves. At the same time, it was held that the Chinese majority were not ready to assume political control, particularly in view of the Colony's economic importance and magnitude of the imperial interests involved. In a shifting society in which Chinese and European alike came to Hong Kong from choice, generally in pursuance of self-interest, the existing government answered essential needs, and provided the necessary minimum framework of control within which the different Hong Kong communities could work and live together.

It was not until the Great War of 1914–18 that the demand for reform was again seriously raised. The important contribution of colonial peoples to the War was acknowledged, and strengthened their claim to a greater degree of self-government within the Empire. The self-governing dominions achieved virtual nationhood in the War when the Imperial Conference of 1917 passed a resolution giving 'a full recognition of the dominions as autonomous nations of an Imperial Commonwealth'. In India, the promise of association of Indians with every branch of the administration and the development of self-governing institutions, made in 1858, was renewed in the Montague-Chelmsford report of 1917. In Africa, Lugard enunciated the principle of the dual mandate, that colonial territories were held in trust to make their products available to the world, and for the benefit of the inhabitants themselves. In the darkest days of the War, Lloyd George's insistence upon fuller consultation with the colonies gave promise of greater freedom to colonial peoples, and this idea gained additional impetus from its concrete embodiment in President Wilson's Fourteen Points.

Hong Kong could not remain untouched by the prevailing ideas and impulses aroused by the War and the agitation for reform revived. Led by H. E. Pollock,[1] an influential lawyer and member of the Legislative Council representing the Justices of the Peace, its demands were broadly similar to those made in 1894 and invited a corresponding fate. It took the form of a Petition dated 19 January 1916, but not sent until the following March, addressed to the Secretary of State, A. Bonar Law (1914–16), from the British residents in Hong Kong. Possibly there was an element of personal pique on the part of Pollock who considered himself unjustifiably passed over for membership of the Executive Council when a vacancy occurred in that body in November 1915. On 23 December 1915, Pollock in the Legislative Council asked[2] what steps had been taken to fill the vacancy and drew attention to his own claims by pointing out that he had been a temporary member of the Executive Council at various times amounting to nearly three years. On that same occasion, he asked two additional questions dealing with reform of the Executive and Legislative Councils; they were:

Question 5. Will the Government recommend to the Rt. Hon. the Secretary of State for the Colonies that the two unofficial members of the Executive Council shall be elected members instead of being nominated by the Government?

Question 6. Will the Government recommend to the . . . Secretary of State for the Colonies that all the Unofficial Members of the Legislative Council shall be elected instead of two-thirds of them being nominated by the Government, and also that the number of Unofficial Members in that Council be increased?

[1] Henry Edward Pollock (Sir) 1864–1953. Prominent Hong Kong Barrister. Called to the Bar, 1887; acting Police Magistrate Hong Kong, 1888–89; acting Puisne Judge, 1892; acting Attorney-General at various times, 1896–1901; Q.C. 1900. Attorney-General in Fiji Islands, 1902; Member of Legislative Council, Hong Kong, elected by the Chamber of Commerce, 1903–04, and elected by the unofficial Justices of the Peace for 36 years 1905–1941. Member of the Executive Council, 1921–1941. Knighted, 1924.

[2] Hong Kong *Hansard* for 23 December 1915.

Pollock was undoubtedly underlining his own claim to membership of the Executive Council by implying that if the vacancy were an elective one, he would be elected, a claim which derived substance from his election to the Legislative Council at different times by both the electing bodies, the Chamber of Commerce and the Justices. The Governor, Sir Henry May,[1] answered that the Governor was alone responsible for making recommendations for appointment to the Executive Council and ruled out discussion by saying 'I am not therefore prepared to permit myself to be catechised as to what action at the present juncture I have taken or shall take to acquit myself of my heavy responsibility'. He assured Pollock that his services had not been and would not be lost sight of. In answer to the two questions relating to alterations in the Constitution of the Colony, May replied,

> The suggestions made do not commend themselves to my judgment, and the season in my opinion is strangely out of joint for even the discussion of such questions, since the energies of both the Colonial and Imperial Governments are at present concentrated on the internecine struggle in which well nigh the whole world is now engaged.[2]

Pollock was not on good terms with the Governor, and in fact he had to wait until May had retired from the governorship before he secured a seat on the Executive Council in 1921.

Pollock did not accept the Governor's verdict and organized the Petition[3] of 19 January 1916, in an appeal to the Secretary of State over the head of the Governor. The Petitioners declared that 'it is fitting and proper that the number of Un-official members on the Executive and Legislative Councils should be increased, and that the principle of election should be extended'. They proposed that two additional unofficial members should be added to the Executive Council, one to be elected by the Chamber of Commerce and one by the non-official Justices of the Peace, these two bodies having 'long been recognized as representatives of the Public for electoral purposes'. Regarding the Legislative Council, the petitioners proposed:

---

[1] Sir Francis Henry May (1860–1922). Born in Dublin; Cadet officer, Hong Kong, in 1881, and Colonial Secretary, 1902–10; appointed Governor of Fiji and High Commissioner Western Pacific, 1910; Governor of Hong Kong, 1912–1919.

[2] Hong Kong *Hansard*, 23 December 1915.

[3] Hong Kong *Sessional Papers* 1916, p. 70.

'(1) That, as regards all the Un-official Members of this Council (other than the Chinese Members who stand on a somewhat special footing), the principle of election instead of Government nomination ought to be applied, and they would humbly submit that it is somewhat inconsistent, whilst trusting the Chamber of Commerce and non-official Justices to elect some of the European members of this Council, to deny the right of election to them in the case of the other European Un-official Members' and '(2) That the number of Un-official Members be increased to 10 by the addition of 4 Un-official members, so as to create an Un-official Majority in the Legislative Council, as in the case of Cyprus and British Honduras'.

They pointed out that the Un-official Members were in 'a permanent and hopeless minority' and that the Legislative Council 'as at present constituted, though consisting numerically of 14 Members, simply carries into effect the individual will and judgment of the Governor or other Presiding Officer'.

In a covering letter[1] dated 9 March 1916, Pollock made some additional points, by way of explanation and 'partly of argument'. He said the Petition had been signed by 566 persons, all British except for 'about one dozen . . . Portuguese and British Indians who . . . were not intended to sign', and the first 28 signatures were those of representatives of the most important shipping, commercial, and financial institutions in the Colony. He explained why some of the influential people including the two non-Chinese nominated members of the Legislative Council, D. Landale of Jardine, Matheson & Co. and E. Shellim of David Sassoon & Co., Ltd., had not signed the petition. Landale, he said, favoured an unofficial majority, but did not sign because it would be an ungracious act since the head of Jardine, Matheson & Co. had always been nominated to a seat on the Legislative Council.[2] E. Shellim, he said, had agreed generally with the petition but thought the time inopportune for any change, a point also made by Sir Paul Chater. He admitted that 'it is fully and clearly recognized, that under war conditions at present prevailing, no definite answer can be expected to this Petition until after the lapse of some months', but urged that a government 'more representative of the wishes of the business men of this Colony, should be established for the

[1] Hong Kong *Sessional Papers* 1916, p. 64.
[2] Landale afterwards claimed that Pollock had misrepresented him, and that he 'made use of my name in a manner which was not warranted by any conversation I had with him . . . with a view to explaining the absence of my signature therefrom'. Hong Kong *Sessional Papers* 1916, p. 78.

purpose of dealing with any trade and shipping problems which may arise at the close of the War'.

Pollock enclosed articles appearing in the press on the subject of the Petition, particularly some comments on documents concerning the 1894 Petition 'which documents were sent by the Hong Kong Government to the Press for publication, on the 25th January 1916, apparently in the hope that they would adversely affect the signing of the petition'. As a result of some criticisms of the Petition arising from this press publicity, Pollock stated that 'in consequence of suggestions made to me, I promised that I would bring to your notice . . . the desire expressed for a more comprehensive electoral body than the Chamber of Commerce or the non-official Justices of the Peace'. The demands contained in the Petition were thus modified in the accompanying letter. He also explained that it had been deemed advisable to limit the signatories of the Petition to those of British race, though a few Portuguese and Indians did actually sign.

In regard to Chinese representation, Pollock suggested that if two more Chinese members were added to the total of ten unofficial members of the Legislative Council suggested in the Petition, the present proportion of Chinese members to the rest of the unofficial members would be preserved. Pollock pointed out the significant differences between his proposals and those of 1894.

> The present Petition does not as did the 1894 Petition, ask for a *British* Un-official majority, and consequently whether the number of Un-officials be 10, or be increased to 12 by the addition of two Chinese members, it would be impossible to get an Un-official majority otherwise than by the combined European and Chinese vote. There would, therefore, be no risk whatever (as there might have been if the Prayer of the 1894 Petition had been granted) of the wishes of the important Chinese community in this colony being over-ruled by the vote of the British non-official members outweighing the combined votes both of the Official and the Chinese Members. The power of the Governor to suspend legislation and of the Secretary of State to veto it are additional safeguards to the rights of the native population.

Pollock also claimed that this Petition was signed by 556 persons, practically all British, whereas the 1894 Petition for greater representation was signed by 363 of whom only 284 were British. Finally Pollock gave instances of the way in which the official majority in the Legislative Council was used to vote down the unofficial members, and he referred to one of his speeches in the Legislative Council in which he accused the Government of treating the unofficial members in an adverse and hostile spirit instead of taking them into their counsel and co-operation.[1]

Sir Henry May criticized the Petition on the ground that no adequate reasons had been given for constitutional change, that popular opinion was not disregarded, and the mercantile community already possessed ample means of making their views known.[2] Bonar Law rejected the Petition without any argument, merely saying:

> I have carefully considered the Petition in question, but I am of opinion that the reasons which led my predecessors, Lord Ripon, in his dispatch No. 135 of 23rd August 1894, and Mr. Chamberlain, in his dispatch No. 119 of the 29th May 1896, to formulate their decisions upon petitions for the amendment of the constitution of Hong Kong are equally applicable at the present time: it is not therefore possible to meet the wishes of the Petitioners as regards the Legislative Council. . . . As regards the Executive Council, I cannot see any sufficient reason for increasing the number, or changing the method of appointment, of the unofficial members who are selected to advise the Governor in Council.[3]

So the Petition failed in its immediate object. Pollock argued ably, yet the case was weak, because it was aimed almost exclusively at giving the British element greater influence in the government. The appeal to the example of Cyprus and British Honduras showed that reform was not sought in the context of the special circumstances of Hong Kong. Pollock's argument, used in his covering letter but not appearing in the Petition, that the interests of the Chinese were safeguarded because the unofficial European votes in the Legislative Council would not outnumber the combined votes of the officials and the Chinese members, merely strengthened the case for continued Crown Colony government which rested on the necessity to protect Chinese interests. Even the British were not happy that political power was vested in the hands of two small and exclusive bodies, the Chamber of Commerce and the unofficial Justices of the Peace, and Pollock undermined the force of the

---

[1] Hong Kong *Hansard* 1914, p. 44.

[2] Sir Henry May to Andrew Bonar Law, 26 May 1916, No. 209, Hong Kong *Sessional Papers* 1916, p. 59.

[2] Bonar Law to Sir Henry May, 15 August 1916, No. 203, Hong Kong *Sessional Papers* 1916, p. 91.

Petition by admitting in his letter that many would like to see the franchise extended to those on the jury lists.

Meanwhile the Home Government had already decided on a revision of the Letters Patent and Royal Instructions in order to bring these constitutional instruments up to date. This decision was taken on its own initiative and was not influenced by the 1916 Petition which arrived at the Colonial Office after the draft revised Letters Patent and Royal Instructions had been sent to Hong Kong for local comment. They were finally issued on 14 February 1917.

The Letters Patent of 1917 'Constituting the Office of Governor and Commander-in-Chief of the Colony of Hong Kong and its Dependencies' and the accompanying Royal Instructions made no change of principle and few changes of detail. The Executive Council still consisted of the Senior Military Officer, Colonial Secretary, Attorney-General, and Colonial Treasurer (the last named was replaced by the Financial Secretary when that office was constituted in 1938) as *ex officio* members,[1] and such other persons as were appointed by Royal Instructions or instructions from the Secretary of State. These latter remained unchanged in number at three, one official and two unofficial, until 1921. The Governor alone determined the Council's business, but a member had the right to have recorded on the minutes his request to submit a question to the Council if it were refused by the Governor, and to have a further record of his opinion if the Governor acted against the advice of the Council. The composition of the Legislative Council remained as it had been fixed by Lord Ripon after the 1894 Petition, that is eight officials including the Governor and six unofficial members, of whom two were elected by the Chamber of Commerce and unofficial Justices of the Peace respectively, and the remaining four, two being Chinese, were nominated by the Governor.

The policy of giving political power to the few British residents in Hong Kong was thus again decisively rejected, but the demand for constitutional change remained. The *China Mail*, in an editorial,[2] admitted that it had anticipated that the Petition would not meet with much success, but it criticized Bonar Law's curt dismissal of the Petition, and urged that there was a case that the

---

[1] The Secretary for Chinese Affairs (up to 1913 known as The Registrar-General) became an *ex officio* member in 1929.

[2] 25 September 1916.

unofficial members of the Council, other than the Chinese, should be elected on a limited franchise, and not be government nominees.

The continued pressure brought into existence a Constitutional Reform Association of Hong Kong which was launched at a well-attended meeting held in the Theatre Royal on 3 May 1917. Its declared objects were, the promotion of greater representation of the public on the Executive and Legislative Councils, the pressing upon the Home Authorities of the claims of Hong Kong to be represented on any imperial council or association to be formed and the expression of its views on post-war trade policy, and generally the active support or promotion or criticism of all reforms and all matters of public interest and importance to Hong Kong.[1]

All British subjects were to be eligible for membership of the Association. The two elected members of the Legislative Council, P. H. Holyoak[2] and Pollock were appropriately elected president and vice-president respectively, assisted by a committee of ten. Holyoak who presided at the meeting declared that the franchise for the election of members of the Legislative Council should be based on the Jury list and not as demanded in the 1916 Petition.

The Association did not show much life until the war was over. In December 1918, it announced a scheme of reform[3] based on the Petition but revised in certain particulars. This proposed that the principle of election instead of nomination by the Governor should, except for the two Chinese members, be applied to the filling of unofficial seats on the Councils, that the number of unofficial members of the Legislative Council should be increased from six to eight; the number of official members reduced from eight to seven, and that all six elected members of the Legislative Council should be British subjects. The revised electoral arrangements provided that the six elected members should be elected, two by the Chamber of Commerce, one by the unofficial Justices of the Peace, and three (one of whom should be Portuguese) by those liable to serve on juries or exempted.

These proposals were discussed at a public meeting held on

[1] *China Mail*, 2 May 1917.

[2] Percy Hobson Holyoak (?–1926) of Reiss & Co., afterwards of Holyoak, Massey & Co., Ltd. Member of the Legislative Council, 1915–1926 as representative of the Chamber of Commerce; Member of the Executive Council, 1924–1926. Chairman of the Chamber of Commerce, 1917–18, 1920–21 and 1925. Died, 25 May 1926.

[3] *China Mail*, 19 December 1918.

9 January 1919, at which Holyoak announced that further amendments were considered desirable because the Chinese had shown enthusiasm for reform and were asking for more Chinese representation, and the Association thought it advisable to make concessions to their wishes. This third revision of the original reform proposals suggested an increase of the number of unofficial members of the Legislative Council to nine, of whom seven should be elected, all being British subjects. Of the seven, two should be elected by the Chamber of Commerce, one by the unofficial Justices of the Peace, three (two of British and one of Portuguese extraction) by British subjects who were liable to or exempt from jury service, and one by the Chinese Chamber of Commerce or other body similarly representative of the Chinese community.

Some criticism was voiced at the meeting, and a motion that, of the seven elected members of the Legislative Council, one Chinese and one Portuguese should be elected by their own communities and the remaining five by British subjects of pure European descent upon a franchise similar to that used for elections to the House of Commons, was defeated, but gave the mover an opportunity to protest against the restriction of voting in Hong Kong to a narrow propertied class. A further motion

> that of the seven elected unofficial members (all of whom shall be British subjects) one shall be elected by the Hong Kong Chamber of Commerce, one by the Justices of the Peace, four (three of whom shall be of British race and one of Portuguese race) by British subjects who are jurymen, or are qualified for but exempt from jury service, and one by the Chinese General Chamber of Commerce or some other body representative of the Chinese community.

was carried by a very large majority. One member of the Portuguese community vainly urged that that community should elect the Portuguese member just as the Chinese member was to be elected by the Chinese; he agreed that some of the Portuguese were not technically British subjects, but he argued some of the members of the Chamber of Commerce were aliens too and yet were allowed to vote in the election of the member representing the Chamber.

A copy of these resolutions was sent to the Governor for transmission to the Secretary of State, who replied that the new Governor, Sir Edward Stubbs,[1] would consider them and make recommenda-

---

[1] Sir Reginald Edward Stubbs (1876–1947), clerk at Colonial Office. Colonial Secretary, Ceylon, 1913–19; Governor of Hong Kong, 1919–26; afterwards Governor of Jamaica, 1926–32; Cyprus, 1932–33 and Ceylon, 1933–37

tions. On 9 December 1920, Pollock, in the Legislative Council,[1] complained of the delay and requested the Governor to ask for a decision in view of the fact that the Secretary of State had raised the question of greater representation in the legislative councils in colonies generally. The Home Government decided against the Constitutional Reform Society's reform proposals, the decision being conveyed to the Society and announced in Parliament on the same day, 22 February 1921. Pollock attempted to keep the issue alive and at a meeting of the Legislative Council on 3 March 1921,[2] asked that all correspondence between the Governor and the Secretary of State on the constitutional reform proposals passed at the public meeting on 9 January 1919, should be published. The request was refused as the correspondence was confidential. Pollock repeated his request which was again refused in a series of written replies dated 22 March 1921.[3] At the next meeting of the Council on 7 April 1921, the Colonial Secretary replied, in answer to a further question by Pollock, that the Secretary of State had given no reason for his view that constitutional change in Hong Kong was regarded as undesirable.[4] The incident was not closed until 7 June 1921 when a new Secretary of State reviewed the question of these reforms in the House of Commons and confirmed his predecessor's decision against making any change.

Meanwhile, another organization with partly political aims, the Kowloon Residents' Association was formed in January 1921. Its object was 'to form a body of residents whose collective and intimate knowledge of this district's requirements would constitute a source upon which such representation as they possess or may possess, on the Legislature, may depend for detailed advice and support'. It criticized the Government because it relied on inadequate sources as to the requirements of the Kowloon people, such as Government officials, or unofficial members of the Legislative Council 'whose knowledge of local conditions was gleaned from a panoramic view of the peninsula from an elevation of 1,200 feet,[5] or wealthy landowners 'whose interests patently conflicted with those of the residents'. The Association demanded the development

---

[1] Hong Kong *Hansard* 1920, p. 83.

[2] Hong Kong *Hansard* 1921, p. 17.

[3] Hong Kong *Hansard* 1921, p. 19.

[4] Hong Kong *Hansard* 1921, p. 25.

[5] The wealthiest Europeans from whom the unofficial members were generally selected, normally inhabited The Peak, 1,200 feet above the City of Victoria.

of motor roads in Kowloon similar to those on the island, a European reserved area, similar to the Peak Reservation,[1] and a hospital for Europeans. In the following November more concrete demands were made regarding amenities such as hospitals, street lighting, improved roads and drainage. The most interesting proposal at this meeting was that the jubilee of Kowloon as a British possession (1861-1921) should be made the occasion of inaugurating a Kowloon Municipal Council with an unofficial majority, whose decisions should at first be subject to the Governor's veto. This plan was never worked out in detail.

The Constitutional Reform Association lingered on for a year or two, but never again recaptured its earlier enthusiasm. In May 1921, a joint meeting of the Association with the Kowloon Residents' Association was held to protest against the recently increased house rates which led to further agitation for elected unofficial members on the Legislative Council. The reform agitation soon died down. A series of strikes of Chinese workers threatened to turn into a general social upheaval which together with an economic recession, made reform inopportune; next, the radicalism of the Kuomintang Party under Sun Yat-sen then influenced by Bolshevik advisers, damped enthusiasm for reform; and besides, the Imperial Government by issuing in 1917 the revised Letters Patent and Royal Instructions made the possibility of further changes remote.

When constitutional change did come it was to give greater representation to the Chinese. As time went on the disparity in numbers between the Chinese and European communities had become greater. The Chinese national feelings were also stirred by the Nationalist Party, the Kuomintang, who now pressed for the abolition of extraterritorial rights, the retrocession of foreign concessions, tariff autonomy, and the general revision of the so-called 'unequal treaties'. In 1926 the Shanghai Municipal Council finally admitted for the first time three Chinese representatives. The upsurge of national feeling among the Chinese was directed mainly against Japan and Great Britain. Japan had incurred China's enmity by taking advantage of the Great War to press on China the Twenty-one Demands in the spring of 1915, deeply encroaching on Chinese sovereignty. Britain with the largest economic and financial interests in China was the aunt sally of the Chinese

[1] The Hill District Reservation of Residential Area Ordinance, 29 April 1904, reserved the Peak district exclusively for European residence.

nationalist feeling against the Western Powers in general. A series of strikes in Hong Kong culminated in 1925 in an economic boycott which paralysed the port.

On 9 July 1926, Sir Chouson Chow,[1] was appointed the first Chinese member of the Executive Council, following the death of Sir Paul Chater who had served on the Council since 1896. The appointment was made on personal grounds and also to disarm anti-British sentiment in China and encourage local Chinese loyalty in Hong Kong. Two years later, the Legislative Council was increased in number to ten officials, including the Governor, and eight unofficials. This change was made on the initiative of the Governor, Sir Cecil Clementi,[2] partly as a result of the rapid post-war growth of Kowloon which he thought merited two additional unofficial representatives of its own in the Council. This increase in their number from six to eight automatically brought about a corresponding increase on the official side. The increases were sanctioned by the Additional Royal Instructions of 15 November 1928, and came into effect in January 1929. The ten official members now consisted of the Governor, the six official members of the Executive Council, and three other officials, the Inspector General of Police, the Harbour Master and the Director of Medical and Sanitary Services. Of the eight unofficial members, two were elected by the Chamber of Commerce and unofficial Justices respectively, as before, and of the remaining six who were appointed on the nomination of the Governor, three were to be Chinese,[3] i.e. one of the two additional unofficial members had to be Chinese. The second additional unofficial member was selected from the Portuguese community, now represented for the first time. The decision to allocate the two new unofficial seats to the Chinese and Portuguese communities was taken on the initia-

---

[1] Sir Chouson Chow 周壽臣 (1861–1959). Born in Hong Kong. Knighted, 1926; Korean Customs Service, 1882–94; Chinese Consular Service in Korea, 1894–96; held various posts in Railways and Customs services in China; Counsellor in the Foreign Ministry in Peking, 1910. Unofficial Member of the Hong Kong Legislative Council, 1921–31, and of the Executive Council, 1926–36.

[2] Sir Cecil Clementi (1875–1947). K.C.M.G., 1926. G.C.M.G. 1931. Cadet, Hong Kong, 1899; Colonial Secretary, British Guiana, 1913–22; Colonial Secretary, Ceylon, 1922–25; Governor of Hong Kong, 1925–30; Governor of Straits Settlements and High Commissioner Malaya, 1930–34. Author of *Cantonese Love Songs*, etc.

[3] Hong Kong *Administration Reports* for 1931, p. 4.

5. SIR SHOUSON CHOW 周壽臣
First Chinese member of the Executive Council, 1926.
By courtesy of the *South China Morning Post*. Hong Kong.

Facing page 146

tive of the Governor. Another change introduced at the same time limited the term for holding an unofficial seat to four years.

This broadening of the Council by greater community representation made further inroads in the monopoly of unofficial seats long held by the British commercial houses. Highly significant of this change, Jardine, Matheson & Co.'s continuous representation since 1850 was interrupted in 1921, and not resumed until 1926.

From 1929 to the outbreak of the Pacific War, circumstances militated against further change in the constitution of the Legislative Council. The severe economic depression of 1931 in Europe spread to the Far East and seriously contracted the commercial activity of the Colony and its revenue. When trade began to recover, Japan's military and economic aggression in China led to open hostilities in 1937 and her alignment with Germany and Italy in a fascist alliance against the Soviet Union and the Western Powers, altered the direction of Chinese nationalist xenophobia.

CHAPTER IX

LOCAL GOVERNMENT 1883-1941

The Sanitary Board and the First Popular Elections, 1883-1898

A SANITARY Board, with local government functions concerned with the maintenance of public health, was set up in 1883. It acquired unofficial members in 1886, two of whom were first elected in 1888. Because of these elections, the Sanitary Board is not without constitutional importance; moreover it later developed into the Urban Council. Since the Second World War, it has been suggested that this should in turn ripen into a fully elective municipal council as the most practical step in the path of constitutional advance.

Among the recommendations made by Osbert Chadwick, in his 1882 Report on the sanitary condition of Hong Kong, was the appointment of a sanitary inspector to carry out necessary public health measures. Pressed by the Secretary of State, who regarded the matter as urgent, W. H. Marsh, then the Officer Administering the Government, recommended in March 1883, H. Macallum, the apothecary at the Government Civil Hospital, for the post. Marsh who considered a new sanitary department unnecessary, suggested that control should be exercised by a Sanitary Board comprising the heads of the three departments most closely concerned, the Surveyor-General, the Colonial Surgeon and the Registrar-General, one of whom, as Chairman, would be responsible for the work of the sanitary officials. Further details were left for the new Governor, Sir George Bowen, to decide.

Bowen accepted Marsh's proposal and the Sanitary Board consisting of the three officials was set up on 5 July 1883, under the chairmanship of J. M. Price, the Surveyor-General. He proposed[1] that the Board should have at least two additional unofficial members, to be nominated by the Governor, but there was so much discussion about its powers that the unofficial element was not added until 1886. The powers of the Board were first defined in the Order and Cleanliness Amendment Ordinance, Number 7 of 13 June 1883. It was given wide powers of inspection and control in accordance with a code of sanitary regulations which were to be

[1] Sir George Bowen to Lord Derby, 29 May 1883, No. 88, CO 129/209.

proposed and discussed by the Board but become operative only after being passed by the Governor in Council, with whom ultimate responsibility therefore rested. The Board thus had the reduced status of an initiating body, able to exercise an independence limited mainly to the control of its own paid officials. Its weakness was revealed almost immediately after its birth, for in the summer of 1883 the Colony suffered a serious outbreak of cholera. The Board made recommendations for more efficient street cleaning and disinfecting of premises by scavenging gangs assisted by a volunteer sanitary corps under the supervision of thirty inspectors. The Attorney-General ruled, however, that a new ordinance would be necessary to carry out these measures and they were held over, though their urgency was great for during the period August 19–26, 1883, when the cholera outbreak was at its worst, 404 tons of refuse were removed per day as against the normal daily average of 83 tons. An Augean task confronted the Board. Quite apart from cholera, the problems of overcrowding, slum clearance, insanitary dwellings, food protection, water-supply and many others that the Chadwick Report had exposed, were aggravated by years of neglect. The Board's proposals for sanitary improvement moreover excited bitter opposition from the property owners, foreign and Chinese. Bowen's draft Public Health Ordinance provoked such determined resistance from property owners that the bill did not even get a first reading in the Legislative Council; with the result that Bowen had achieved practically nothing by the time of his departure in December 1885.

The following year, 1886, to allay criticism, the Board took the initiative in proposing that representatives of the community be added to its number as unofficial members. W. H. Marsh, once more serving as Officer Administering the Government, accepted the Board's proposal[1] and appointed four unofficial members[2] as representatives of the ratepayers and also added two officials, the Captain Superintendent of Police and the Sanitary Inspector; the

---

[1] W. H. Marsh to Secretary of State, 11 August 1886, No. 159, CO 129/228.

[2] The four unofficial members were A. P. MacEwen, Dr Patrick Manson, Dr Ho Kai and N. J. Ede. MacEwen was an unofficial member of the Legislative Council, elected by the Chamber of Commerce, and a partner of Holliday, Wise & Co. Dr Manson was an authority on tropical diseases and one of the founders of the Hong Kong College of Medicine for the Chinese (1887) and later a founder of the London School of Tropical Medicine. Dr Ho Kai, the only Chinese, was qualified in law and medicine and soon became an influential spokesman of the Chinese. N. J. Ede was Secretary of the Union Insurance Society of Canton.

re-organized Board now consisted of nine members, five official and four unofficial. Marsh explained to the Secretary of State that he sought to strengthen the Board's authority by making it more representative.

The new Board's first task was to revise the draft of the proposed Public Health Ordinance left over by Bowen; in a protracted debate, the main issue was whether the desired improvement in housing standards could be imposed without compensating the owners of property, and the draft was not ready before December 1886. Insistence upon minimum standards of housing with adequate space for ventilation alone was calculated by the Board to cost $1,582,192 in compensation to property owners.

The draft bill proposed amongst other things that the Board itself should be reorganized. It suggested a Municipal Board of Health consisting of four officials, the Surveyor-General, Registrar-General, Colonial Surgeon and Captain Superintendent of Police, and four unofficial members of whom two were to be appointed by the Governor and two were to be elected by those whose names appeared on the jury lists; the Governor was also to nominate the president, vice-president and secretary of the Board. It was to have wide powers to make bye-laws on virtually all aspects of public health. However, the Executive Council amended the bill to limit the Board's power to make bye-laws, on the ground that the more important public health regulations ought to appear in the Ordinance itself, and not be left to the Board.[1] The Executive Council wished to keep ultimate control over all the sanitary legislation in its own hands, as against the Board's desire for elected and nominated unofficial members to strengthen its own position on controversial matters. Dr Ho Kai supported the idea of a municipal council to deal with health questions and wanted all discussions to be held in public, but he took a very strong line against the proposed sanitary improvements, arguing that they would shake public confidence, and entail sacrifice of valuable building space, which would result in more cramped housing, higher cost of land and higher rents. He thought that the government was making the great 'mistake of treating Chinese as if they were Europeans'[2] and protested that the Chinese did not need or

---

[1] W. H. Marsh to Sir Henry T. Holland, BT. (later, Lord Knutsford), 28 February 1887, No. 62, CO 129/231.
[2] Ibid.

desire more living space. He complained that the bye-laws were based on those of English cities and declared, 'I protest loudly against this kind of indiscriminate and servile legislation'. In view of the opposition aroused, the Sanitary Board's draft bill was drastically amended and made to apply only to new houses and not to existing property; but even then Ho Kai's opposition was not appeased. The Secretary of State refused to sanction the payment of compensation to owners: 'Owners could not fairly claim compensation for being prevented by the law from building houses without regard to the requirement of the health . . . [of the people]', was his verdict. In the autumn of 1887 all the contentious clauses concerning property and housing space and back yards were removed from the Public Health Bill and in this emasculated form the Ordinance was passed. Dr Ho Kai maintained bitter opposition for which he sought support by organizing a petition against the Ordinance among the Chinese. Every effort was made by the property owners to shelve the bill. As Major General Cameron, the Officer Administering the Government, pointed out, the trouble was the apathy of the general public over the bill, for the Europeans were not permanently resident, and the Chinese wanted only to be left alone, and so the initiative had to come from the government in face of opposition from interested parties who 'wanted to repudiate the first principle of sanitation'.[1]

The Executive Council, though it had rejected the proposal to set up a municipal board of health, did accept, in the Public Health Ordinance, a thorough-going re-organization of the Sanitary Board, including its proposal to have an elected element among its membership. It was to be composed of four official members, Surveyor-General, Colonial Surgeon, Registrar-General and Captain Superintendent of Police, and not more than six additional members of whom four, including two Chinese, were to be nominated by the Governor, and two were to be elected by those ratepayers whose names were on the special and common jury lists. As before, the Governor appointed the president, vice-president and secretary. The Board's sessions were to be in public. This re-organization did not pass without opposition, mainly over a demand that all six unofficial members should be elected and not merely two, giving the Board an elected majority and not merely an

[1] Major General Cameron to Sir Henry T. Holland, BT., 27 September 1887, No. 331, CO 129/234.

unofficial majority. All the unofficial members of the Legislative Council voted against the Public Health Bill, not merely on account of those clauses dealing with the constitution of the Sanitary Board, and it was carried only by recourse to the official majority.

The Chinese petition against the Public Health Ordinance, organized by Ho Kai, was supported by 47,000 signatures. It referred to the Elliot Proclamation of 1841 which promised the Chinese the free enjoyment of their customs, and it declared that since there had been no epidemic or plague and since the Chinese were prosperous, they wanted no disturbance or change. The petitioners asked that four members of the Board should be elected instead of two, and that the Board should be empowered to appoint its own officials. The Secretary of State considered the petition but the Ordinance came into force in June 1888[1] despite the Chinese protest.

The reconstituted Sanitary Board was now set up. The first elections to the Board in accordance with its new constitution were held on 12 June 1888, and the local press remarked that 'the day would be ranked as a day of note by the future historian of Hong Kong; for the first time the ratepayers of the Colony had been given a voice in the management of their own affairs'.[2] Of four candidates for the two elective seats, J. D. Humphries and J. J. Francis, Q.C., were elected with 71 and 55 votes respectively, the other two candidates, R. K. Leigh and A. MacConachie polled 43 and 18 respectively. The total poll was 187 votes out of the 669 persons on the jury lists for that year, not all of whom were qualified as ratepayers to vote. Humphries entered the lists at the last moment and conducted a vigorous campaign with processions of rickshaws; and yet less than one elector in three voted.

The nominated unofficial members were Wong Shing (Chinese member of the Legislative Council), Dr Ho Kai, Dr James Cantile and N. J. Ede. Osbert Chadwick, then in the Colony to advise on sanitary works, was made a member of the Board by a special ordinance.

---

[1] The contentious clauses of the Public Health Ordinance were left to a Buildings Ordinance No. 15 of 1889, but here again the opposition was such that Des Vœux omitted its contentious property clauses, and eventually a Crown Lands Resumption Ordinance was passed later in the same year by which sanitary improvements were to be effected by using the power of resumption.

[2] The Daily Press, 16 June 1888.

The unofficial members held their seats for three years, and on 17 June 1891, a second election was held. There was much excitement and the three candidates made election speeches, though questions were not allowed by the presiding officer. Humphries and Francis were again elected with 217 and 198 votes respectively, and the third candidate, A. Shelton Cooper, secured only 77 votes. The jury lists numbered 738 and the total number of votes cast was 492, a reasonably heavy poll, bearing in mind that not all those qualified to serve on the jury were necessarily qualified to vote as ratepayers. The third election took place on 16 June 1894 but aroused very little interest or excitement. J. J. Francis and R. K. Leigh were the only candidates, nevertheless there being no provision for declaring unopposed candidates duly elected, balloting was necessary as a matter of form.

Election by those whose names appeared on the jury lists meant election by those who could speak English. A juror was a 'male person between the ages of 21 and 60 . . . who is a good and sufficient person resident within the Colony and is not ignorant of the English language . . . .'[1] The jury lists do not give the nationality of the juror, but the lists for 1888 and 1891 both showed 30 Chinese names, and the impression gained from reading the lists is that many nationalities were represented, with a majority, certainly not overwhelming, of English.

The bubonic plague in 1894 inevitably raised once more the issue of the composition and powers of the Sanitary Board. Sanitary improvement made little headway against the opposition of the Chinese and of the property owners with the result exactly as Chadwick had prophesied—an outbreak of plague. The Sanitary Board drew up more stringent bye-laws dealing with compulsory visiting and cleansing of houses and the isolation of infected cases; it set up a special housing committee to deal with resumption of land in the stricken areas.

In the discussions on constitutional reform, it has already been noted that one proposal to meet the desire for more self-government was that the Sanitary Board should blossom into a municipal council, something which the Board itself had proposed eight years before, in 1886. The unofficials on the Legislative Council opposed the creation of a municipal council. The Retrenchment Committee of 1894 even suggested that the Sanitary Board

[1] Juries Ordinance No. 6 of 1887.

should be abolished and its work taken over directly by the Government through a government official. In 1895 Robinson reported[1] that the Executive Committee had agreed to its abolition and that he favoured this because he could not find any suitable Chinese to serve on the Board, since all the Chinese members had resigned from it. He suggested that the head of the Medical Department should take over the work of the Sanitary Board with four assistants. It was because of a new appointment of a Medical Officer of Health in 1895, whom the Board naturally wanted under their own control, but who was attached to the Medical Department at the instance of the Governor, that the unofficial members of the Board all resigned except one, N. J. Ede. So from 1895 the Board was in a state of suspended animation.

On the question of the Board becoming a municipal council, Robinson told[2] Lord Ripon that there was no general desire for a municipal council, and he again gave the misleading instance that at the Board elections in June 1894, only 25 out of 500 electors took the trouble to vote. He said four unofficial members of the Board resigned because he would not place the Medical Officer of Health under the Board, and the latter now comprised the Director of Public Works, the acting Colonial Surgeon, the Captain Superintendent of Police and the acting Medical Officer of Health and was working smoothly and efficiently. Chamberlain, who became Colonial Secretary in 1895, refused to agree to the Board's abolition without a further specific recommendation from the Legislative Council. The latter refused to recommend its abolition and it was once more reconstituted, on the advice of four of the unofficial members of the Legislative Council. There were to be three official members, the Colonial Surgeon, the Captain Superintendent of Police and the Director of Public Works, and two unofficial members elected by the ratepayers. Robinson admitted to Chamberlain that while he did not regard this as satisfactory, he had agreed so as not to oppose the unofficial members of the Legislative Council. Robinson now also agreed that the Medical Officer of Health should be attached to the Sanitary Board, and not to the Medical Department as he had first recommended, as its chief adviser and executive officer. As the re-organization aroused

[1] Sir William Robinson to Lord Ripon, 18 May 1895, No. 163, CO 129/267.
[2] Sir William Robinson to Lord Ripon (Confidential), 22 May 1895. CO 129/267.

6. The Old City Hall until its demolition in 1933.
By courtesy of the Hong Kong Government Information Services.

Facing page 155

opposition amongst the British residents, Robinson, in June 1896 conducted a plebiscite of the British community, based on the jury lists, as to whether the Sanitary Board should contain an official or unofficial majority; the result was that 331 (including '3 or 4 Chinese') voted for an unofficial majority and 31 against. In reporting this to Chamberlain, Robinson urged once more his view that the Sanitary Board should be abolished, and all sanitary work placed directly under government. Chamberlain was annoyed by this plebiscite, and commented that 'it is inconsistent with crown colony government to seek the guidance of a plebiscite', that it was unsatisfactory since it gave the views of one section only of the community, and moreover, in this case it had led to a result which was opposed to the Governor's own advice. He refused to make any further change in the constitution of the Board until the new governor was able to advise on the question. Chamberlain's stand saved the Sanitary Board.

The Urban Council

The introduction of elections in 1887 portended the change of the Sanitary Board into a full municipal council. It seemed imminent in 1894 with the blessing of the Marquis of Ripon, but Joseph Chamberlain, who succeeded to the Colonial Secretaryship in 1895, set himself against a municipality in Hong Kong 'for this reason among others: that the Colony and the Municipality would be in great measure co-extensive, and it would be almost impossible to draw the line between colonial and municipal matters'.[1] At the same time he opposed Robinson's proposal to abolish the Sanitary Board unless this were clearly demanded by public opinion. Thus the Board endured another forty years before the expectations of 1887, and indeed those of 1842, received a measure of fulfilment in the creation of an Urban Council in 1936.

Sir Henry Blake tried to revitalize the Board. It was six years since elections had last been held, and he arranged for them to be resumed. He also nominated two Chinese as two of the four nominated members of the Board under the 1887 Ordinance. Elections were held on 18 December 1899 but aroused little interest or excitement. Though only two nominations were received, Dr William Hartigan and James McKie, a ballot had to

[1] Joseph Chamberlain to Sir William Robinson, 29 May 1896, No. 119, CO 129/271.

be taken nevertheless because the Ordinance made no provision for formally returning unopposed candidates and 19 votes were cast as a formality.

The naval and military authorities complained of the insanitary state of the Colony; Major General W. J. Gascoigne reported the town to be in a filthy and insanitary condition, a charge which Blake indignantly denied,[1] but in 1899 Blake had to concede a demand that a representative of the Military have a seat on the Board.

Dissatisfaction with the powers of the Board, and the recurrence of plague every spring continued to breed discontent and, in April 1901, the two elected members resigned on the ground that the Board could and would do nothing until it received adequate and independent powers of its own with direct responsibility to the Governor.[2] This feeling must have been widely shared for when the elections were due to be held on 15 April 1901 to fill the vacancies caused by the resignations, not a single nomination was received. The presiding officer J. W. Norton-Kyshe[3] complained of public apathy regarding municipal affairs, stating that he had found similar conditions in Penang and Singapore. One member of the general public who attended the proceedings retorted that it was not apathy but disgust at the attempt by government officials to browbeat the public, as a result of which no candidate had come forward, and the presiding officer and officials 'were left to their own devices'.[4] The public opposition expressed itself in a Petition, dated 25 June 1901, signed by over 1,000 persons, mostly European, which was sent in July of that year to Joseph Chamberlain, asking for a special commission of enquiry into the sanitary condition of Hong Kong; it alleged that in the 19 years since the Chadwick Report, little had been done to implement its findings. The Governor in reply called attention to the Public Health Ordinances, which had been placed on the statute-book, despite the bitter and sustained opposition of the unofficial members of the Legislative Council and other influential members of the community, including the Chinese. He roundly accused the

[1] Sir Henry Blake to Joseph Chamberlain, 21 July 1899, No. 197, CO 129/292.
[2] Sir Henry Blake to Joseph Chamberlain, 30 April 1901, No. 170, CO 129/304.
[3] Registrar of the Supreme Court and author of *The Laws and Courts of Hong Kong*, 2 volumes, Noronha & Co., Hong Kong 1898.
[4] *China Mail*, 15 April 1901.

sponsors of the Petition of making sanitary problems the excuse for agitating for a municipal council. The whole affair was started by the Chamber of Commerce which wrote to the Governor to complain about Hong Kong's sanitary conditions and the almost yearly recurrence of plague.[1] As the Governor replied that the Chamber was accepting reckless and exaggerated statements published in the press without due investigation or adequate knowledge, the Chamber in its resentment organized the Petition to vocalize public discontent.

As a result of the Petition, The Secretary of State sent Osbert Chadwick, already well-known in Hong Kong, and Professor W. J. Simpson, of the London College of Tropical Medicine, to enquire into Hong Kong's sanitary condition. They considered that the Sanitary Board was ineffective and that efficiency demanded its replacement by an expert sanitary commission armed with full authority, but the Governor would not recommend the change. On their advice a new draft Public Health and Buildings Ordinance was drawn up, but again there was a great outcry from the property owners who petitioned against it, and gained some concessions. The Ordinance was delayed until 1903 and was amended in December 1903. In the amended ordinance, the Principal Civil Medical Officer who had become president of the Board under the earlier ordinance of that year, was given full control of all sanitary affairs, with direct responsibility to the Government. This put an end to the prolonged experiment of giving the Board authority to make and administer its own bye-laws, subject only to their being passed by the Executive Council. The Ordinance created what was in effect a sanitary department under a government official, and the Board became little more than a consultative committee. Chadwick and Simpson had their way at last.

Sanitary administration continued to be criticized on three main points. It failed adequately to provide for public health as witness the annual visitations of plague, its officials were accused of bribery and corruption, and thirdly, popular support for sanitary measures was lacking because the Board had no real control over policy.

[1] Printed together with the Petition in *Sessional Papers*, 1901, p. 501–564. In an article in *Twentieth Century Impressions of Hong Kong and the Treaty Ports*, edited by Arnold Wright and H. Cartwright, London 1908, p. 100, reference is made to a plebiscite taken by the Chamber of Commerce, which is presumed to refer to this 1901 Petition but there is no evidence of any formal plebiscite.

Allegations of corruption were so insistent that a Commission of Enquiry into the sanitary administration of the Colony was set up in 1906 under the chairmanship of Henry Pollock[1] which issued its report in March 1907.[2] It uncovered widespread evidence of corruption among sanitary officials, British and Chinese alike, which shocked public opinion; it was sympathetic to the complaints of property owners against the 1903 Ordinances which had insisted on improvements without compensation, and it criticized the constitution and powers of the Sanitary Board. It accused the Principal Civil Medical Officer of deliberately engineering the passing of the Amending Ordinance of December 1903 with the sole object of stripping the Sanitary Board of its power and vesting it in himself. The commission also stigmatized this loss of the Board's authority as a disfranchisement of the people.

The Commissioners *inter alia* recommended a Sanitary and Buildings Board working in four sections—secretarial, medical, engineering and veterinary—consisting of four official and six unofficial members; of the latter, two British and two Chinese should be nominated by the Governor and two elected by the ratepayers; the Board should have power to elect its own president and have complete control over sanitary policy and administration with direct responsibility to the Governor for the expenditure of funds voted by the Legislative Council. These particular recommendations regarding the structure of the Board were not accepted; instead, by a Public Health and Buildings Ordinance passed in July 1908, the composition and powers of the Sanitary Board, so often the subject of debate, were finally settled and assumed a form which lasted the remaining 20 years of its life. The Board was to consist of four official and six unofficial members, and, as before, of the latter, two were to be elected by those whose names appeared on the jury lists, and four, two being Chinese, were nominated by the Governor. The Principal Civil Medical Officer was replaced as president by a cadet officer. The Captain Superintendent of Police also ceased to be a member and was replaced by the Medical Officer of Health. The electorate was slightly increased by removing the stipulation that those qualified for jury service had also to be ratepayers before being qualified to vote. In addition, all building matters were placed under a separate

---

[1] He was soon succeeded in the chairmanship by E. A. Hewett.
[2] Hong Kong *Sessional Papers* 1907, p. 185.

Building Authority, and the Board was confined to less contentious and more purely sanitary matters. The Board continued in name, but only as a consultative committee, the cadet officer who became the administrative head of the Sanitary Department being responsible directly to the Governor. He was obliged to lay his departmental estimates and proposals before the Board for discussion before March 31st each year; he had to consult the Board on all changes giving effect to sanitary bye-laws and on all staff appointments, dismissals, and organization, and to bring all complaints before it, but the Board had no means of enforcing its opinion. The administrative head of the Sanitary Department could not be dismissed by the Board; nor did it have control over its finances. The principle of an unofficial majority on the Sanitary Board was conceded because of precedent, but made nugatory by whittling away the Board's powers. The electoral principle remained, but under the circumstances the elections aroused little public interest and were in fact quite frequently uncontested.

Despite the election fiasco of 1901, elections were held in 1903 but as only two candidates appeared there was no opposition, and this happened again in 1906. The first election following the 1908 re-organization, held on 20 January 1909 was one of the few in the election series to be keenly contested. A total of 1,327 votes[1] were cast for four candidates by a total number on the jury lists of 943; if each had two votes for the two seats there was a maximum vote of 1886, so that 70% of the total votes were cast in this election, a very high poll allowing for the usual high proportion of absentees. In the election due to be held on 19 January 1912 there was no contest, the two candidates being returned unopposed. The election of 22 January 1915 produced a close contest, in which 806 votes were cast for three candidates, out of a total voting strength of 1,325 or nearly 61%. In the following year, on 18 February 1916, an election took place to fill a vacancy, in which the two candidates polled 415 votes out of a total possible vote of 1,148 or 35·3%. In 1919 again only one candidate was nominated for one seat. In 1920 an election was held in which the retiring member was challenged by a candidate who was backed by the Kowloon Residents' Association; the latter was narrowly defeated in a close contest by 191 votes to 164, and though the election caused more excitement than usual, the poll was small. After that no election aroused any

---

[1] *China Mail*, 21 January 1909.

excitement or contest until that of 1932, on which occasion, one of
the candidates, Dr Li Shu-fan, conducted an electioneering campaign using motor-cars carrying posters and supported by European
and Chinese canvassers. 'It was a campaign such as was never before
seen in Hong Kong and deserved to succeed because of its thorough-
ness' wrote one press report.[1] He defeated his opponent, Mr F.
C. Mow Fung by 936 to 161. On this occasion, when all the
electioneering arts were employed the total vote was 1,099 out of
a possible 1,568, or 70%. At the second election held that same
year in November, only one candidate was nominated for the one
vacant seat, and up to the abolition of the Sanitary Board in 1936,
there were no further elections, the candidates being returned
unopposed on each occasion.

Looking over these election results, the conclusion is that there
was no great keenness; the 1932 excitement was due to the energy
and personality of one candidate. There were few contested
elections. The 1909 election was alone remarkable for any mani-
festation of civic spirit. In 1919 and 1920, at the height of the
reform agitation conducted by the Constitutional Reform Association, when great public interest in elections might have been
expected, there was little excitement over the elections and only
a relatively small percentage of voters voted in 1920. Probably no
great importance was attached to membership of the Sanitary
Board because it had so little power.

The demand for a municipal council in Hong Kong never
wholly died, the Kowloon Residents' Association for example put
it forward in 1920. Eventually in 1936 the Sanitary Board became
the Urban Council; yet it came into being as a result of criticism
from within the Government and not as a result of pressure from
without. The Sanitary Board in spite of having an elected element,
never became a popular body upon which the demand for wider
municipal powers could be focussed.

The Sanitary Department functioned side by side with the
Medical Department in an uneasy partnership. The chief critic of
the public health administration of the Colony was the Director
of Medical Services, and particularly the incumbent of that office
from 1929–1937, Dr A. R. Wellington.[2] He complained that though

---

[1] *China Mail*, 12 May 1932.

[2] Memorandum on the changes in the Public Health Organization of Hong
Kong by Dr A. R. Wellington, Hong Kong *Sessional Papers* 1937, p. 103.

he was called the Director of Medical and Sanitary Services, he had in fact no responsibility for sanitary services which were under the control and supervision of the Sanitary Department: he pointed out that in none of the Public Health Ordinances was there any reference to the head of the Medical Department. The old office of Colonial Surgeon as originally created in 1843 was charged only with the health of the Police, the inmates of the prison and junior ranks of the government service for whom Government assumed this liability, and originally had no responsibility for the health of the community as a whole. Dr Wellington criticized the existing sanitary administration because there was no one authority which controlled all public health activities. The Secretary for Chinese Affairs, for example, controlled restaurants and Chinese dispensaries amongst other things; the Police dealt with hawkers of foodstuffs and food stalls; the Public Works Department dealt with buildings, sewage and drainage; and the Education Department dealt with school hygiene.

The Director of Medical Services condemned this division of responsibility among various 'independent lay authorities' as he called them, and he argued that all public health activities should come under the control of the Medical Department. He thought that public health problems would normally be best administered by a municipal government, but that in Hong Kong there was no room for a municipality side by side with the Colonial Government. He submitted a scheme of re-organization in 1930. This was considered by the Sanitary Board in 1932, which accepted it but proposed that the functions of the Board should be enlarged, and become a Public Health Board. In the ensuing discussion, the principle of an Urban Council was accepted; legislation was passed in 1935, and the Council came into being on 1 January 1936.

By the 1936 re-organization, the Sanitary Board was replaced by an Urban Council, under the chairmanship of a cadet officer. The Director of Medical and Sanitary Services became the official adviser to the Council on all matters pertaining to public health, and occupied the position of vice-chairman of the Council *ex officio*, and he controlled the Council's technical staff including health officers, veterinary surgeons and sanitary inspectors.

The new Urban Council consisted of not more than thirteen members, of whom five were official members, and eight unofficial members. The former were the chairman and head of the Sanitary

Department, the Director of Medical Services as vice-chairman, Director of Public Works, Secretary of Chinese Affairs, and the Inspector General of Police. Of the unofficial members two were elected by those whose names appeared on the jury list or were exempted by the nature of their occupation from jury service, the remaining six, of whom three were to be Chinese, were nominated by the Governor. The unofficial members serving on the old Sanitary Board were to continue during their terms, and all unofficial members were to hold office for three years. The powers of the Council were not enlarged so as to be commensurate with its new high-sounding name, but subsequent legislative amendments did give it more consultative powers, and widened the scope of its work.

The creation of the Urban Council did not stimulate any renewed interest among the electorate in the choice of its elected members. Only one candidate was nominated at the first election fixed for 22 January 1936. The first contested election did not occur until 29 February 1940, and there was another contest in 1941, in each case the two opponents were members of the Portuguese community.

The main interest in membership of the Urban Council, as of the old Sanitary Board, lay in the opportunity of serving an administrative apprenticeship, with the reasonable expectation of a reversionary right to membership of the Legislative Council.

CHAPTER X

ADMINISTRATIVE DEVELOPMENTS

The Administrative Departments, 1841–1941

WHEN in 1841 Captain Charles Elliot took over Hong Kong, he made a number of appointments, e.g. magistrate, harbour master, assistant harbour master, clerks of works and land officer, to form a skeleton administration, but as the cession of the Island had not yet been provided for by a definitive treaty these appointments were not confirmed by the Home Government. Only in September 1843 did the Secretary of State, after consultation with Sir Henry Pottinger, decide on the principal administrative officers required and their annual salaries. They were: Governor (and Superintendent of Trade) £6,000, Colonial Secretary £1,800, Colonial Chaplain £700, Chief Justice £3,000[1] Attorney-General £1,500, Chief Magistrate £1,200, Colonial Auditor £1,000, Surveyor-General £1,000 and Harbour Master £600. They became heads of small departments[2] and with their staffs formed the first civil service in Hong Kong. The top officials were recruited in England[3] and the assistants and junior staff were recruited locally. The staff of all grades envisaged in 1843 totalled 28 persons. The staff of the Superintendent of Trade was kept separate, except that responsibility for the finances of the treaty ports rested with the Colonial Treasurer, and appeals from the consular courts lay in the Supreme Court of the Colony. The naval and military forces and the Post Office remained under direct British Government control.

Almost immediately three more officials were needed, a medical officer, an officer in charge of registration of the Chinese, and a police superintendent.

Pottinger, who had asked for a medical officer, was told to make use of local practitioners to attend to prisoners and police—the only people for whose health the Government assumed responsibility. However, in 1844 the prevalence of sickness, especially fever, led Davis to appoint a Dr Dill as Colonial Surgeon, and this

---

[1] The salary had to be raised to this amount to attract any candidate for the post.

[2] Except the Auditor who was attached to the Colonial Treasurer's department.

[3] Except that Lt. W. Pedder, R.N., Harbour Master and Major William Caine, Chief Magistrate, had their appointments by Elliot confirmed.

was accepted by the Colonial Office; five years later a small hospital was sanctioned for which the post of Medical Superintendent was created before 1864. A port health officer had to be appointed in 1869 following cases of infection brought by visiting ships. The Colonial Surgeon was renamed Principal Civil Medical Officer in 1897, and in 1928 became Director of Medical Services, and in 1936 Director of Medical and Health Services with a corresponding widening of his responsibilities.

A Registrar-General was appointed by Davis in 1844 to register all the Chinese in order to combat triad societies and assist in the better maintenance of law and order. The first to hold the office was Samuel Fearon, an interpreter on the staff of the Superintendent of Trade who later became the first professor of Chinese at King's College, London. This official's close contact with the Chinese demanded a proficiency in the Chinese language, which in turn, led him gradually to assume responsibility for all questions relating to the Chinese and to be the channel of communication between them and the Government. In 1858, this side of his duties received statutory recognition and the additional title 'Protector of the Chinese'. As the Chinese community grew, so did his duties and status, and in 1884 he became an *ex officio* member of the Legislative Council. In 1913, he became known as Secretary for Chinese Affairs. In 1938 a Labour Officer was added to his staff to deal with trade unions, wages and conditions of work.

The third office Davis created was that of Superintendent of Police. In 1845 Charles May was recruited from England to organize a police force and a police department came into being. From superintendent, the title was elevated to Captain Superintendent on the appointment of M. W. Deane, one of the first cadet officers, to that post in 1869; in 1929 it became known as Inspector General of Police and ten years later in 1939 as Commissioner of Police.

Davis was responsible for the origins of the Education Department, which grew up haphazardly from humble beginnings in 1847 when three Chinese vernacular schools were each given a grant of $10 per month, and a committee was appointed to report and administer these sums. The first appointment of Inspector of Schools was made in 1856 and then in 1862, a headmaster for the Government Central School was recruited from Britain who also combined the duties of Inspector of Schools.

The government printing press was authorized in 1853 and under Bowring, began to operate under the supervision of the government printer, D. Noronha; it never evolved into an independent government department.

An Auditor had been appointed to the staff of the Colonial Treasurer in 1844, but when economies were effected in accordance with the recommendations of the 1847 Parliamentary Select Committee, the Colonial Secretary combined the duties of the post with his own. In 1857 this arrangement was ended, and an Auditor-General was appointed to audit the colonial and consular accounts; he had to submit all accounts in detail to the Colonial Office for further audit. His duties were again merged with those of the Colonial Secretary in 1870 on the retirement of W. H. Rennie, and the audit became purely local. In 1890 at the instance of the Colonial Office, audit by the Colonial Audit Department in London was resumed and an auditor (not auditor-general), was appointed, and though he was employed locally, his main responsibility was to his departmental superiors in Whitehall.

A new government department came into being on 1 May 1860 when a Postmaster General was appointed to take over the Post Office from the British authorities at a salary of £800 a year.

Another department, the Import and Export Department, was set up in 1886 as a result of an agreement with China which ended the Hong Kong 'blockade'. The Hong Kong Government undertook to supervise, control and report on the import and export of opium in order to assist the Chinese customs officials to check smuggling in that commodity. The Import and Export Department provided the machinery to carry out the terms of the agreement, and as Hong Kong was a free port, its work was necessarily confined to the control of the opium trade. It became more important in 1909, when import duties were first imposed on luxury articles such as wines and spirits, to make up for revenue lost as a result of restrictions imposed by the Secretary of State on the opium trade. Its responsibilities were much increased in 1919 when details of imports and exports into and out of the Colony had to be declared and the Department had the duty of compiling the annual trade statistics.

In 1883 the beginnings of a Sanitary Department came with the appointment of a Sanitary Inspector and the setting up of the Sanitary Board; its history has already been given and need not be repeated. In 1883 an assistant Colonial Secretary was appointed. The Public Works Department expanded with the growth of the Colony and in April 1892 the name of the head of the department was changed from Surveyor-General to Director of Public Works.

A Superintendent of Government Gardens was appointed in 1861, and a government gardens and tree planting department attached to the Surveyor-General's department came into existence in 1872; seven years later it became an independent government department under a Botanical Superintendent. In 1905 it became known as the Botanical and Forestry Department.

In one respect there was some retrenchment. The practice had been to support the Established Church in the Colonies by contributing to the salaries of Anglican clergy and to the cost of Anglican churches from public funds.[1] In Hong Kong the Colonial Chaplain was a salaried government official and the building of the Anglican cathedral was assisted by a Hong Kong government grant of £4,639 which paid for two-thirds of the costs. The Anglican bishop was also given official recognition by being appointed under Letters Patent, though no part of his salary came from local public funds.[2] Following the great Colenso controversy in South Africa, all Anglican colonial bishoprics were disestablished: in Hong Kong this took effect with the appointment of Bishop Burdon in 1874, from which date the Anglican bishopric became a purely ecclesiastical appointment. In 1882 it was further decided that the Colonial Chaplaincy should no longer form part of the official establishment; this was carried into effect on the retirement of the existing incumbent in 1892, when his successor became Cathedral Chaplain with a salary provided out of cathedral funds. Since 1892, all churches in Hong Kong have been on the same footing in relation to government.

Before the end of the 19th century, other small departments were created. A Gunpowder Department apparently existed for a short time,[3] and the Lighthouses Department was established in 1875 following the erection of lighthouses at Cape D'Aguilar and Green Island in that year and the Observatory came in 1883. The

---

[1] Grants of land and occasionally building grants were made to other Christian denominations and charitable bodies, e.g. the Morrison Education Society.

[2] A pension from public funds was voted to the first Bishop of Victoria, Bishop George Smith, when he retired in 1864.

[3] See Sir Charles Collins, *Public Administration in Hong Kong*, London 1952, p. 130.

Gaol and Land Registry were also organized as separate departments. The Gaol was first built in 1843 and placed under a sheriff responsible to the Police Magistrate. A governor of the gaol was appointed in 1858 and in 1863 became known as the Superintendent of Victoria Gaol. The head of the department became Superintendent of Prisons in 1920 and Commissioner of Prisons in 1938. The land registry was first organized as a department of the Surveyor-General's office and became independent in 1883 under a Land Officer and Official Receiver, who in 1912 became known simply as Land Officer.

The organization of the New Territories as a separate department under two District Officers, North and South, has already been referred to.

The 20th century saw a great expansion in the government services, largely because governments have undertaken more functions. In 1901, the total number of employees of all grades in the government service was 715; in 1938 the figure was 2,886.

The Colonial Treasurer was replaced in 1938 by an administrative officer, the Financial Secretary, who was responsible for all financial questions and policy. In 1938 an Inland Revenue Department was set up to deal with income tax which was then being imposed for the first time. Further expansion arose from technical developments, for example, a Civil Aviation Department was set up in 1931, attached to the Harbour Master's Department.

In education, the Inspector of Schools became the Director of Education in 1909. The Kowloon-Canton Railway was completed in 1910 and was operated directly by government under a Manager appointed in 1911 and who became known as Manager and Chief Engineer until the Second World War.

When war came in 1939, certain departments relating to the war were created including Air Raid Precautions Officer, Custodian of Enemy Property, Controller of Trade, Controller of Food, and Censor and Detaining Officer.

Arrangements for the administration of justice have grown steadily through the Colony's history. A magistrate was appointed in 1841 and became Chief Magistrate when an assistant was found to be necessary in 1843. The Supreme Court under a Chief Justice was set up in 1844, with civil and criminal jurisdiction and with a registrar and interpreters. A summary court under a judge was established in 1861, and in 1873 this became part of the Supreme

Court and a puisne judge appointed. Arrangements for a Court of Appeal were made in 1912 to consist of three judges, the two Hong Kong judges being joined for this purpose by the British judge in Shanghai or by a local barrister of high standing.

The first magistrates appointed had no specific legal qualifications, though Caine had had considerable army experience in the judge-advocate general's department. The first qualified barrister was appointed magistrate in 1858. Some effort was made to associate the unpaid Justice of the Peace with the work of the lower courts, but generally, all magistrates have been stipendiary. In 1861, the two magistrates were made co-equal and the post of Chief Magistrate disappeared. By 1938 there were two magistrates in Kowloon and two in Victoria.

The appointment of government law officers followed the usual British pattern. Pottinger appointed a temporary legal advisor in 1843 until an attorney-general appointed from home could arrive in 1844. A Crown Solicitor was first appointed in 1851 to act also as deputy sheriff and coroner.

A most important development, carried out under Sir Hercules Robinson, was the inauguration in 1861 of the cadet scheme, by which young men of promise were recruited in Britain by competitive examination, and who, after further training in the Chinese language (Cantonese) were to be regarded as candidates for promotion in due course to the highest administrative posts. The term cadet officer to denote the administrative grade of officers in the Hong Kong Government service remained in use for almost a century, until 1960. The scheme was dropped by Sir Arthur Kennedy, Governor 1872–1877, but was reintroduced by Sir George Bowen.

Sir Hercules Robinson was also responsible for the first comprehensive review of salaries of those grades recruited locally in which government had to compete with local commercial firms, as a result of which the first general advance in salaries had to be conceded. Up to 1862 superannuation arrangements were on a haphazard basis. A private contributory superannuation scheme was operated, and pensions for retiring officers were voted by the Legislative Council on the recommendation of the Governor, each case being considered individually. In that year, the Pension Ordinance, No. 10 of 1862, established pensions for senior officials on a non-contributory basis. Robinson had proposed a contributory scheme but the Secretary of State ruled against this, in order to bring the pension arrangements in Hong Kong into line with those being adopted in other British colonies at this time.

Under Sir Arthur Kennedy a system of recruitment by public examination for the lower ranks of the civil service was begun in 1875, and thus opened the way to a greatly extended and systematized recruitment of local personnel. The depreciation in the value of the dollar led to much discontent among the officials over the diminishing value of their salaries which were paid in silver dollars. In 1902 salaries were placed on a sterling basis, in a salary scheme which for the first time put salaries, except for certain senior officers, such as the Chief Justice, Colonial Secretary and Attorney-General on an incremental basis and arranged for more clearly defined grades.

One important feature of the inter-war years was a demand for the appointment of local people to more senior posts in the government service. There were Retrenchment Commissions in 1909 and 1932, set up to suggest economies. That of 1932 urged the appointment of Asians to positions of greater responsibility and pointed to the Medical and Sanitary Departments as those most likely to offer opportunities for non-European graduates being produced by the University of Hong Kong.[1] It also suggested the appointment of Chinese nurses. This policy, vigorously advocated in the Legislative Council by Sir Man Kam Lo, was accepted by the Governor, Sir Andrew Caldecott, not solely on ground of economy. In the 1935 budget debate the acting Colonial Secretary declared that the 'Government has fully and frankly accepted the policy of replacing wherever possible European by Asiatic employees'. In 1936 the principle was laid down that before any vacancy was advertised in the United Kingdom, local candidates with the necessary qualifications were to be considered. The expansion of the government services thus began to bring improved opportunities to local people for employment in the government service, though this policy was not carried as far nor pursued as rapidly as many would have liked.

[1] Hong Kong *Sessional Papers* 1932, pp. 52–3.

The Office of Lieutenant-Governor

In his dispatch of 29 May 1896, Joseph Chamberlain referred to the decision that the Senior Military Officer would in future administer the government in the absence of the Governor. In this connection a brief history of the office of Lieutenant-Governor might be of interest.

The Hong Kong Charter of 5 April 1843 provided that if the Governor were absent from the Colony or were from any cause unable to act, then his powers should devolve upon a Lieutenant-Governor, or if no Lieutenant-Governor were appointed, upon the person holding the office of Colonial Secretary. In 1843, the intention was that the office of Lieutenant-Governor should be held by the senior military officer. Anglo-Chinese relations had been uncertain and difficult, and the fear remained that despite the treaty settlement of 1842, British commerce might still need protection. Hong Kong therefore had a military importance which pointed to the advantage of the garrison commander acting as the deputy for Governor and Superintendent of Trade. In 1844 General D'Aguilar assumed this post, and he and his successors took control of the administration in the absence of the Governor as a matter of course.

This arrangement continued until 1854 in which year Sir Samuel George Bonham retired. Then mainly as a measure of economy as has been explained above, it was decided to separate the post of Superintendent of Trade from that of Governor of the Colony, and replace the latter post by a lieutenant-governor. But this could not be done without fresh legislation, so as a practical solution Sir John Bowring, the next Superintendent of Trade, became nominal Governor of Hong Kong, and William Caine, the Colonial Secretary, became Lieutenant-Governor, with full control over the Colony's administration. The arrangement broke down and, Bowring was made Governor with full powers, but without any increase in salary. Caine retained the position of Lieutenant-Governor and naturally deputized for Bowring as required. For most of the five years that Caine held it, the post was a sinecure.

When Caine retired in 1859 the post of Lieutenant-Governor was not filled, but held temporarily by the Governor himself during the period between his appointment and his actual arrival in the Colony. Thus Sir Hercules Robinson was commissioned as Lieutenant-Governor in June 1859 and assumed the governorship on his arrival in September 1859. When Robinson returned home on leave, W. T. Mercer,[1] the Colonial Secretary, was chosen in preference to the Senior Military Officer to deputize for the Governor and administered the government from July 1862 until February 1864, and again, when Robinson left to take up the governorship of Ceylon, from March 1865 until the arrival of Sir Richard MacDonnell in March 1866. This was probably due to Mercer's own senior position in the Colony, as well as to the return of more peaceful conditions after the treaties of 1858 and 1860 which made it less likely for serious calls to be made on the military. Another factor in the change was the introduction of civil service recruitment by examination in 1861 aimed at building up a professional civil service in the Colony, which could hardly be done without offering opportunities of promotion.

Three years later, in 1868, the Imperial Government after much discussion of the principle involved, decided to revert to the original practice of giving the Major General in Command of the Hong Kong garrison a commission as Lieutenant-Governor. In October of that year, MacDonnell applied for leave and recommended J. Gardiner Austin, the Colonial Secretary, as the Officer Administering the Government following the precedent set by Mercer. He was informed that a General was being sent out with a commission as lieutenant-governor and as a temporary measure Major General J. R. Brunker came from Japan in January 1869 to take temporary charge of the government for the forty-two days that the Governor was away. He died three months later, in April, and his successor, Major General H. W. Whitfield, arrived armed with a lieutenant-governor's commission. Thus when MacDonnell returned to England on leave in April 1879, Whitfield accordingly deputized for him.

This reversion to a military deputy for the governor was not a success. Whitfield made many mistakes, among which he criticized the Secretary of State himself over the disposal of the special gambling fund;[2] he suspended senior police personnel as a

[1] William Thomas Mercer (1800–?). Nephew of Sir John Davis, whom he accompanied to Hong Kong in 1844 as his private secretary. Colonial Treasurer in 1847 and Colonial Secretary 1854 on the promotion of William Caine to be Lieutenant-Governor.

[2] MacDonnell had licensed gambling houses and incurred great criticism. The Liberal Government at home ruled that money from vice should not be regarded as normal revenue, and the gambling licence fees had therefore to go into a special fund to be used for police and other special purposes.

preliminary to police reform; and he completely reversed Mac-
Donnell's licensing of gambling. Whitfield had bluntly to be told
to make no change of policy while MacDonnell was away. When
Whitfield resigned in June 1874, a change was decided upon and
the War Office was informed that the Hong Kong Colonial
Secretary would in future administer the government in the
absence of the Governor.[1] This change was supported by the
arguments that a senior Hong Kong civil servant was more conver-
sant with the questions that might come up, and also it was
important that members of the civil service should not feel
themselves debarred from assuming the highest positions. Major
General Colborne who followed Whitfield was given a special
commission, specially worded, to administer the government only
in exceptional circumstances and for special civil reasons. So when
in October 1874, Kennedy was invited by Lord Carnarvon to
return to England for consultations, J. Gardener Austin, the
Colonial Secretary, administered the government. Colborne was
extremely annoyed at being passed over and Kennedy reported
that it 'has nearly caused General Colborne a fit. He has fairly
exploded . . .'. The General argued that as he took precedence
next to the Governor he should have been the Officer Administering the Government. Because of this incident, the clause in the
Hong Kong Charter dealing with the position of lieutenant-
governor was revised in 8 June 1875.[2] The amendment provided
that the Lieutenant-Governor should deputize for the Governor
should the latter be unable for any reason to act, or, if no one were
appointed Lieutenant-Governor, then the Colonial Secretary should
act for the Governor, 'subject to such instructions as the Governor
may have received'. These words were specially added to keep
control firmly in the hands of the Colonial Office in London.
On 9 April 1877, this section was further amended; the lieutenant-
governor was to act for the governor if the latter were for any
reason incapacitated, but if none were appointed, the Colonial
Secretary was to act for him; 'until Her Majesty's pleasure should
be made known and in accordance with any instructions received'.
Colborne remained sullen and unco-operative and refused to take
his seat on the Executive Council. Austin administered the

---

[1] Minute on private letter from Kennedy to Herbert, October 1874, CO
129/168.
[2] CO 381/35.

government from March to December 1875 as Colonial Secretary. This remained the settled government policy in the matter until the governorship of Sir George Bowen (1883–1885).

Bowen with twenty years as a colonial governor assumed the role of an elder statesman, and there were no colonial institutions upon which he did not regard himself qualified to pass judgment. In 1883 his plans for constitutional reorganization led him to pronounce upon this question of the Lieutenant-Governor. There had been much shuffling of offices each time the Colonial Secretary administered the government, so he proposed[1] that the General Officer commanding the troops in Hong Kong should administer the government in the absence of the Governor, as had been the original practice. But he went even further and argued that the General ought to be the Governor as at Gibraltar and Bermuda. 'Hong Kong is the Gibraltar of the East' he kept repeating, and asserted that 'In fact neither Gibraltar nor Hong Kong is a Colony in the proper sense of the term'. Derby replied[2] agreeing that there would be some disturbance of work if the Colonial Secretary acted as deputy for the Governor but that this was not peculiar to Hong Kong; he said that the matter had been carefully discussed in 1864 and 1866 and 1871 and it had ultimately been decided that it was preferable to have the Colonial Secretary as deputy for the Governor because it helped to train future governors and gave men a chance to show their ability. Probably the decision in 1871 in favour of the Colonial Secretary was influenced by the Civil Service reform of 1870, which opened the Home Government service to examination and created a professional spirit and the opportunity of a professional career.

Bowen continued to press the claims of the General, and Derby eventually agreed that in the absence of the Governor and the Colonial Secretary, the General should administer the government, and that he would in future be given a dormant commission to this effect. This was adopted, and so when Bowen went on short leave to Japan in summer of 1885, and Marsh, the Colonial Secretary being also at that time on leave, Major General W. G. Cameron administered the government; but when later in that year Bowen retired and Marsh had returned, it was the latter who took over. Marsh himself left on retirement before Bowen's successor, Sir

[1] Sir George Bowen to Earl of Derby, 23 May 1883, No. 82, CO 129/209.
[2] Earl of Derby to Sir George Bowen, 23 August 1883, No. 174, CO 129/209.

William Des Vœux, arrived, and Major General Cameron again took over. In May 1891 Des Vœux returned to Britain on retirement, and Fleming,[1] the Colonial Secretary, being also on leave, Major General Digby Barker assumed the government. He urged that he should continue to be the officer administering the government, even after Fleming returned to the Colony, as he was expected to do, before the new Governor, Sir William Robinson arrived. In his reply, Lord Knutsford repeated the ruling that in the absence of the Governor, the Colonial Secretary should be the officer administering the government, when he was in the Colony. To avoid arguments, Fleming's leave was extended so that he would arrive with the new governor, leaving Barker in charge until then.

In 1895, the question of having the General as the Governor's deputy to act in his absence was again considered by the Home Government. Joseph Chamberlain, the Unionist Colonial Secretary of State wrote confidentially to Robinson[2] asking if it were preferable to have the General or the Colonial Secretary as the officer administering the government in the absence of the Governor and suggesting that there was something be said for the former 'in the present state of affairs in the Far East'. In his reply[3] Robinson wrote that in view of the unsettled conditions in the Far East, his view was that the General should assume the government in the absence of the Governor. As a result, the change was made, and when Robinson left the Colony in February 1898, Major General Wilsone Black became the acting governor. There was indeed, as Chamberlain urged, 'something to be said' for restoring the general to his previous position as acting for the governor in his absence. The whole Far East was in a state of tension. Military works, fortifications, accommodation and land to strengthen the Colony's defences posed serious problems. The military contribution had been doubled and created constitutional issues. It was therefore reasonable that the General should be more closely associated with the administration. He had been a member of the Executive Council since 1844 and his position as prospective officer administering the government made it logical that he should be a member of the

---

[1] Sir Francis Fleming (1842–1922). Governor of Sierra Leone, 1892, Governor of the Leeward Islands, 1895–1901.

[2] J. Chamberlain to Sir William Robinson (Confidential), 21 October 1895, CO 129/267.

[3] Sir William Robinson to J. Chamberlain (Confidential), 4 December 1895, CO 129/269.

Legislative Council and this was done in 1896. With the easing of
the tension after the Boxer troubles of 1900 and the Anglo-Japanese
Alliance of 1902, defence needs were less insistent and the practice
of having the Colonial Secretary as the officer administering the
Government was revived in December 1903, when the Colonial
Secretary F. H. May, became Officer Administering the Govern-
ment on the departure of the Governor, Sir Henry Blake. The last
General to act as deputy was Sir William Gascoigne, February to
September 1902. Indeed this practice had only been departed from
with some reluctance and because the tenseness of international
relations made it advisable. It was recognized that the Colonial
Secretary had some claim in the matter, and Lockhart, the Colonial
Secretary who had been the victim of the change of 1895 was
consoled by being appointed the first civilian Commissioner of
Weihaiwei in 1902.

After 1902, the Colonial Secretary has invariably deputized for
the Governor when necessary and the office of Lieutenant-
Governor has lapsed.

Part III

THE CONSTITUTION IN THE POST-WAR PERIOD
1945-1962

7. The Central District, 1963. The City Hall is in the foreground; the domed Supreme Court building is in the centre, the Anglican Cathedral of St. John in the upper left, with the Central Government Offices just behind. Government House is in the top centre.
   By courtesy of Crown Lands and Surveys, Hong Kong Government.

8. The procession of Judges at the ceremonial opening of the Assizes, January 1960.
   By courtesy of the Hong Kong Government Information Services.

Between pages 178–179

CHAPTER XI

THE YOUNG PLAN OF CONSTITUTIONAL REFORM

The Restoration of British Authority

DURING the First World War and the inter-war years, Japan's industrial development and military power gave her the dominant role in the Far East, despite the attempt made at the Washington Conference in 1922 to limit her naval armaments. With the outbreak of the Second World War in Europe, the Japanese military and naval leaders saw an opportunity of establishing Japan's hegemony over the whole Pacific area. On the 7 December 1941 Japan struck at Pearl Harbour and on the same day, allowing for the international date line, attacked Hong Kong, which surrendered on Christmas day, after a stubborn fight of 17 days.

For the next three years and seven months the Japanese were in control. War shortages caused great distress to a Chinese population which had been swollen to double its size by refugees from the area of Japanese military operations around Canton, and which the new Japanese rulers proceeded to reduce by harsh methods to less than 600,000, less in fact than the 1931 census figure, one third of whom were farmers and fishermen living on their own resources. The Allied blockade denied supplies to Hong Kong and led inevitably to the neglect of public services such as communications, malarial control, and medical services. Trade dwindled. All British institutions were abolished. Under General Rensuke Isogai a military government was set up. It introduced some Japanese administrative institutions such as the District Administrative Offices headed by Japanese in consultation with local Chinese residents, which were responsible for such measures as food-rationing. Two councils, the Chinese Representative Council, and the Chinese Co-operative Council, were set up. They were entirely Chinese bodies having consultative status only and it is doubtful if they influenced Japanese policy as they were primarily agencies through which the instructions of the Japanees were made known; likewise no Chinese served on the supreme Japanese governing body. Under war conditions little else was to be expected. Many Chinese preferred obscurity to collaboration though some took the view that it was better to work with the Japanese in the hope of mollifying the severities of the occupation. Behind the Japanese administration stood the dreaded *kampetei*.[1]

Japan's collapse in 1945 mercifully spared the Colony the ordeal of a military reconquest. The restoration of British authority was by no means assured and its fate was the subject of some desultory discussion among the Allies. American sentiment was strongly anti-colonial by tradition and President Roosevelt, to whom the war was a crusade against the enemies of human freedom, was influenced by it. Clause 3 of the Altantic Charter dealing with 'the right of all peoples to choose the form of government under which they will live', and the restoration of 'sovereign rights and self-government to those who have been forcibly deprived of them', was intended by him to apply as much to former colonial peoples as to those liberated from Nazi and Japanese militarism. United States opinion over-simplified the colonial problem by arguing that it was illogical to represent the war as a struggle for human freedom and to deny it to colonial peoples. The President therefore '. . . once or twice urged the British to give up Hong Kong as a gesture of good will'.[2]

At the Yalta Conference in February 1945, at which China was unrepresented and British not fully consulted in that part of the discussions which concerned the Far East, Roosevelt urged in private conversations with Stalin that Hong Kong should be given back to China or internationalized as a free port.[3] United States official opinion did not favour British retention of Hong Kong. A further factor against the British keeping Hong Kong lay in the hopes aroused by the 1943 treaty undertakings by Britain and the United States to end the 'unequal treaty' system and give up their special privileges and concessions in China.[4] The Chinese hoped

[1] This brief account is based on conversation with Chinese who were resident in Hong Kong during the Japanese occupation.

[2] R. E. Sherwood, *The White House Papers of Henry L. Hopkins*, London 1948, pp. 719-9.

[3] E. Roosevelt, *As He Saw It*, New York 1946, pp. 223-4.

[4] Treaty between the United States and China for the Relinquishment of Extra-territorial Rights in China and the Regulation of Related Matters signed at Washington, 11 January 1943, with Accompanying Exchange of Notes. See *United States Relations with China*, Department of State Publication 3573, Far Eastern Series 30, 1949, p. 514. A similar Sino-British Treaty was signed at the same time.

this would include Hong Kong, though the treaties made no reference to the rendition of ceded territory.[1]

The administration of territory reconquered during the War was under the control of the Allied Combined Civil Affairs Committee which ruled that the Chief Allied Commander was to follow in a liberated country such policy as was laid down by the government which exercised authority over it before the enemy occupation. Since 1943 a small planning unit which had been working in the Colonial Office on plans for the resumption of British administration in Hong Kong, assumed the functions of a British Civil Affairs Staff, all with military rank, under the above Allied arrangements. But there was some doubt if this British military administration would be allowed to function in Hong Kong because the latter came within the area in which Generalissimo Chiang Kaishek was the Allied Commander-in-Chief, and he had grounds for hoping that the Colony would be retroceded to China as part of a general settlement in the Far East. Further, the Allied Combined Civil Affairs Committee's ruling regarding policy to be followed in a liberated country, applied only to territory recovered 'as the result of an operation'. This was interpreted by the United States to mean that it did not apply in such cases as Hong Kong where the territory was recovered as a result of the general Japanese surrender and not as the result of a specific military operation.[2]

The surrender of Japan came sooner than expected and a naval squadron under Rear-Admiral Sir Cecil Harcourt was detached from the British Pacific Fleet to receive the surrender of the Japanese at Hong Kong and restore British authority. When Chiang Kaishek protested, the surrender was received in the name of both British and Chinese Governments, on 30 August 1945. Two weeks earlier, on 16 August the Colonial Secretary of Hong Kong, Mr (later Sir) F. C. Gimson, who had been interned at Stanley, assumed temporary control until 7 September when the British Civil Affairs Unit arrived to set up a military administration under the Admiral. The normal civil administration was restored on 1 May 1946 by the return to Hong Kong of the Governor, Sir Mark

[1] China was included in the Four Power Declaration on General Security signed at Moscow on 30 October 1943 recognizing the right of China to participate in the peace negotiations and in the establishment of machinery for postwar international co-operation. *Ibid.*, p. 37.

[2] See F. S. V. Dennison, *British Military Administration in the Far East 1943-6*. H.M.S.O., London 1956, p. 147.

Young,[1] who had been interned in Formosa during the War. His first announcement was to promise a measure of constitutional reform, whereby the people of the Colony might be given a fuller and more responsible share in the management of their own affairs. The restoration of British rule was not therefore intended to be a simple restoration of conditions as they had been before the War.

The Young Plan

On 1 May 1946 civil government was restored in Hong Kong when Sir Mark Young returned to the Colony to resume his interrupted governorship. At the ceremony which marked that occasion, he broadcast the following important statement on a revision of the Hong Kong constitution:

His Majesty's Government has under consideration the means by which in Hong Kong, as elsewhere in the Colonial Empire, the inhabitants of the Territory can be given a fuller and more responsible share in the management of their own affairs. One possible method of achieving this end would be by handing over certain functions of internal administration, hitherto exercised by the Government, to a Municipal Council constituted on a fully representative basis. The establishment of such a Council, and the transference to it of important functions of government might, it is believed, be an appropriate and acceptable means of affording to all communities in Hong Kong an opportunity of more active participation, through their responsible representatives, in the administration of the Territory. But before a decision is taken on the methods of giving effect to the intentions of His Majesty's Government, it is considered essential that the important issues involved should be thoroughly examined in Hong Kong itself, the fullest account being taken of the views and wishes of the inhabitants. The Governor has accordingly been instructed to examine the whole question, in consultation with the representatives of all sections of the community, and to submit a report at an early date, bearing in mind the policy of His Majesty's Government that the constitution should be revised on a more liberal basis as soon as possible. The aim will be to settle and to announce NOT later than the end of the year the principles on which that revision should be based.[2]

[1] Sir Mark Aitchison Young. G.C.M.G., 1946. Colonial Secretary, Sierra Leone, 1928; Chief Secretary to the Government of Palestine, 1930; Governor of Barbados, 1933; Governor of Tanganyika, 1938; Governor of Hong Kong, September 1941. Prisoner-of-war 1941–45. Resumed Governorship of Hong Kong, 1946–47. (Who's Who, 1961)

[2] South China Morning Post and The Hong Kong Telegraph, 2 May 1946.

Not only was there a clear intention of liberalizing the constitution, but the method of achieving it was also to be liberal, namely through consultation with all sections of the community; and it should be noted that the aim was to give 'a fuller and more responsible share in the management of their own affairs' to 'the inhabitants', and not only to those of British nationality.

There were many factors making for the granting of a greater measure of self-government to the colonies. The Charter of the United Nations Chapter XI, Art. 73, demanded that member nations, in

> the administration of territories whose peoples have not yet attained a full measure of self-government recognise the principle that the interests of the inhabitants of these territories are paramount, and accept as a sacred trust the obligation to promote to the utmost . . . the well-being of the inhabitants of these territories, and to this end . . . to develop self-government, to take due account of the political aspirations of the peoples, and to assist them in the progressive development of their free political institutions according to the particular circumstances of each territory and its peoples and their varying stages of advancement. . . .

Quite apart from this international obligation under the Charter of the United Nations, British policy had long sought this same objective, and there was a genuine desire to continue to carry overseas the British traditions of constitutional freedom on the model of Westminster, and of respect for the rights of all peoples. A very important factor was the degree to which colonial peoples supported Britain with men and material in the struggle against militarism and dictatorship during the War. This unsolicited tribute to British colonial rule by the colonies themselves evoked in response a willing assumption by Britain of the duty of preparing colonial peoples for self-government. The Colonial Development and Welfare Act of 1940, for example, arranged for financial aid to the colonies in the form of outright grants for capital projects and also for recurrent expenditure on important services such as education, agriculture, health and research. The aim as expressed in this Act, was material welfare and development as 'the primary requirement upon which advance in other directions is largely consequential'. It was realized that besides the Victorian ideal of law and order, government action was demanded in many fields previously left to private enterprise, the cost of which could only be met from increased economic development. Government was becoming more complicated and more expensive, and self-government in underdeveloped areas was therefore correspondingly more difficult to achieve. The ideal of self-government needed to be restated in the light of modern conditions; this was defined by Colonel Oliver Stanley speaking in the House of Commons on 13 July 1943:

> We are pledged to guide colonial people along the path to self-government within the British Empire. We are pledged to build up their social and economic institutions, and we are pledged to develop their natural resources.[1]

In 1948, British colonial policy was expressed in these words:

> The central purpose of British colonial policy is simple. It is to guide the colonial territories to responsible self-government within the Commonwealth in conditions that ensure to the people concerned both a fair standard of living and freedom from oppression from any quarter.[2]

All the British political parties shared these views.

The end of the War in 1945 was therefore the signal for important evolutionary change in the structure of the British Commonwealth. India, Pakistan and Ceylon were granted independence and elected to remain within the Commonwealth, Burma demanded and secured complete independence. They were but the first of a number of British dependent territories to secure self-government. The announcement by the Governor of Hong Kong on 1 May 1946 therefore reflected the prevailing view which encouraged colonies to aim at sharing a partnership of free nations within the British Commonwealth.

In June 1946, representative bodies, Chinese and non-Chinese, were invited in accordance with the May 1st announcement, to state their view on the question of 'the form which the revision of the constitution should take, and on some of the questions which would be involved if they favoured the establishment of a municipal council. At the same time those members of the public who felt that they were in a position to express the opinion and wishes of any part of the community were also invited to express their view'. The interests of all sections of the community were to be considered and safeguarded. There was a wide response to this important

---

[1] Quoted by J. S. Furnival, *Colonial Policy and Practice*, Cambridge 1948, p. 315.
[2] Cmd. 7433, 1948 quoted in Sir Charles Jeffries, *The Colonial Office*, Oxford 1956, p. 38.

invitation in the form of representations to the Governor from private individuals and public bodies and discussion in the public press. These were considered by the Governor, in accordance with his instructions, and in a broadcast address to the people of the Colony on 26 August 1946, he gave an outline of his views, which became known as the 'Young' Plan.

From the comments he had received, the Governor said that the general trend of opinion in the Colony seemed to favour the establishment of a municipal council, and he outlined some tentative proposals as a basis for further discussion. Briefly, he proposed that the council should control only the urban area and that two-thirds of its members should be elected in equal numbers by Chinese and non-Chinese voters respectively, and the remaining one-third, again in equal numbers, by Chinese and non-Chinese representative bodies. He indicated some of the problems that would have to be faced, such as the franchise, qualifications for a councillor, and the powers and functions of the Council. He held out the prospect that it would have complete control over its own municipal finances, which would enable it to pursue a genuine independent policy in the sphere of administration entrusted to it. In addition to the municipal council, the Young Plan proposed a reform of the Legislative Council by which the number of un-official members would be increased by one and the number of official members decreased by two. The reformed Legislative Council would therefore consist of seven official members and eight unofficial members, in addition to the Governor who, as president, would retain his original and casting votes and so hold the balance between the official and unofficial elements. To make the eight unofficial members more representative, it was proposed that four should be nominated by unofficial bodies, one each by the Justices of the Peace and Chamber of Commerce as before, and two by the new municipal council. The municipal reform scheme and that for the reform of the Legislative Council were therefore closely related. Parallel constitutional development was also envisaged for the New Territories which were administered independently.

The plan was well received and during September and October of that year further views were expressed by local people, public bodies and various communities on the proposed municipal council and on the broad question of constitutional reform.

Sir Mark Young sent his considered proposals to the Secretary of State for the Colonies in October 1946. He earmarked $1,500,000 in the 1947 budget towards the cost of setting up the municipal council[1] but left the Colony on retirement on 17 May 1947 before any further step could be taken. In July 1947 an announcement was made simultaneously in the House of Commons and in Hong Kong, that the Secretary of State, had, subject to certain reservations, approved the proposed revision of the constitution embodied in the Young Plan.[2]

Once the general principles of the plan had been decided, its details remained to be worked out and embodied in bills to be placed before the Legislative Council. All through the discussion, it was clear that there was no intention on the part of the Colonial Office in London, nor of the local British authorities in Hong Kong, to impose reform on the Colony against its wishes. Further, and in the event this proved decisive, the intention was that that part of the constitutional reform plan which required legislation should be enacted by the existing Legislative Council, which should have an opportunity of giving its opinion on the plan as a whole. The views of the community had been desired and considered, but it is quite clear that the British colonial authorities retained confidence in the traditional mode of assessing public opinion through the unofficial members of the Legislative Council.

Progress was slow because a great deal of detail had to be worked out. The new Governor, Sir Alexander Grantham,[3] referred to this in his address to the Legislative Council before the presentation of the 1948 budget:

> I believe that all of us were guilty in the beginning of an underestimate of the amount of detailed work to be done before the municipality could become a reality. The technical and legal framework which has to be laid is new in Hong Kong and it is moreover extremely complicated. In addition, much preparatory work has to be done, as it were, on the ground; voting wards have to be carefully delineated, voting registers compiled and the whole election machinery created.[4]

---

[1] Hong Kong *Hansard* 1957, p. 51.

[2] *Annual Report 1947*, p. 2.

[3] Sir Alexander William George Herder Grantham, G.C.M.G., Colonial Administrative Service, H.K. 1922; Colonial Secretary, Bermuda, 1935–38; Colonial Secretary, Jamaica, 1938–41; Chief Secretary, Nigeria, 1941–44; Governor, Fiji and High Commissioner for the Western Pacific 1945–47; Governor of Hong Kong 1947–57. K.C.M.G. 1945. (*Who's Who*, 1961)

[4] Hong Kong *Hansard* 1948, p. 57.

Almost two years elapsed before the plan was ready.

On 3 June 1949, the *Government Gazette* published three bills dealing with the municipal council: The Municipal Corporation Bill, The Municipal Electors Bill and the Corrupt and Illegal Practices Bill,[1] and they laid down the scheme for a municipal council in great detail.

The proposed municipal council consisting of a mayor and councillors, was to administer only the urban area comprising the Islands of Hong Kong, Ap Lei Chau and Stonecutters, with Kowloon and New Kowloon. There were to be thirty councillors, of whom half were to represent the Chinese community and half the non-Chinese sections of the population. Two-thirds of the total council, that is twenty, were to be directly elected, and one-third nominated by various public and professional bodies. Membership was open to qualified electors of either sex and was not restricted to persons of British nationality, but since the English language was to be the language of the council, members had to be able to speak, read and write that language; a residence qualification of ten years out of the previous fifteen was additionally demanded, except that special consideration was given to those who left the Colony because of the Japanese occupation. Elected and nominated members were to serve for three years and be eligible for further terms. The council was to have the right to elect the mayor and deputy mayor from among its members, both appointments being held for one year only. The mayor was to be paid such renumeration as the council thought fit.

The franchise was to be extended to all those of the age of 25 years or above, men and women alike, capable of reading and writing either English or Chinese. There was to be a residence qualification; for British subjects this was to be one year since reaching the age of 23; for persons of all other nationalities, it was to be six years' residence in the Colony out of the preceding ten, with the special qualification that a period of absence during the Japanese occupation could be counted as residence provided a voter could show that he was resident in the Colony for four years between 1936 and 1941, or for one year since August 1945. In addition only those with the above qualifications whose names

[1] The Bills of Hong Kong for 1949, pp. 225–335, 336–358 and 359–374 respectively. Supplement No. 3 to the Hong Kong *Government Gazette*, 3 June 1949.

were on the jury lists, or who were exempted by their occupation from jury service, or alternatively who held property of a certain annual value, could exercise the vote. Elections were to be held in the first week in March every three years and at other times as vacancies on the council occurred; at each election a voter had as many votes as there were councillors to be elected. All members of the council had to retire on 31 March every three years.

With regard to the distribution of seats among the Chinese and non-Chinese communities, there were to be ten wards for the Chinese, six on the Island and four in Kowloon each returning one member to the council; the non-Chinese were grouped together in one ward having ten seats. The representation of the Portuguese and Indian communities in this non-Chinese electorate was contrived by providing that, if a Portuguese and an Indian candidate did not receive enough votes respectively to bring them among the ten candidates at the head of the poll, then the Portuguese and Indian candidates who secured the highest number of votes cast for Portuguese and Indian candidates respectively, were to be declared elected, and displace from the ten persons at the head of the poll, the two obtaining the least number of votes.

Ten councillors were to be nominated by recognized unofficial bodies as follows: The Chinese Chamber of Commerce, 1 Chinese; the Registered Trade Unions, 2 Chinese; the University of Hong Kong, 1 Chinese; the Hong Kong General Chamber of Commerce 2 non-Chinese; the Kowloon Residents' Association, 1 non-Chinese; and the unofficial Justices of the Peace, 1 Chinese and 1 non-Chinese. The body responsible for electing the tenth (non-Chinese) member was left undetermined in the bill. The names of persons nominated by these bodies had to be published in advance, and objection on grounds of disability could be lodged by any elector. A candidate for the council was to be disqualified if he held an office of profit under the Crown or were financially interested in a council contract, or had been convicted of felony in the previous ten years, or were guilty of corrupt practices as defined in one of the three bills, or were a member of an assembly or council of any foreign power, or were under 25 years of age.

The declared intention was that the municipal council should take under its control all the functions of the existing Urban Council plus the Fire Brigade, parks, gardens and recreation grounds, the licensing and control of places of amusement and the licensing of vehicles. On these subjects it had power to make its own bye-laws. At a later stage, it was to take over control of education, social welfare, town planning and other important services. The municipal council was to become the rating authority and to have its own funds from the rates, and also act as agent for the Colonial Government in the collection of certain revenue. The council was to have as officials, a municipal secretary, treasurer, health officer and engineer, and their deputies and staffs, but it was not to have its own police force.

The Young Plan was still-born. Before the municipal bills were published on 3 June, criticism from a very influential quarter made itself heard. The Hon. D. F. Landale, the senior unofficial member of the Legislative Council, in the course of the 1949 Budget debate objected to money being earmarked for the municipal council, and urged that reform of the Legislative Council should come first. He said:

> There is I believe a strong body of opinion that does not favour this reform, and would rather see a larger and more representative Legislative Council working in conjunction with a larger and more representative Urban Council than through the cumbersome machinery of the proposed Municipal Council which, of necessity, would overlap a lot of the functions of the Colonial Government.[1]

Sir Alexander Grantham replied in his summary of the budget debate that if this were so, then he hoped that the Hon. D. F. Landale and his colleagues would bring forward alternative proposals. He added

> I can however assure this Council that it is not the intention to steam-roller through the Legislative Council the existing proposals and any alternative proposals that have the backing of the unofficial members of this Council will be forwarded to the Secretary of State with my recommendations. While I am on this subject I should just like to say that I welcome the quickening interest in the matter of constitutional reform. That contrasts very pleasingly with the apathy that was displayed when these proposals were first published in July 1947.[2]

The unofficial members accepted this invitation and at the meeting of the Legislative Council on 27 April 1949, Hon. D. F. Landale gave notice of the following resolutions which, after many meetings, the unofficial members had agreed upon, and which

[1] Hong Kong *Hansard* 1949, p. 91.
[2] Hong Kong *Hansard* 1949, p. 137.

were to be moved after an interval of two months to allow for discussion.

Since the publication of the dispatch of the Rt. Hon. the Secretary of State for the Colonies dated 3 July 1947, in which he gave general approval subject to minor modifications to the recommendations submitted by Sir Mark Young and contained in his dispatch No. 145 of 22 October 1946, it has become increasingly evident that in the view of the general public of Hong Kong:

a. The proposals of Sir Mark Young involving the creation of a Municipal Council and a minor modification of the constitution of the Legislative Council are no longer considered to be the best means of giving to the inhabitants of the Colony a fuller and more responsible share in the management of their own affairs.

b. Sufficient consideration was not given to alternative methods of achieving this object.

c. The most effective means of achieving this object is a more fundamental modification of the constitution of the Legislative Council.

Therefore in order to make known to His Majesty's Government as soon as possible the present views of the Colony, it is hereby moved that for the purpose of affording the inhabitants of the Colony a fuller and more responsible share in the management of their own affairs.

1. The present proposals for the establishment of a Municipal Council be abandoned.

2. The constitution of the Legislative Council should be constituted as follows:

A Council of 20 with an official membership of 9, including H. E. the Governor and an unofficial membership of 11 consisting partly of members elected by qualified residents of British nationality and partly of members nominated by the Governor. The Governor to have an original and casting vote and the usual reserve power.

3. After the constitution of the Legislative Council has been modified as above indicated, the new Legislative Council should consider whether and, if so to what extent, the constitution of the Urban Council should be modified with the view to securing for the Urban Council a greater measure of direct representation and an increase in its financial and administrative powers in municipal affairs.[1]

The whole basis of the Young Plan was undermined by these resolutions which gave priority to the reform of the Legislative Council and left the reformed Council to decide on the nature of the reforms to be introduced in municipal affairs.

[1] Hong Kong *Hansard* 1949, p. 150.

The resolutions were brought up on 22 June 1949 in a slightly amended form by the late Sir Man Kam Lo[1] in the absence of Mr Landale. It was now proposed that the Legislative Council should consist of 17 members instead of 20, by reducing the number of official members from nine to six. At the commencement of this decisive debate, the Governor announced that the officials would not vote or take part except to supply any information required.

The speeches of the unofficial members on that occasion[2] make a valuable commentary on the problem of constitutional reform in Hong Kong. Sir Man Kam Lo dealt with the difficulty of estimating public opinion in the Colony and stated that the aim of the resolutions was to get the opinion of the inhabitants on whether the Young Plan should be abandoned, or as an alternative, whether the Legislative Council should be reconstituted along the lines of the resolutions he was proposing. He admitted that the views of the Chinese Chamber of Commerce, the Kowloon Residents' Association and the Kowloon Chamber of Commerce were 'certainly not at one in regard to either of the points', and that the two Reform Clubs (see p. 204 ff.) also disagreed. He doubted how far these public bodies represented the views of a substantial section of the community. He thought that on the whole the majority wanted the present proposals, but in any case he rightly claimed that the unofficial members were not absolved from giving their views. There were three questions on which opinions differed; they were, whether all members of the Legislative Council should be elected or not, the nature of the electorate, and thirdly, whether the Young Plan should be abandoned. On the last point, Sir Man Kam pointed out that the intention was not to abandon the idea of a municipal council but only that of its immediate creation. He pointed to the duplication and expense and argued that it would be more satisfactory if the Urban Council evolved in a more orderly way by gradually expanding its functions until it grew into a municipality. He allowed that the virtue of the Young Plan, which was conceived as an experimental prelude to more sub-

---

[1] Sir Man Kam Lo (1893–1959). Knighted 1948. Educated in England. In 1915 passed the Solicitors' Final Examination taking the first place in the First Class Honours. Has served on many commissions and public committees. Member of the Legislative Council, 1935 to 1949. Member of the Executive Council from 1946 to his death in 1959. (*Who Was Who* 1951–60)

[2] Hong Kong *Hansard* 1949, pp. 188–204.

stantial reform, would be lost if the more far-reaching proposals now being moved, were carried.

On the question of elections, Sir Man Kam Lo argued that since the British occupation, the fundamental conception was that the Government should concern itself with the welfare of the Colony as a whole without sectional or racial prejudice or distinctions. He thought no electorate could be devised to do justice to all sections and interests; the unofficial members of the Legislative Council represented the interests of the Colony as a whole and this remained the justification for the nomination of members. According to the 1931 census the number of British subjects divided according to their racial origins was: Chinese, 61,604; Europeans, 6,636; Eurasians, 717; Portuguese, 1,089; Indian, 3,331; others 453; totalling 73,782, and he considered that probably the same proportions remained. He thought that the difficulty about the electorate lay in the lack of homogeneity; and though the announcement of 1 May 1946 promised a great measure of control over their own affairs to the inhabitants of the Colony and not to British subjects alone, nevertheless in his view any other than an electorate of British subjects would involve long argument and delay. He argued that there must be some incongruity even in this restricted electorate of 73,000 persons which could not claim to represent a community ten times as large, and observed, 'but to suggest that members elected by a fractional electorate and pledged to discharge the mandate of this fractional electorate can and will more adequately represent the Colony as a whole than nominated members is a proposition with which I profoundly disagree'. Hence he argued for the retention of a partly nominated element in the Legislative Council. But he thought that the realistic approach was to introduce a new elective element into the constitution of the Legislative Council, as a recognition of its fundamental basis and as 'a step in the right direction along its road of progress and evolution'. He considered communal electorates were undesirable but thought they might be inevitable to avoid a non-Chinese candidate strongly supported by non-Chinese voters being defeated by another non-Chinese candidate receiving the support of Chinese electors only. He summed up saying that it was the unanimous view of the unofficial members 'that whilst it is impracticable to devise a scheme of constitutional reform which will completely satisfy aspirations of all the inhabitants, their proposals represent a fair and acceptable compromise'. To those who demanded that all the members should be elected, he replied that it was better to get substantial advance by agreement than to stand out for some yet unattainable ideal.

The remaining speakers emphasized the difficulty of ascertaining the wishes of the community in the matter of constitutional reform and many doubted if any demand for reform existed at all. The Hon. M. M. Watson, who seconded the motion, said he was quite unable to find any definite trend of opinion one way or the other on the reforms which had been suggested, and said, 'However there seems to me to be a somewhat surprising lack of interest in the subject amongst the population generally which is perhaps due to the pressure of more absorbing events'. The Hon. (later Sir) Chau Tsun-nin[1] said 'It is by no means easy . . . to assess with accuracy the public feeling on such an important matter'. One speaker went so far as to state 'I can see no evidence over the last six weeks since this motion was first tabled that the large majority of residents of long standing in this colony want any reform at all', and he doubted if there would have been any demand for reform had it not been for the initiative taken by the British Government.

The Hon. M. M. Watson put the view that if the municipal council had elected members and the Legislative Council not, there might be difficulties between the two councils, and the general opinion of the unofficial members was that it was safest and more in accord with constitutional precedent to begin with the Legislative Council rather than to embark on the experiment of a new municipal council which would be expensive, complicated and partly overlapping. There was little argument against a municipal council; the argument was that there should be delay and that the Legislative Council should be reformed first as befitting its position of authority in the community. One member, Dr. The Hon. (later Sir) Chau Sik-nin,[2] alone argued against

[1] Sir Tsun-nin Chau. C.B.E., 1938, knighted 1956. Member of the Legislative Council, 1931–53, and senior unofficial member 1950–53; Member of the Executive Council, 1946 to 1959 and Senior Unofficial member 1948–59. (*Who's Who* 1961)

[2] Sir Sik-nin Chau. Kt. 1960, C.B.E. 1950. Chairman, Federation of Hong Kong Industries, United College of Hong Kong, Hong Kong Chinese Bank Ltd., etc. Director of numerous companies. Hong Kong, London and Vienna Universities. Member of the Urban Council 1936–41. Member of Legislative Council 1946–59 and senior unofficial member 1953–59; member of the Executive Council since 1948 and senior unofficial member since 1960. Permanent Director of Tung

restricting the vote to British subjects. The motion was carried by the unanimous vote of the unofficial members,[1] and Sir Alexander Grantham undertook to send the views with his comments to the Secretary of State, 'who must give the final decision'. The Young Plan was therefore temporarily in abeyance putting the basis of constitutional reform once more in the melting pot.

The issues were again discussed in the press and other proposals were made. In 1949 two organizations demanding reform came into existence, the Reform Club and the Chinese Reform Association, which helped to canalize some sides of public opinion.

A Chinese petition signed by representatives of 142 Chinese organizations among whom were the Chinese Manufacturers' Union, the Kowloon Chamber of Commerce, the Chinese Chamber of Commerce, the Hong Kong Chinese Reform Association, and Chinese Trade Unions, altogether representing a membership of 141,800 Chinese, was presented to the Governor on 18 July 1949 requesting more thorough-going reform.[2] It asked for an enlarged Legislative Council to be set up as an interim measure, composed of eleven unofficial members, and such official members as the Governor chose provided that they were in a minority of at least two; it urged that the system of nomination be discontinued in favour of all unofficial members being elected, and that of the eleven, six should be Chinese, irrespective of nationality. It expressed the view that the electoral roll for the interim Legislative Council 'might well be based on the tax-payers' list without discrimination as to race and nationality, since the Chinese people cannot be held to be aliens and have for traditional and geographical reasons long regarded themselves as being indigenous to Hong Kong . . . '. The petitioners also asked that the Government's pledge to establish the municipal council based on the Young Plan, should be implemented before 1 May 1950, that all 30 members of the council should be elected, that nomination of some members by designated bodies should be abandoned, and that the qualification for voting should be the same for Chinese and

---

Wah Hospital Advisory Board, Chairman of Hong Kong Anti-Tuberculosis Association. Chairman of Hong Kong Model Housing Society, etc., etc. Hon. President or Vice-President of numerous associations. (*Who's Who* 1961)

[1] In 1949 there were seven unofficial members, three Chinese, three British and one Portuguese.

[2] *South China Morning Post*, 19 July 1949.

non-Chinese alike with no racial, national, residential or any other
discrimination between the two sections of the community. They
requested that a commission should be appointed by the Governor
to improve upon the draft of the Municipal Council Ordinance
along the lines suggested. The proposal of the unofficial members
of the Legislative Council to reform the Council was supported
but their proposal to delay the setting up of the municipal council
was deplored.

On 8 March 1950[1] Sir Alexander Grantham referred in the
Legislative Council to the many societies and other bodies which
had sent him their views on constitutional reform, or had published
them. He stated that he had sent all these opinions with his own
comments to the Secretary of State; they were being studied, but
the General Election of 1950 and events in China and Korea had
caused some delay. In July 1952, Sir Alexander went to the United
Kingdom and the question of constitutional reform was discussed
at the Colonial Office. On 20 October 1952 the Secretary of State,
Mr Oliver Lyttelton, announced in the Commons that the numbers
of elected representatives on the Urban Council would be increased
from two to four, but that the time was inopportune for other
constitutional changes of a major character. This view was repeated
by the Governor when he referred to the Secretary of State's
announcement in addressing the Legislative Council on 22 October.
He also added 'I should like to take this opportunity of supple-
menting that statement by an assurance that I am at all times ready
to consider further proposals for constitutional change provided
they are not of a major character'.[2]

---

[1] Hong Kong *Hansard* 1950, p. 41.
[2] Hong Kong *Hansard* 1952, p. 252.

CHAPTER XII

CONSTITUTIONAL DEVELOPMENTS IN THE POST-WAR YEARS, 1945–62

The Transfiguration of Hong Kong Society

IN his statement in the House of Commons on 20 October 1952 sanctioning minor constitutional changes only, the Secretary of State for the Colonies explained briefly and without further elucidation that after consultation with the Governor, he had decided that the time was inopportune for other constitutional changes of a major character. There was no indication that the British Government had altered its mind about the desirability of reform in principle; the argument was that the time, 1952, was inopportune. The explanation must be sought in the general situation in the Far East, which had undergone a radical transformation in the six years between 1946, when the promise of a greater degree of self-government was given, and 1952, when the decision against major changes was announced.

Up to 1949 the Hong Kong Government maintained close and friendly relations with the Nationalist Government of China as the recognized government of that country, e.g. it assisted that Government in its attempt to introduce and stabilize the gold yüan currency, and in January 1948 the British Government allowed the Chinese Maritime Customs to operate in British waters and maintain collecting stations in Hong Kong and Kowloon, the agreement being embodied in a local ordinance of October 1948.

In 1949 the situation in the Far East was completely changed by the setting up of the Chinese People's Republic in Peking on 1 October 1949. On 15 October Canton fell and the next day Chinese Communist forces appeared on the Hong Kong border.

The effect of the Chinese communist success on Hong Kong was profound. Trade with the mainland suffered. More important, political refugees particularly from Shanghai, poured into Hong Kong and there was also a mass exodus of Cantonese from Kwangtung province coming, as they have always done, to seek greater security and a higher standard of life in the Colony, where most had relatives to assist them in settling down. This Cantonese invasion of Hong Kong was no unusual phenomenon, and the

T'ai P'ing Rebellion, the Chinese Revolution of 1911 and the Japanese attack on Canton in 1938 had all brought a flood of refugees. The chief difference on this occasion was the size of the flood.

In 1945, on the resumption of British control, the population was estimated at 'about 500,000'.[1] After the liberation, people began to return at a rate approaching 100,000 a month until by the end of 1946, the pre-war figure of 1,600,000 was probably reached. From the beginning of 1949 to the spring of 1950, that is during the period of the establishment of the Chinese People's Republic, it is estimated that 776,000 refugees crowded into the Colony and that by 1950 the population had risen to 2,360,000.[2] The Colony was faced with the problem of resettling these newcomers who strained public services and material resources, created difficulties in housing, public hygiene and water-supply, and subjected the Colony to the continual hazard of fire by the mushrooming of their squatters' shacks. They brought a dangerous factionalism[3] into the life of the Colony and created special problems such as preventing clashes between refugees and communist sympathizers; maintaining order on their respective national days and keeping the schools free from the struggle between the rival parties for control of education for propagandist purposes.

In February 1950, the British Government recognized the Chinese People's Republic but relations between Britain and China did not become normal and there were incidents over shipping in neighbouring waters and over the disposal of Chinese Nationalist Government property which had sought refuge in the Colony.

In 1950 hostilities in Korea began by the attack of North Korean communist forces on South Korea, and when the United Nations intervened, Hong Kong became the scene of more military activity. In December 1950, the United States placed an embargo on trade with China, in which Hong Kong was included, and the Colony was seriously affected because of its close economic links with the mainland of China. In May 1951, the embargo was adopted by the General Assembly of the United Nations. The result was that at the very time that the Colony was faced with the towering problem of absorbing three-quarters of a million refugees, its ability to do so was weakened by the necessity of extending controls over a wide

[1] *Annual Report 1952*, p. 27.

[2] *Annual Report 1951*, p. 23.

[3] *Annual Report 1949*, p. 2.

range of commodities and introducing import licensing of controlled goods.[1] Hong Kong which lived by unrestricted trade and close economic relations with the mainland, had to turn to manufactures and in this it was helped by imperial preferences in the United Kingdom market. In 1952 the United States allowed the import of goods manufactured or processed in the Colony, and so helped to break down the identification of the Colony with China.

In all these circumstances, it was indeed difficult to go on with the discussion of the Colony's constitutional reforms. Any wide enfranchisement of the Chinese inhabitants might well have led to bitter factional disputes and it was clearly unrealistic to talk about the representation of communities when one person in three was a refugee.

There can be no doubt of the difficulty of any far-reaching and important social and constitutional experiment under these circumstances and there can be no surprise that the time was judged to be 'inopportune'. But this does not mean that nothing was attempted.

Post-war Constitutional Development, 1946-62

The Executive Council was reconstituted in May 1946 with a membership of eleven, seven official and four unofficial; the former included five *ex officio* members,[2] together with the Director of Medical and Health Services who resumed the seat to which he had been appointed in 1939, and Hon. T. M. Hazlerigg appointed provisionally for one year.[3] The four unofficial members comprised two Chinese and two Europeans.[4] In 1948 the Executive Council was increased to twelve, six official and six unofficial members with the Governor himself holding the balance. This was done by adding the Commissioner of Labour to the already existing five *ex officio*

---

[1] *Annual Report 1951*, p. 9.

[2] The Senior Military Officer, Colonial Secretary, Attorney-General, Secretary for Chinese Affairs and Financial Secretary.

[3] T. M. Hazlerigg, who first occupied his seat temporarily for the Director of Medical and Health Services on leave. He had retired from the Hong Kong Government service in 1937 and returned in 1945 as the Political Adviser to the Military Administration, the post being later renamed Special Adviser.

[4] They were Hon. (later Sir) Arthur Morse, of The Hongkong and Shanghai Banking Corporation, D. F. Landale of Jardine, Matheson & Co., Sir Tsun-nin Chau, a member of the Legislative Council since 1932, and Sir Man Kam Lo, a member of the Legislative Council since 1936.

9. Refugees on the Border, May 1962.
By courtesy of the Hong Kong Government Information Services.

Facing page 198

10. Old Colonial Secretariat, demolished in 1954.

11. Central Government Offices, East Wing, 1963. The end of the West Wing can be seen on the left. By courtesy of the Hong Kong Government Information Services.

Facing page 199

members, and adding two unofficial members,[1] one European and one Chinese to the existing four. The next year, one European member was replaced by a leading British barrister of Portuguese origin[2] and this balance among the unofficial members has since remained unchanged. The numerical equality between the official and unofficial elements manifested the Government's intention that the Governor should be advised by a body in which the official vote was not the determining factor.

The Legislative Council was reborn on 1 May 1946 with nine official and seven unofficial members. The former were the five *ex officio* members of the Executive Council who were automatically members of the Legislative Council, and the Director of Medical and Health Services, plus three others who were appointed provisionally only, namely, Hon. T. M. Hazlerigg, the Government's Special Adviser, the Chairman of the Urban Council and the Director of Public Works. Six of the seven unofficial members one of whom was nominated by the Chamber of Commerce, were given provisional appointments on 18 May 1946, and a seventh was elected by the unofficial Justices of the Peace in the following October; they comprised three Chinese, three British and one Portuguese. In 1947 Hazlerigg resigned leaving eight official and seven unofficial members.

In 1951 the Legislative Council was increased from fifteen to seventeen members, by the addition of the Director of Education on the official side and of a fourth Chinese on the unofficial side. In 1953, the unofficial Justices elected a member of the local Indian community, thus reducing the European element. There were then four Chinese, one European and one Portuguese as nominated members and one European and one Indian as elected members. In 1958, the Justices nominated a European[3] in place of the Indian member, but the latter was nominated by the Governor to a seat in 1959 and in the same year the Portuguese member was replaced by a Chinese. There has been no change in this balance among the unofficials, viz. five Chinese, two British and one Indian, and no

[1] Hon. Dr D. J. Sloss, Vice-Chancellor of the University, and Sir Sik-nin Chau.

[2] Hon. Leo D'Almada e Castro, Q.C.

[3] Hon. H. D. M. Barton, of Jardine Matheson & Co., Ltd. With the departure of D. F. Landale in 1949, the Legislative Council was again without a member of the 'Princely Hong' until Mr Barton's appointment in 1958, but it continued to supply a member of the Executive Council until 1956.

material change in the general structure of the Legislative Council, up to 1962.[1]

A joint delegation of members of the Reform Club and Civic Association went to London in August 1960, but their interviews with Colonial Office officials failed to convince the Secretary of State of the desirability of substantial constitutional change. Lord Perth, Minister of State for Colonial Affairs visited the Colony, and in a statement, issued on his departure on 29 October 1960, he confirmed that

> 'Her Majesty's Government consider it undesirable that there should be any radical or major change in the present constitutional position in Hong Kong', adding that 'This does not, however, preclude the possibility of minor modifications, within the framework of existing principles, in the composition of the Legislative Council or the Urban Council'.[2]

Perhaps the most significant constitutional development which has been introduced since the war has been the granting to the Colony of a wide measure of financial autonomy. This was announced by the Governor, Sir Robert Black,[3] in the course of his annual address to the Legislative Council on 6 March 1958.

> Before concluding, I have to report a decision recently taken by the Secretary of State. He has approved a considerable relaxation in the financial control which he exercises over Hong Kong. In 1948 the Colony was released from Treasury control and given a large measure of autonomy over its own finances. The control which the Secretary of State still retained at that time was that his approval was required for the annual Estimates, for supplementary provisions exceeding $1 million in the case of capital expenditure and $\frac{1}{4}$ million in the case of recurrent expenditure, and for the issue of any loan and for any expenditure involving important points of principle. The Secretary of State has now informed me that, in view of the good standing, financial and administrative, of the Colony, he will further relax his control and will no longer require the Estimates to be

[1] On 12 June 1964, the membership of the Council was increased to 13 unofficial members and 12 officials plus the Governor as President. Since the Governor has a casting vote in addition to an original vote, the official view can still be made to prevail if required.

[2] *South China Morning Post*, 30 October 1960.

[3] Sir Robert Brown Black. K.C.M.G., O.B.E. Colonial Administrative Service, Malaya, 1930; Assistant Colonial Secretary, Trinidad, 1939; Secretary, Malaya, Foreign Exchange Control, 1940; Prisoner-of-war, Japan, 1942–45; Deputy Chief Secretary, North Borneo, 1946; Colonial Secretary, Hong Kong, 1952; Governor of Singapore, 1955; Governor of Hong Kong, 1958–1964. (*Who's Who* 1964)

submitted for his approval; nor will be require supplementary provisions to be authorized by him. On the other hand, he wishes to extend the principle of demi-official consultation which is already in use, and I have agreed that the Financial Secretary will keep the Finance Department of the Colonial Office regularly and fully informed about this Government's financial policy and about the way that this policy works out in practice. The Financial Secretary will take account of the views of the financial advisers of the Secretary of State in advising this Government on policy.

This is a very important and considerable extension of our financial independence, and of course it brings with it its responsibilities; but I am confident that honourable Members will gladly share in these responsibilities, particularly in the sphere of examination of the Government's proposals for expenditure in Appropriation Bills, so as to ensure that we employ the Colony's resources in the best possible manner for its development and for the benefit of its people.[1]

The control of the Secretary of State is now reserved only in the cases of raising loans and of financial matters involving important points of principle. The Finance Committee of the Legislative Council, on which the unofficial members have a majority, has accordingly become a more influential body, although it will be realized that under the ultimate constitutional authority of the Letters Patent, the Secretary of State through the powers of disallowance and legislation by the Crown, could still if he chose, exercise complete control. In normal circumstances such intervention by the Home Government must be regarded as only a theoretical possibility.

The Urban Council was resuscitated in May 1946 with five official members, viz. the chairman of the Council, the Director of Medical and Health Services, the Secretary for Chinese Affairs, the Director of Public Works and the Commissioner of Police, all *ex officio* and six unofficial members appointed by the Governor for one year from 25 May 1946. Of these latter, three were Chinese, one Indian and two European. In 1947 there were three Chinese, one Indian, one Portuguese and one British, and the Council retained this balance in its unofficial membership until 1952. The Chairman of the Urban Council assumed the concurrent title Director of Urban Services in 1953 at the head of an Urban Services Department. Amongst the *ex officio* members, the Social Welfare Officer replaced the Commissioner of Police in 1953, and the

[1] Hong Kong *Hansard* 1958, p. 46.

following year, 1954, the Commissioner for Resettlement was added on a temporary basis making six officials holding their seats *ex officio;* in 1955 the Deputy Director of Health Services who had acted as vice-chairman was renamed Assistant Director of Health Services.

The question of resuming popular elections to seats on the Urban Council was raised at a meeting of the Legislative Council on 9 April 1952, by Sir Tsun-nin Chau. He asked if, in view of the delay in reconstituting the Legislative Council and the postpone-ment of the modification of the Urban Council, the Government would consider holding elections under the Urban Council Ordinance. In reply the Colonial Secretary said that arrangements would be made for the election of two additional members to the Urban Council. Elections were accordingly held on 30 May 1952, for the first time since 1941. The two elected members held their seats for one year only.

In September 1952, the unofficial members of the Urban Coun-cil made proposals which included increasing the number of elected members to four, enlarging the electorate, and improving the voting arrangements. These suggestions were approved by the Secretary of State, and as a result, when he made his statement in the Commons on 20 October 1952, deferring major constitutional change, he announced at the same time that the number of elected representatives would be increased from two to four.

The Hong Kong Government carried the proposals into effect in two Ordinances, passed in March and December 1953. The first increased the number of elected members of the Urban Council from two to four, increased their term from one to two years, one half retiring in alternate years, and similarly increased the term of the nominated members to two years. The second ordinance enfranchised, subject to certain qualifications, teachers, those assessed for salaries or personal tax, civil servants and the auxiliary defence services. The roll of electors was increased from 10,798 to an estimated 18,500.

These ordinances did not introduce any new principle, and their main and probably intended effect was to soften the blow caused by the decision to postpone all major constitutional change. The importance of the Urban Council was enhanced in 1956 by the addition of six unofficial members, two nominated and four elected, making altogether eight nominated and eight elected unofficial members which, with the six officials, made up a Council of 22 members. This change was initiated by the Council itself, in a debate which took place on 27 September 1955.[1]

The official members, on that occasion, as on a similar occasion in the Legislative Council, refrained from speaking and voting. The initiative came from the nominated side of the unofficials, though all agreed that an increase in the size of the Council was essential in order to lighten the amount of committee work which was then bearing heavily on the members. The mover argued that since the electorate was less than 20,000, some nominated members should remain, that reform should be gradual, and that the increase should be limited to the six proposed, making the elected and nominated members equal in number. He also asked the elected members to express their views on the possibility of conducting the elections through wards. The elected members accepted the motion though protesting that it fell short of that extension of the electorate and of the electoral principle generally that they had advocated. They rejected the ward system as a basis of the elections.

The Government accepted the change,[2] and the six additional members were sanctioned by the Urban Council (Amendment) Ordinance, No. 1 of 1956. Elected members were normally to hold their seats for four years, instead of two, and transitional arrangements were devised[3] so that four members were to be elected every two years, and similarly four nominated members were to be appointed every two years in those years when elections were not held, thus arranging for the alternate filling of four elected and four nominated unofficial members each year.

Another important change was also then made. By the Urban Council Ordinance of 1955 three of the appointed members had to be of Chinese origin. This provision was omitted from the 1956 Ordinance, and the Colonial Secretary, speaking on the first reading explained that, 'It is considered that statutory provisions as to a member's race are inappropriate and that the public interest would

---

[1] *South China Morning Post*, 28 September 1955. In order to comply with the Urban Council Ordinance which does not give the Council power to discuss its own constitution, the Council had to resolve itself into committee for the purpose of the debate.

[2] Hong Kong *Hansard* 1956, p. 30.

[3] Those members elected in 1954 were to hold office until 31 March 1956 and those elected in 1955, 31 March 1957. In March 1956, the election was to be for six members, four with the greatest number of votes were to hold their seats until 31 March 1959, and the remaining two until 31 March 1957.

be in no way damaged if Your Excellency were to be left with complete discretion as to the race of the appointed members'.

The discussion of constitutional changes and the reintroduction of Urban Council elections brought into existence political associations, the chief of which were the Reform Club and the Civic Association.

The Reform Club of Hong Kong was founded in 1949 by a group of British and Chinese professional people to urge a programme of constitutional reform. Among its principal objects, as stated in its annual report for 1952–53, were: to assist in creating a healthy public opinion; to stimulate interest in public affairs by constructive criticism; to bring about an improvement in the machinery of government; to devise means of closer contact between Government and citizen; to remodel the Legislature with due regard to the existing necessity for a Government majority; to foster an effective opposition in the Legislature; and to assist the Legislature by helping to keep it fully informed of public opinion on all aspects of current problems.

The Reform Club outlined its proposals for constitutional reform in a Petition to the Governor presented in June 1949. Briefly, it supported the demand of the unofficial members of the Legislative Council for an unofficial majority, in the ratio of 11 to 9, the eleven unofficials were to be five British, one Portuguese, and five Chinese, all of British nationality; three were to be nominated by the Governor and eight elected by a joint roll of British subjects and Hong Kong citizens. The latter had to possess a residence qualification, to sign a declaration to uphold the interests of the Colony and be willing to be conscripted in its service to safeguard its security. After an interim period of 12 to 18 months, all the unofficial members were to be elected. The Reform Club also wanted a wholly elected municipal council instead of the partly elected one suggested under the Young Plan. In a more moderately worded petition to the Queen presented in October 1953, it demanded the addition of two unofficial members elected by the same electorate as that for the Urban Council. With the Young Plan in abeyance the Reform Club concentrated on the Urban Council elections when these were re-established in 1952, with the proviso that, 'The Reform Club will of course contest these elections but it must be stressed that no real constitutional advancement can be expected until there are reforms in the Legislature and the elections to the Legislative Council'.[1]

The Chinese Reform Club was set up at the same time with a similar programme, but as the Reform Club, being non-racial, embraced the Chinese, separate advocacy of similar reform interests was unnecessary; in addition its external affiliations prejudiced its appeal as a local party.

The Hong Kong Civic Association was founded in 1955 and its objectives as stated in its Constitution were: to promote the economic social cultural and political welfare of the people of Hong Kong; to encourage industrial, commercial, and agricultural development; also housing education medical and health services; to help the underprivileged; to encourage greater interest in public affairs; and to promote closer understanding between the government and the public. It did not advocate any major change in the existing form of government and was of the opinion that the vast majority of the electorate were not in favour of any drastic constitutional reform; but it urged that civic interest should be encouraged and guided, and that expansion of the electoral franchise should be made gradually as civic education progressed. But it took warning from other colonies 'whose drastic constitutional reforms have been introduced contrary to the best interests of the people concerned and often with serious consequences'.[2]

On 30 January 1961, the Reform Club and Civic Association joined forces for the purpose of contesting the Urban Council elections with a common platform based on the joint memorandum on constitutional reform presented by their combined delegation to the Colonial Office in August 1960. The agreement, which was to run for four years unless mutually varied, allowed each to maintain its separate identity and to work for parity in elected members. The memorandum demanded eight additional elected members to the Urban Council and a widening of the Council's responsibilities; the addition of eight elected seats to the Legislative Council, possibly in two stages; the inclusion by the Governor, of a number of elected members of the Legislative Council in the Executive Council; and it asked that the existing electorate should be enlarged not by a complete re-organization, but by adding new

[1] Reform Club of Hong Kong, Annual Report 1951–52.
[2] See also Hong Kong Civic Association Annual Report for 1957.

categories of voters such as nurses, property taxpayers and business profit taxpayers.[1]

In the absence of any change in the composition of the Legislative Council, interest tended to be concentrated on the Urban Council elections. The first election, that of 1952, for two seats, was dominated by the Reform Club; after a vigorous campaign, it was successful in getting one of its candidates returned at the head of the poll, the other seat being secured by a candidate nominated by the Kowloon Residents' Association. There were nine candidates, but the six of them, who were independent of any organization, all fared badly. Only 3,368 persons voted out of a total of 9,704 on the register; and the most successful candidate secured only 30% of the vote and only 8% of the electorate. In 1953, there were eight candidates for four seats, which were secured by the four Reform Club candidates by large majorities. Again the number voting was small, only 2,536 out of 10,798 voters,[2] and led to the comment: 'The poor display of civic spirit is thus either a deplorable exhibition of apathy or a stupid refusal to take a little trouble—and in any case is a grave reflection upon the population's desire for and title to any degree of self-government'.[3]

In 1954 there were five candidates for only two seats and the Reform Club again secured both against independent opponents in an election in which 4,957 people voted out of a total electoral roll of 13,700.[4] In the 1955 election, at which only 1,914 voters recorded their votes,[5] the Reform Club was again successful in securing the two available seats against the opposition of a single independent candidate. In 1956 there were six vacant seats; the Civic Association entered the lists against the Reform Club and no independent candidate came forward. The Reform Club secured the first four places and the Civic Association the remaining two. The vote was 6,048 out of a total of 14,682,[6] In 1957 the two organizations again monopolized the elections and on this occasion the success of the Reform Club was checked; it gained one seat and its opponents three, with 6,916 people casting their votes out

---

[1] *South China Morning Post*, 31 January 1961.
[2] Hong Kong *Hansard* 1953, p. 337.
[3] *South China Morning Post*, 22 May 1953.
[4] *ibid.*, 24 March 1954.
[5] *ibid.*, 31 March 1955.
[6] *ibid.*, 8 March 1956.

of 19,305.[1] In the 1959 elections three Reform Club and one Civic Association candidates were successful in a poll of 7,236 out of a total roll of 23,584,[2] or 33% of the electorate. In January 1961, the Reform Club and Civic Association formed a coalition and jointly nominated four candidates for the 1961 elections, and since no other candidates appeared, no elections took place. This was repeated in 1962. By these developments, the Chinese members have secured half the seats on the Urban Council; in 1962 there were two European and six Chinese elected members, three European and five Chinese nominated members, and six *ex officio* members, five European and one Chinese.

The elections have had the advantage of enabling some residents to undertake public administrative work who would not otherwise have that opportunity. To justify their election the elected members have to be active and exert pressure; they tend to be progressive, challenging, responsible and constructive. The electorate is limited to English speaking people, and is comparatively small. The compilation of the electoral register for Urban Council elections is the responsibility of the Commissioner of Registration of Persons. According to the register of electors given in the Annual Report of the Commissioner for the year 1961-62, dated 18 June 1962, 26,039 persons were entitled to vote, a little over 0·7% of the total population, 22,621 in Hong Kong (Victoria) and 6,599 in Kowloon. They consisted of 15,330 jurors, 2,131 exempted from jury service, 6,599 teachers, 47 taxpayers and 1,932 members of the Defence Force and Auxiliary Services. The elected members therefore cannot claim to represent the people but only some of the people, and probably the influential and intelligent section of it. The interests of the mass of the Chinese-speaking people are still the responsibility of the nominated unofficial members.

Post-war conditions also called for administrative changes in the New Territories. Under Sir Henry Blake's arrangements of 1899, each village or group of villages had its village elders to assist and advise the British officials, but they had declined in status and usefulness. There was no clearly defined way of electing them and they 'were often self-appointed persons who happened to be the most substantial or vociferous individuals of their village or district. Age which is revered in China, counted for a good deal'. The

---

[1] *ibid.*, 9 March 1957
[2] *ibid.*, 4 March 1959

Japanese occupation brought changes, and bitter dispute between those who would and those who would not collaborate. Many fled to the interior and returned after the war to find it difficult to resume their position of influence in the village.

A rough-and-ready system of representation was devised whereby the heads of families of the old-established New Territories villages nominated or elected village representatives at the rate of one for every fifty families, with a minimum of one and a maximum of three for each village. In many cases village representatives were not formally elected and when, due to death or resignation, a vacancy occurred, representatives were appointed on the recommendation of a letter signed by the heads of the majority of families. Elections were first held in some districts in 1946, and by the end of that year the system of village representatives had been accepted over the larger part of the New Territories. The next step was the setting up of rural committees composed of, or elected by, village representatives in the twenty-eight[1] subdistricts into which the New Territories were divided for the purpose. This development took time and even by 1957, only 24 had been formed.[2] The committees had no statutory existence or power, whatever authority they exercised was by delegation from the District Commissioner; but they helped in the administration of the territories by being the natural organ of consultation between the officials and the people; they assisted in the settlement of village and—what often amounted to the same thing—clan disputes.

The Heung Yee Kuk was recognized by the Government as reasonably representative of responsible opinion in the New Territories, but in the spring of 1957 it made certain changes in its constitution which gave rise to controversy among its members. The result was that many of them resigned, and 21 chairmen of Rural Committees and 18 other prominent local citizens put forward alternative proposals. The main issue was whether membership of the Heung Yee Kuk should continue to be based on the Rural Committees or have a more popular structure. Efforts to reach a compromise failed, and the Government, which did not accept the changes made, withdrew recognition from the Heung Yee Kuk, on the ground that it was no longer representative of

---

[1] Later reduced to 27.
[2] *Annual Report 1957*, pp. 360–61.

12. The New Territories Magistracy at Fan Ling, opened in 1961.
By courtesy of the Hong Kong Government Information Services.

Facing page 209

opinion in the New Territories. The Heung Yee Kuk was thus reduced to the status of a private society subject to the Societies' Ordinance; however, it refused to register as a society and a petition to the Governor to exempt it from registration was rejected in a reply in which the Government's objections were stated at length. The Government insisted that the law must take its course; so in November 1958 the Heung Yee Kuk began legal proceedings against the District Commissioner for the New Territories and Registrar of Societies. When, in November 1959, the Government introduced a bill in the Legislative Council to provide the Heung Yee Kuk with a new constitution, there were demonstrations outside the Central Government Offices against the bill, but the ordinance was passed in December 1959. The Kuk was to consist of a Council and an Executive Committee. The Council was composed of chairmen and vice-chairmen of the 27 Rural Committees, the unofficial Justices of the Peace for the New Territories and 21 councillors elected by the foregoing. The Executive Committee which was to meet monthly, consisted of the chairmen of the Rural Committees, the New Territories unofficial Justices of the Peace and 15 ordinary members elected by the full Council. The threatened legal proceedings were dropped and after protracted discussions the scheme was accepted and the first elections were held in January and February 1961 respectively. In 1960, the Rural Committees were for the first time given a small monthly subvention for routine expenses.

After the war, the old division of responsibility for the New Territories between District Officers North and South respectively, was revised and one District Officer was made responsible for the whole area with assistants. In 1948 he became known as District Commissioner and was assisted by a District Officer in each of the three districts into which the whole was divided; in 1957 there were four Districts, Yuen Long, Tai Po, Tsuen Wan and Islands; in 1960, the latter district was divided into two, Sai Kung and Islands respectively, each with its own District Officer, making five altogether. In 1954[1] the District Officers were relieved of their general court duties for which a special magistrate was appointed, but they retained their small debt courts and land courts, until 1961 when their jurisdiction was transferred to the District Courts.

[1] *Annual Report 1954*, p. 274.

CHAPTER XIII

THE STRUCTURE OF GOVERNMENT IN 1962

The Executive: The Governor in Council

THE office of Governor and Commander-in-Chief of the Colony of Hong Kong is constituted and his powers defined in general terms by the Letters Patent and Royal Instructions of 14 February 1917, with subsequent amendments, and which are referred to briefly as the Hong Kong Letters Patent 1917 to 1960. These require him to act 'according to such instructions as may from time to time be given him under our Sign Manual and Signet, or by Order in our Privy Council, or by us through one of our Principal Secretaries of State, and to such laws as are now or hereafter shall be in force in the Colony'.[1] This last important provision states explicitly the principle that the Governor of Hong Kong, as with all other British officials, cannot act despotically or arbitrarily, but is subject to law in much the same way as any other citizen. In Hong Kong the law is sovereign. The Governor's powers are further defined in the Colonial Regulations, Part II, Chapter V. 'The Governor is the single and supreme authority responsible to, and representative of, Her Majesty. He is by virtue of his Commission . . . entitled to the obedience, aid, and assistance of all military, air force, and civil officers.' He is Commander-in-Chief of the Colony but does not command the regular forces stationed in the Colony; he can demand information from the senior Military and Air Force Commanders, but by tradition does not issue any orders to officers of the Royal Navy, and recommendations for the movement of warships are made through the Secretary of State for the Colonies. The Governor has to supply information on the Colony to the Secretary of State in the form of 'the annual returns for the Colony, commonly called the Blue Book, relating to Revenue and Expenditure, Defence, Public Works, Legislation, Civil Establishments, Pensions, Population, Schools, Course of Exchange, Imports and Exports, Agriculture, Produce, Manufactures and other matters . . . with reference to the state and condition of the Colony'.[2] As the personal representative of the Sovereign, he exercises the

[1] Letters Patent, 14 February 1917, Section II.
[2] Ibid., Royal Instructions, 14 February 1917, Section XXXV.

royal prerogative of pardon in capital cases; the decision to pardon or not must be taken on his own responsibility, but if he acts contrary to the advice of the Executive Council, he must enter his reasons at length in its minutes.[1] The Governor can also pardon offenders who give information regarding crimes, but except in the case of a political offence, he is not permitted to make banishment from the Colony a condition of pardon. The Governor may suspend or dismiss any official, subject to the prescribed procedure being complied with.

The powers and influence of the Governor cannot be precisely defined. He is the chief executive officer and exercises a general influence over the whole administration in virtue of his ultimate responsibility for the peace order and good government of the Colony. All government decisions are promulgated in his name and his views are therefore invested with great consequence.

The Governor is advised by an Executive Council consisting of the Senior Military Officer for the time being in command of the regular forces, the Colonial Secretary, Attorney-General, Secretary for Chinese Affairs and the Financial Secretary, all these being *ex officio*, and such other persons as may be appointed by the Crown or on instructions from the Secretary of State. The membership of the Council in 1962 consisted of six official members namely the five *ex officio* members mentioned above, and one nominated official, and six unofficial members, appointed by the Crown on the nomination of the Governor for a period of five years, and eligible for appointment for further terms. In the case of a vacancy the Governor makes a provisional appointment. In effect, the Governor chooses his official advisers except the five *ex officio* members. As the sixth official, he normally selects a senior administrative officer of staff grade, but not necessarily the most senior. The unofficial members of the Executive Council are usually chosen from past or present members of the Legislative Council with an established record of public service.

The Executive Council advises the Governor and he is bound to consult it except in such cases as, in his judgment, the public service would 'sustain material prejudice by consulting the Council thereon' or on unimportant matters. He can act without the advice of the Council in case of emergency, but must then communicate to the Council at the earliest practicable moment the measures

[1] *Ibid.*, Sect. XXXIV.

taken and his reasons. The Governor determines its agenda and business according to the following rule: 'The Governor shall alone be entitled to submit questions to the Executive Council for their advice or decision; but if the Governor decline to submit any question to the Council when requested in writing by any member so to do, it shall be competent to such member to require that there be recorded upon the Minutes his written application, together with the answer returned by the Governor to the same'.[1] The Governor may act in opposition to the Executive Council's wishes, but in this case, he must report to the Secretary of State with his reasons, and any member of the Council can insist that his opinion on the matter be entered at length on the minutes. The Governor has to 'communicate these Our Instructions to the Executive Council, and likewise all such others, from time to time, as We may direct, or as he shall find convenient to our service to impart to them'.[2] The Council which meets and deliberates in private cannot proceed to business unless summoned by the Governor, and unless at least two members attend exclusive of himself or the member who is presiding. The Governor presides unless prevented. Minutes are kept and sent to the Secretary of State each six months. Theoretically, the Executive Council has no powers of its own, it is the body from which the Governor seeks advice, but the Governor in Council has certain statutory duties, e.g. to make regulations in accordance with certain ordinances.

The Legislature: The Legislative Council

The unicameral Legislative Council is the supreme law-making authority for the Colony. According to Section VII of the Letters Patent 'The Governor, by and with the advice and consent of the Legislative Council, may make laws for the peace, order, and good government of the Colony'. There are certain limits to this law-making power. The Crown retains the power of disallowance of any ordinance through the Secretary of State, and a bill passed by the Legislative Council may also be reserved for the signification of the royal assent. The Crown has the right of concurrent legislation by order in council, and further, 'the Governor and Legislative Council shall conform to and observe all rules, regulations, and

[1] *Ibid.*, Section XI.
[2] *Ibid.*, Section VI.

directions in that behalf contained in any Instructions under Our Sign Manual and Signet.'[1] On the passage of a bill through the Legislative Council, the Governor has to declare that he assents, or refuses his assent, or that he reserves the bill for signification of the royal pleasure.

The Legislative Council consists of the five *ex officio* members of the Executive Council and not more than four other officials, 'as We may from time to time appoint by any Instructions or warrants under our Sign Manual and Signet, or as the Governor in pursuance of Instructions . . . may from time to time appoint by an Instrument under the Public Seal of the Colony . . .', all of whom are styled official members; and, further, of not more than eight unofficial members, 'as the Governor, in pursuance of Instructions . . . may from time to time appoint by an Instrument under the Public Seal of the Colony . . .'. The unofficial members hold their seats for four years but are eligible for re-appointment for further terms. Vacancies are filled by provisional appointments made by the Governor. If an unofficial becomes bankrupt, or is convicted of a criminal offence or is absent from the Colony for more than three months without permission from the Governor, his seat is declared vacant; any member of the Legislative Council except an *ex officio* member, may resign but such resignation cannot take effect unless accepted by the Governor. The Governor or, in his absence, the senior official member present presides—but the Senior Military Officer is not considered an official member for this purpose—and has an original and a casting vote. The quorum is five. The Legislative Council makes its own standing orders but they must not be repugnant to the Letters Patent or the Royal Instructions. An individual member may propose any subject for debate, and if seconded it is debated, except that financial resolutions may be initiated only by the Governor or only with his permission. All ordinances are enacted 'by the Governor of Hong Kong with the advice and consent of the Legislative Council thereof'. All ordinances passed in any one year must be assented to by the Governor, if he proposes to assent to them, in that year.

There are a number of specified subjects, legislation upon which must not be assented to by the Governor, except on special instructions from the Secretary of State, or without a suspending clause

[1] *Ibid.*, Section XII.

permitting reference to the colonial authorities at home, or unless the matter is of urgent necessity. Among the subjects so restricted are those arranging for divorce; relating to the currency of the Colony or the issue of bank notes or establishing a banking association; imposing differential duties; proposing any action inconsistent with British treaty obligations, interfering with the British armed forces, affecting the royal prerogative or the interests of British subjects not residing in the Colony; and imposing any restriction 'whereby persons not of European birth or descent may be subjected or made liable to any disabilities or restrictions to which persons of European birth or descent are not also subjected or made liable'.

Private bills are allowed subject to safeguards, and if introduced by a private member must be published before being introduced for a first reading. Copies of all ordinances must be sent to the Secretary of State with any necessary explanations and they must be collected and published each year. The Council's minutes must also be sent to him after each meeting at which they have been passed.

Under the Standing Orders, all members of the Legislative Council must take the oath of allegiance, and must therefore be British subjects, and must be English-speaking as the proceedings are in English. The meetings are fixed at the discretion of the Governor, and he may adjourn or suspend any meeting. The order of business in the Legislative Council is: confirmation of the minutes, swearing of the oath (or affirmation) by a new member, announcements, papers laid upon the table and not debated, petitions, questions, Government business, and unofficial members motions.

Papers are presented only by official members, who may be questioned on the work of their own departments or on matters for which they are responsible; other members may also be questioned, but only on matters for which they are responsible, and prior notice must be given unless waived by the Governor as president. The Governor can send messages to the Council to which consideration must be given and he may address the Council at any time. Notice must be given of any motion, with certain procedural exceptions.

Voting is by voice, but if a division is called for, the unofficial members vote first. The legislative procedure follows that of the

House of Commons, namely, a formal first reading at which, apart from the mover and seconder, the Governor may speak but no other discussion allowed, a second reading in which general principles only may be debated, a committee stage dealing with the detailed clauses and a third reading at which the bill is passed as amended in committee. The public are admitted to the meetings of the Council, but strangers may at any time be ordered to withdraw.

The Governor has considerable say in the personnel of the Council since four official members and six of the eight unofficial members are appointed on his direct nomination, that is ten out of seventeen members. The official members in 1962 were the five *ex officio* members and the Director of Education, Director of Public Works, Director of Medical and Health Services and Director of Urban Services. The last three have regularly occupied seats on the Council since 1946, and are virtually *ex officio* but the ninth seat seems to be awarded on more personal grounds. There might be some advantage if all heads of departments were members of the Legislature and liable to be publicly questioned there, in accordance with English constitutional practice, but this would necessitate a corresponding increase in the number of unofficials. In any case, all the official members must support the official policy by their votes.

Of the eight unofficial members, six are directly nominated by the Governor and two are elected respectively by the Justices of the Peace and the Hong Kong General Chamber of Commerce for the Governor's subsequent formal nomination. Of the six unofficials nominated by the Governor there were in 1962 five Chinese, and one Indian. In the past, the number of Chinese members to be nominated by the Governor was laid down by the Secretary of State; the Letters Patent and Royal Instructions of 1917 are silent on the point, but it may be inferred that convention now governs the point although the Queen's instructions in any case are necessary for substantive appointments and she may disallow provisional appointments when reported.

The representative of the Hong Kong General Chamber of Commerce on Legislative Council was, up to 1961, elected at a special general meeting of the Chamber; since that date the election is by the General Committee. Since the War the Chamber has elected its chairman as its nominee on the Council; before the War this was not the usual practice. The Hong Kong General

Chamber of Commerce is an international body comprising some 760 firms, and by its Articles of Association, the General Committee must be British and members of British firms; since this body elects the chairman, he is invariably an important British business man, and has usually had long experience in the Colony before reaching the chair. An electorate of 760 is small enough, but it is racially mixed and very influential because representative of a vitally important side of Hong Kong life.

The unofficial Justices of the Peace have shown faith in their nominee by normally re-electing him for long periods. During the 57 years, 1884 to the Pacific War in 1941 they elected only three men, F. D. Sassoon, 1884–87, C. P. Chater, 1887–1906, and H. E. Pollock, 1906–41, and since the War only four, the Hon. M. M. Watson 1946–53, Dhun Ruttonjee 1953–58, H. D. M. Barton 1958–62 and S. S. Gordon 1962. They have nominated on occasion members of communities which might not otherwise be represented on the Council, and in this way paid regard to the broad interests of the community at large. The remaining unofficial members nominated by the Governor are selected, it would seem, from prominent members of the business community, especially those of them who have proved themselves by public service.

The Legislative Council normally meets once a week on Wednesday afternoons. Its proceedings have become formal and one of the most important reasons for this is the existence of a committee system in which issues that would normally be debated in public in the Legislative Council, are argued in private in committee. By section 4 of the Standing Orders of the Legislative Council of Hong Kong, dated 19th December 1929, there are three standing committees.[1] They are the Finance Committee, consisting of the Colonial Secretary as chairman, the Financial Secretary, the Director of Public Works and all the unofficial members; the Public Works Committee comprising the Director of Public Works as chairman, the Financial Secretary, and all the unofficial members of the Legislative Council; and the Law Committee, consisting of the Attorney-General as chairman, and four other members appointed by the President at the first meeting each year of the Legislative Council. Any member of the Council is entitled to attend any meeting of any of these committees, but is not entitled to take part in the proceedings of a committee of which he is not a

[1] Hong Kong Civil Service List 1958, p. 11.

member. The Committees meet and debate in private and there is no published record of their proceedings. This committee system has been in being with emendations since 1883, and the Finance Committee since 1872. The Finance Committee meets normally every other Wednesday afternoon after the meeting of the full Council, but it can and does meet as often as required. The unofficial members have a majority and it is safe to say that Government measures involving some financial provision must, in general, satisfy them. In the absence of any published proceedings it is impossible to be dogmatic, but there is reason to believe that it is in this Committee that the influence of the unofficials is perhaps most felt.[1]

The other two standing Committees, those of Public Works and Law, meet seldom, if ever, are of little importance, and continue largely in name only. These two Committees have their business remitted to them from the Legislative Council, and so cannot examine proposals before they are brought before the Council. The result is that, except in regard to Finance, the system of standing committees is modified in practice and replaced by a much more flexible committee system. Much of the Public Works programme is discussed in a Public Works sub-committee of the Finance Committee, since public works are normally dependent upon financial provision being found possible. This sub-committee produces an annual printed report; the first appeared for the year 1955–56, and it is presumed that this sub-committee began to function then. A Government Public Works Review Committee examines all public works proposals and a New Buildings Schemes Committee, consisting of the Deputy Colonial Secretary, chairman, Deputy Financial Secretary, three unofficial members of the Legislative Council and two other officials, the Assistant Secretary (Lands) and the Assistant Director of Public Works, considers all new public works before they are submitted to the Council. These three Committees meet as necessary, and much of the ground work of legislation is debated in them, in private. It is understood that most recently a further sub-committee has been formed to discuss proposals for staff increases, etc. before their inclusion in the draft estimates of expenditure for the annual budget.

---

[1] This was confirmed by an unofficial member at the budget debate on 16 March 1964.

Similarly the Standing Law Committee, virtually unused, has its work performed by a Law Reform Committee, consisting of the Chief Justice or his representative as chairman, the Attorney-General or his representative, an unofficial member of the Legislative Council selected by the unofficial members, the Registrar-General or his representative, the chairman of the Hong Kong Bar Association or his representative, the president of the Hong Kong Law Society or his representative, a member of the Attorney-General's Department (member and secretary), and such other persons as may from time to time be co-opted by the Committee either generally or for any particular purpose.[1]

There is one further important modification of the standing committee system. The draft estimates of revenue and expenditure (the budget), are referred each year to a Select Committee, consisting of the Colonial Secretary, the Financial Secretary and all the unofficial members. This is almost the same membership as the standing Finance Committee, but it is presumably felt that the annual estimates should be the subject of a special committee for that sole purpose. This procedure has been adopted since the War.

This Committee system must not be confused with the quite different committee stage in the legislative process taken between the second and third readings in the full council.

Administration: The Urban Council

There has been no traditional division of functions between central and local government authorities in Hong Kong such as is found in Britain and the United States because the limited size of the Colony permits the central government itself to perform all the necessary tasks.

The Urban Council is not a municipal council after the English pattern. Its responsibilities, which are limited to the urban areas, are laid down by ordinance and include environmental hygiene, supervision of markets and hawkers, public cleansing, cemeteries, and the provision of recreational facilities. It operates through an Urban Services Department, the functions of which 'shall include the doing of such acts and things as may be necessary for the purpose of implementing any decision of the Council . . . '. The head of the Urban Services Department is an administrative officer,

[1] *Government Gazette*, No. 12, 16 March 1956.

13. Urban Council Meeting, 6 August 1963. By courtesy of the Hong Kong Government Information Services.

14. Voting in the Urban Council elections held on 7 March 1963.
By courtesy of the *South China Morning Post*, Hong Kong.

employed and paid, like his staff, by the Hong Kong Government and responsible to it.

The Urban Council consists of *ex officio* members and ordinary members; there are five *ex officio* members, the chairman, appointed by the Governor, who is the Director of Urban Services, the Deputy Director of Medical and Health Services as vice-chairman, Director of Public Works, Secretary for Chinese Affairs, and the Director of Social Welfare; the Commissioner for Resettlement also sits as a temporary *ex officio* member.[1] There are 16 ordinary members, of whom eight are elected and not more than eight are appointed, giving them a clear majority over the official members. The ordinary members must not hold office under the Crown or have been sentenced to any period of imprisonment exceeding one year; or have been convicted of treason; or have been disqualified under any corrupt practices ordinance; or be a member of the legislature of any foreign power or a salaried functionary of any foreign power; or be an undischarged bankrupt. Ordinary members may be of either sex and must give proof of ability to speak and write English and must sign a declaration of acceptance of office. The eight appointed ordinary members comprised in 1962, five Chinese, two British and one Portuguese,[2] and they hold office normally for four years and are eligible for re-appointment.

The eight elected members are elected for four years by voters possessing any of the following qualifications; *(a)* liability to serve as a special or common juror, *(b)* exemption from jury service on certain specific grounds, *(c)* qualified teachers under the Education Ordinance, *(d)* payment of tax under the Inland Revenue Ordinance, and *(e)* membership of the Defence Force or Auxiliary Services, except that members of the Police Force and of the regular Armed Forces are not qualified to vote. A voter must be over 21 years of age and not have been found guilty of corrupt practices or have been convicted and imprisoned for a term exceeding six months. The maximum scale of election expenses is prescribed by the Governor and must not exceed 'during the election . . . after such election or within the nine months before

---

[1] *Annual Report 1957*, p. 358. In March 1964, the Governor announced an increase of unofficial members of the Urban Council, two appointed and two elected.

[2] The Urban Council Ordinance of 1956 does not follow precedent set by the earlier ordinances dealing with the Sanitary Board or the Urban Council in binding the Governor to nominate a minimum number of Chinese.

On the occasion of the formal opening of the
City Hall on 2 nd March 1962 His Excellency
Sir Robert Black, Knight Grand Cross of the
Most Distinguished Order of St. Michael &
St. George, Officer of the Most Excellent Order
of the British Empire, Governor & Commander in
Chief of the Colony of Hong Kong, presented this
scroll to the Urban Council upon whom the
management of the City Hall had been vested
by Ordinance on Wednesday, 29th March 1961.
It was received on behalf of the Urban Council
by the Chairman the Honourable Kenneth
Strathmore Kinghorn, Justice of the Peace.

Scroll presented to the Urban Council by the Governor on the occasion of
placing it in control of the City Hall at its opening, 29 March 1961

the date of such election', $5,000, plus 20 cents for each entry
in the register of voters in excess of 25,000.

An election agent's fee is not to exceed $1,000. In the case of
two or more joint candidates, i.e. having the same election agent,
the maximum permitted expenditure is reduced by one quarter,
and in the case of more than two joint candidates, by one third.[1]

The Urban Council's position may be anomalous, but there can
be no question of its influence and importance. It has no direct
control over its chairman, the Director of Urban Services and his
staff, but its public discussions do in practice carry great weight,
and its decisions are normally implemented. Its value is that
administrative action, which closely touches the lives of the people

[1] Corrupt and Illegal Practices (Urban Council Election Expenses Order
1955, GNA B4 of 1955).

is discussed in public and helps to create an informed public opinion. The work of the Council is onerous. It meets for formal business at least once a month, but the chief work is done in its 15 select committees and 4 sub-committees; the Chairman presides over the policy committees, and unofficial members may occupy the chair of other committees and assume responsibility for a particular part of the Council's work. Membership of the Council is no sinecure, and carries on an old British tradition of unpaid service to the community. There is considerable pressure from the unofficial members of the Council gradually to increase the scope of its activities, and the Young Plan may yet be implemented, though in piecemeal fashion. The Resettlement Department created early in 1954, operates under its general direction,[1] though here again the Commissioner for Resettlement and his staff are not under its control. The Housing Authority set up by the Housing Ordinance No. 18 of 1954 consists of all members of the Urban Council, *ex officio*, and not more than three members appointed by the Governor.[2] The Housing Division which consists of Government staff lent to the Housing Authority is also part of the Urban Services Department. The Council controls parks and playgrounds as well as such new amenities as the swimming pool, and the recently excavated Lei Cheng Uk Tomb of pre-T'ang times.

The administration and management of the new City Hall which was completed in 1962 also comes under the Urban Council.

Administration: The Government Departments

The administrative functions of Government are discharged, under the general superintendence of the Colonial Secretary, by some thirty-five departments, the staffs of which form the Hong Kong Civil Service. The Colonial Secretariat under the general control of the Deputy Colonial Secretary co-ordinates the work of the other Departments and acts as the link between the policy-making authorities and the administrative bodies who have to implement their decisions.[3] Generally, the departments administer ordinances coming within their sphere, in addition to any specific statutory

---

[1] *Annual Report 1957*, p. 196.

[2] *Ibid.*, p. 188. Up to 1962, only one such member had been appointed.

[3] This account is based on information given in the *Annual Report 1962*.

duties, carry out policy decisions, prepare departmental estimates for the budget and put up proposals for future legislation or administrative action. The heads of departments might be deputed to answer questions in the Legislative Council, if they are members, but generally are responsible to the Governor through the Colonial Secretary.

The Colonial Secretariat is organized in four divisions, general administration, finance, defence and establishment. The first is controlled by the Deputy Colonial Secretary. The Financial Secretary prepares the annual budget and deals with financial and economic policy. The Defence Secretary is responsible for the Royal Hong Kong Defence Force, the Auxiliary Police Force and the Essential Services Corps and is the link between the Hong Kong Government and the British Armed Forces stationed in the Colony.

The establishment is controlled by a Public Services Commission, which is an independent statutory body, set up in 1950, to advise on pensionable posts, appointments and promotions in the Government service.

The Legal Department under an Attorney-General is responsible for advising the Government on legal matters, drafting legislation and conducting public prosecutions.

The Secretary for Chinese Affairs advises on all matters connected with the Chinese population in the urban area and presides over statutory committees of special importance to the Chinese, controls the District Watch Force, and co-ordinates the policy of other departments in relation to the Chinese, e.g. in connection with measures against drug addiction.

The Social Welfare Department has six sections dealing with Child Welfare, Youth Welfare, Community Development, Welfare of Women and Girls, Special Welfare Services e.g. to the Blind, Relief and Public Assistance, and Probation, and it has close relations with the Council of Social Service and many voluntary bodies concerned with social welfare.

The Accountant General is responsible for the government accounts and a Director of Audit is responsible, under the general supervision of the Director-General of the Overseas Audit Service in London, for auditing them. A Commissioner of Rating and Valuation is responsible for the assessment of rates and questions concerning the value of real property. The Commissioner of

Inland Revenue concerns himself with internal revenue such as the Earnings and Profits Tax, Stamp Duties, Estate Duty, Entertainment Tax, Dance Halls Tax and the Betting and Sweeps Tax.

The Director of Commerce and Industry is responsible for trade development, collection of import and excise duties, the working of the Preventive Service, the production of trade statistics and of any other statistics required by the Government, certificates of origin, trade licensing, etc. He controls the Hong Kong Government offices in London and Sydney which are mainly concerned with trade promotion.

The Public Works Department has nine sub-departments dealing with waterworks, Crown Lands and Surveys, administration of the Buildings Ordinance, electrical and mechanical works, architecture (government buildings), development, port works, drainage, and roads. The Director of Public Works is also responsible for town planning.

The Urban Services Department under a Director is responsible for sanitary services in the whole colony and for certain services in the field of public health in the urban area such as standards of cleanliness in the preparation of food, control of slaughter houses, administration of pest control measures, and supervision of hawkers; it controls public parks, playgrounds, bathing beaches, car parks and the City Hall. It operates in association with the Urban Council which ensures that decisions which touch the daily life of citizens are debated in public by a body composed of officials and representatives of the community. The Urban Services Department also comprises a Housing Division under a Commissioner who works in association with the Housing Authority.

Resettlement Department became necessary with influx of refugees. The Urban Council working through the Department its responsible for the clearance and resettlement of squatters, the administration of resettlement estates and areas, and the department works in close association with the Housing Authority and the Commissioner for Housing.

The Police Department and the Prisons Department, each under a Commissioner, need little comment. The duties regarding control of immigration which used to be performed by the police have now been placed under an independent Immigration Department; the problem is to control illegal immigration, for the ordinary community services cannot bear the strain of continued mass immigration into the Colony, and the long-maintained open frontier with China has had to be abandoned.

The Medical and Health Department is responsible for providing hospital and clinical facilities in the whole colony, including the New Territories and also provides maternal and child health facilities, a school medical service and port health services, and is responsible for preventive measures against epidemics. The department also supplies medical staff for the Urban Services Department, the industrial health section of the Labour Department, and the Prisons Department. The Urban Council, through the Urban Services Department is the authority for environmental and food hygiene for the urban area, and is in process of taking over similar responsibilities in the rural areas. Government policy aims at providing medical facilities at low cost for those unable to afford the expense of consulting medical practitioners on their own account, and with this in view, in addition to various hospitals, Government provides out-patient clinics or assists voluntary associations or medical missionary bodies to provide them. The normal charge at a clinic is one dollar for each attendance, but tuberculosis, leprosy and venereal disease treatment is free as are maternal and child services.

The Education Department concerns itself with primary, secondary and post-secondary education and directly maintains schools and assists by grants or subsidies approved schools run by missionary and other voluntary agencies.

The Labour Department is responsible for initiating labour legislation, for the registration and inspection of factories with a view to promoting industrial health and safety; it undertakes conciliation in industrial disputes, advises on the formation and management of trade unions and has statutory duties in the protection of women and young persons in regard to conditions of labour, and administers the Workmen's Compensation Ordinance. The Commissioner of Labour is also the head of another smaller department as Commissioner of Mines.

The Registrar-General's Department deals with land registration, births and deaths, marriages, registration of companies and trade marks and patents. It also contains the offices of the Official Receiver in Bankruptcy, the Official Trustee and Judicial Trustee and of the Official Solicitor in Lunacy; for these highly specialized duties it has a staff of solicitors.

The Marine Department under a Director is responsible for co-ordinating and controlling the harbour services assisted by various port committees on which the local commercial interests are represented.

The Airport administration and operation are controlled by a Director of Civil Aviation.

The British section of the Kowloon-Canton Railway is run directly by Government through a Manager and Chief Engineer.

A Postmaster General controls the Post Office and the Radio Station, but telephone and cable services are privately organized by a public utility company.

The Director of the Royal Observatory is responsible for providing meteorological information and warnings.

The Director of the Information Services Department is responsible for official publicity.

The Agriculture and Forestry Department covers land utilization and provides technical advice to farmers in the use of scientific techniques and conservation of soil and water through afforestation. The Government fosters the fishing industry and encourages co-operative marketing schemes through the Co-operative Development and Fisheries Department, which is responsible for a Fisheries Research Unit.

The Fire Brigade under a Chief Officer provides protection against the hazard of fire in the urban area and more populous parts of the New Territories.

A Stores Department buys and distributes government stores.

The Government Printer at the head of the Printing Department is responsible for all government publications.

A Quartering Authority provides accommodation for Civil Servants.

A new department set up in 1961, the Government Public Enquiry Service, assists the general public by answering enquiries concerning government departments.

The New Territories Administration, under a District Commissioner, has been described in an earlier chapter.

On 1 January 1962 the total actually employed in the Hong Kong Government service was 49,902, almost treble the number employed on 1 April 1949, at which date the figure was 17,554; the authorized establishment including unfilled posts was 56,910. The estimated cost of salaries and wages for the year 1962–63 was about

378 million dollars, or 31% of the total estimated government expenditure for the year. Monthly paid officers form four broad categories, one includes administrative and professional officers; a second, junior grades with monthly salaries above $360 for men and $275 for women; a third, staff subject to discipline below the rank of police sub-inspector or equivalent rank; and finally non-pensionable officers with initial monthly salaries up to $360 for men and $275 for women.

Local Recruitment

Much progress has been made in encouraging local recruitment to the government service. This policy, which was designed to be complementary to plans for constitutional progress, was laid down in a British Government White Paper, Colonial No. 197 of 1946: 'If progressive advancement along the road to self-government within the frame work of the British Commonwealth of Nations is to be a reality, the public services of the colonies must be adapted to local people. It is already a fully accepted principle that there should be no barrier to the appointment of a Colonial candidate or a locally recruited public servant to any post which he is qualified to fill . . . '. It also urged the appointment of an independent public services commission in each Colony to supervise this policy. A Public Service Commission was set up in Hong Kong in 1950.

The Retrenchment Commission of 1932 had urged this policy, but there was little progress until after the War. In 1946 Admiral Sir Cecil Harcourt, head of the temporary Military Administration praised the Chinese and Portuguese staff without whom, he said 'the personnel position would have been untenable, and it can hardly be denied that they thereby established credentials which it would be hard for any future government to ignore'.

Sir Man Kam Lo, who made himself the spokesman of the demand for extended local recruitment, complained in the Legislative Council[1] that little was being done to implement the policy. Sir Mark Young, in his address to the Legislative Council during the budget debate in September 1946, replied by giving a definite undertaking that 'The policy of Government is to ensure that every opportunity shall be given to locally recruited persons not only to enter but to rise in the service of the public up to the highest posts

[1] Hong Kong *Hansard* 1946, p. 117.

and to fulfil the highest responsibilities of which they are capable
or can be assisted to become capable' by any means at the disposal
of the Government.[1] The first post-war Salaries Commission of
1947 implemented this policy by making the payment of expatriate
allowance to an overseas officer conditional upon there being no
person with the requisite qualifications being available for local
recruitment. An immediate start was made in the Medical Department where the Director was an enthusiastic supporter of the new
policy, and before the year was out the grades of medical officer,
nursing sister and health inspector which had up till then been
restricted to expatriate officers were thrown open, and in the
Education Department the grade of master was similarly opened.
Of even more significance was the appointment in 1946 of the first
Chinese, born in the Colony, to be a cadet officer and in 1952 for
the first time a locally recruited officer was promoted to be the
head of a government department. The same policy was adopted
in the Police Force and in the technical departments such as the
Kowloon-Canton Railway and the Public Works Department,
opening the way to greater advancement of Chinese staff. In 1951
there were 54 locally recruited officers in the then classes I and II
of the civil service, comprising administrative and senior professional technical officers and others with a minimum basic monthly
salary of $1,750;[3] or 10·75% of the total employed in these classes.
On 1 January 1962, there were 730 local officers and 950 expatriate
officers, that is the percentage of the former had risen to 43·5 in
the equivalent of these classes. To implement this policy much
depended upon the provision of education and training facilities,
and progress was slow until the flow of graduates from the University began once more. As evidence of the new policy, the Central
British School giving secondary education, which had been
restricted to European children, was renamed King George V
School in 1947 and thrown open to all children who could benefit
by the instruction given.

It has been recognized that the policy of local recruitment for
the government service must be supplemented by opportunities for
advancement in the service. Local officers have been assisted in

[1] Hong Kong *Hansard* 1946, p. 128.

[2] Report of the Salaries Commission, Hong Kong *Sessional Papers* 1948.
Part I, p. 12.

[3] Slightly lower for women.

this respect; in 1962, for example, 92 local officers were sent overseas to attend courses of instruction, at a total cost, including that
of other expatriate officers who attended courses while on leave,
of $1,550,000. In 1961 a start was made with more systematic
schemes with the object of enabling locally recruited officers to
qualify themselves by training or examination for the highest posts
they are capable of filling.

CHAPTER XIV

GOVERNMENT BY DISCUSSION—HOW THE CONSTITUTION WORKS

Public Opinion and Lawmaking

LITTLE electoral machinery exists to enable opinion in the community to be reflected in the Government through elected representatives in the Legislature. The Governor and his professional civil service colleagues, backed by the Colonial Office in London, are in control. Yet the appearance of bureaucratic rule is misleading. An examination of the working of the Hong Kong constitution shows that interested opinion is consulted continuously prior to any important government decision, and that on occasion, where the interests of the whole community are concerned, as for one example only, the validity of Chinese marriages, the general public at large is invited to express its views. Indeed, consultation as practised by the Government is so extensive that the term 'government by discussion' aptly describes one of its leading characteristics and is taken as a fitting title to this chapter.

Even with electoral machinery, it is not always easy to find out public opinion or be certain that a government acts in accordance with the popular will. One criterion is the presence or absence of political unrest. Organized opposition to the government in Hong Kong is conspicuously absent and demands explanation. It may be due to apathy, repression or to Government and people being broadly in step. Some degree of apathy comes from the realization that decisions vitally affecting the future of Hong Kong may be taken in London, Peking, New York or elsewhere. There is also among the Chinese a tendency to political acquiescence, which stems from a Confucian respect for the official and which should not be mistaken for apathy. The police do have wider powers than for example in Britain, but generally, freedom of speech, conscience and association are enjoyed by the individual under the constitution and these rights are incompatible with repression. Again, there is a mass of government publications regarding government business which creates the impression of willing accountability to the public.

In fact, the Government in Hong Kong commands respect by a policy of serving the common interest. This is not the same thing as governing in accordance with the general will, but it is accompanied by some effort to elicit the views of the public as to what the general interest is.

The unofficial members of the Legislative Council are most influential because their function is to represent the community. Examination of the working of the Council shows the sensitiveness of Government to their views.

The proceedings of the Council have become formal; it has almost ceased to be a debating assembly. Government measures are rarely challenged and the unofficial members have not formed an opposition party as they threatened to do fifty years ago under the inspiration of Thomas Whitehead. The one exception is the full-dress debate on the annual budget. The Governor addresses the Council reviewing the work of the administration during the previous year and outlining some of the main problems to be faced in the coming year. The Financial Secretary presents his budget in detail and, at the next meeting, all the unofficial members pass comment with speeches in which traditionally they are free to range over the whole compass of public affairs. At the subsequent meeting, replies are made by the Colonial Secretary and other departmental heads dealing with the issues raised. There is little debate even here, and the occasion is one marked by a series of speeches which afford the unofficial members an opportunity to catch the public eye and justify themselves. They are fully reported in the daily press. The Council's normal proceedings have diminished in interest because in practice they do little more than formally record assent to bills which have been debated elsewhere.

There are many reasons for this formality. The existence of an official majority which can always be used to carry government bills means that debate may be without effect on the final vote. Moreover, as society becomes more complex, legislation deals more with technical issues than with matters of broad popular interest. As an example, in the year 1957, chosen at random, the first twenty ordinances passed, given in alphabetical order were:

Births and Deaths Registration (Amendment), Board of Trustees of the United College of Hong Kong Incorporation Bill, Business Regulations (Amendment) Bill, Commonwealth Preference (Motor Vehicles), Crown Proceedings, Custodian of Property (Termination

of Functions), Defences (Firing Areas) (Amendment), Dutiable
Commodities (Amendment), Education (Amendment), Enemy Pro-
perty Legislation Repeal, Fatal Accidents (Amendment), Franked
Instruments (Validation), Hawkers (Amendment and Validation),
Hong Kong Airport (Control of Obstructions), Hong Kong Airport
(Control of Obstructions) (Amendment), The Hongkong and Shanghai
Banking Corporation (Amendment), Hong Kong Tourist Association
Bill, Housing (Amendment), Kowloon City Baptist Church, Landlord
and Tenant (Amendment), Law of Property (Enforcement of Coven-
ants), Masonic Benevolence Fund Incorporation.

It is clear that they are not so much policy measures as technical
administrative measures, where expert views must ultimately
prevail. They are inherently non-contentious, unless it be amongst
the experts themselves and have to be voted as a necessary part of
efficient administration. The working of the committee system in
the Legislative Council, where the unofficial members have a
majority or are well represented, makes it difficult to pass ordinances to which they were strongly and collectively opposed. They
can therefore secure concessions before the final vote in the
Council. Much informal consultation also takes place between the
members and heads of departments quite apart from the discussions in committee. Thus in various ways differences are ironed
out at an early stage and lengthy debate in the Council is obviated.

The precise degree of influence exercised by the unofficial members is difficult to estimate. On important issues, their opinion has
obvious weight and their opposition is avoided. Their vote against
the Young Plan in 1949 was decisive, for neither the British
Government nor the local British authorities were willing to make
constitutional changes over their heads; yet their proposal for an
amended Legislative Council was not accepted. In deference to
local Chinese opinion Chinese custom is safeguarded and legislation concerning it is unlikely to be proposed except on the initiative
of the Chinese unofficial members. The Government, having
nominated all but two of the unofficial members, naturally has
confidence in its choice and normally heeds their advice.

It is on those rare occasions when the normal consultative
processes break down or fail for some reason to reconcile the
differences that the reality of the influence wielded by the unofficials is brought into the open. The following examples, taken
from recent proceedings of the Legislative Council:

The Education (Amendment) Bill, 1958,[1] part of the object of which was to ensure the structural soundness of school premises and prevent the use of schools for propaganda purposes, aroused opposition for fear the bill would lead to the closure of private schools and reduce much-needed educational facilities. The first reading was taken on 18 December 1957 and the second was delayed until 8 January 1958, on which occasion the Attorney-General moved an amendment. The one unofficial member who spoke, referred to the need for various safeguards 'sufficient to ensure that Government stands no chance of getting away with undesirable restrictions'. Similarly, in 1957 a Medical Registration Bill,[2] directed against those holding medical qualifications but not registerable in Hong Kong, chiefly refugee doctors, aroused opposition. When the second reading was taken on 22 May, the Director of Medical Services referred to 'much evidence of public apprehension both as to its purpose and possible effects. There have been many representations to Government and to Unofficial Members . . .' and on behalf of the Government he himself moved eight amendments.

In the case of the Landlord and Tenant Bill, 1955,[3] the first reading was on 6 July and the second was delayed until 17 August, because of opposition. The Attorney-General's speech on the latter date acknowledged that 'many representations and suggestions have been put forward by the honourable Unofficial Members of this Council and by various bodies and associations in this Colony'; he said 'All suggestions, representations and comments have been most carefully considered . . .'; as a result, he himself proposed a number of amendments.

In 1956 a debate developed in the Legislative Council on the future of broadcasting in Hong Kong.[4] The Government had outlined five recommendations in a Sessional Paper and the Colonial Secretary moved that they be accepted. Amendments were proposed by an unofficial member and supported by his colleagues, and at the end of the debate, the Colonial Secretary announced that the amendments would be accepted by the Government.

---

[1] Hong Kong *Hansard* for 1958, p. II.
[2] *Ibid.*, 1957, pp. 142, 182
[3] *Ibid.*, 1955, pp. 214, 239.
[4] *Ibid.*, 1956, p. 45

One of the most conspicuous examples was the defeat of the Football Pools Betting Bill in June 1960. Following a move to introduce football pools into Hong Kong, a committee was appointed to consider possible amendments to the law regarding gambling. Towards the end of 1959, the committee was asked to consider the question of the pools separately and replied that they would probably recommend that the law be amended to allow their operation. On 23 December 1959, Government announced its intention, with the approval of the Executive Council, to introduce legislation to this effect, and the Football Pools Betting Bill received its first reading on 4 May 1960. The Officer Administering the Government on that occasion made the following special statement. '. . . Unofficial Members of the Executive Council and of this Council have informed me that in their view there is a large body of opinion in the Colony which is opposed to this measure, and certain Unofficial Members have expressed their own personal misgivings as to the desirability of proceeding in the manner proposed.' He suggested a debate on the second reading in accordance with standing orders. This took place on June, and the bill was defeated by the opposition of seven unofficial members, in a vote in which all the eight official members and one unofficial member abstained. Government preferred to go back on its announcement rather than override the unofficial members.

The evidence is that opposition to the Government's legislative proposals, constitutionally expressed through the unofficial members of the Legislative Council, is listened to with respect, and that Government is clearly anxious to avoid a head-on conflict with the unofficials.

The structure of two committees of the Legislative Council, those of the Finance Committee and the Select Committee for the annual draft Estimates of Income and Expenditure, gives the unofficial members a substantial majority. It may be assumed—in the absence of any published proceedings this cannot be confirmed—that financial proposals go forward to the full Council in a form acceptable to them.

The conclusion must be if that the largely formal proceedings of the Legislative Council recorded in the Hong Kong *Hansard* provide no index of the degree of influence in fact exercised by the unofficial members representing the community at large; the evidence is, not that there is little consultation with the unofficials but much profitable consultation, not less debate but more effectual debate. This takes place during the preparatory stages of legislation when amendments can be more easily examined and accepted. Whatever disadvantage there may be attaching to influence exercised in private, behind the scenes, is possibly offset by the greater persuasive power of the unofficial members which allow a settlement of disputed points being arrived at without the Government exposing itself to public rebuff if the measure is not amended in accordance with public feeling.

In such a system of nominated unofficial members of the Legislative Council, much depends on the criteria used by the Governor in making his nominations. Under existing conditions his choice is limited. The candidates must be British subjects, otherwise they could not take the oath of allegiance. They must be men of some substance, otherwise they could not afford time to attend the meetings of the Council or of its committees, or attend to the various duties inseparable from membership or avail themselves of invitations from departmental heads to inspect government projects. The British tradition of unpaid service to the community has much to commend it, but few can afford to give the necessary time. In any case, the Governor nominates only six members, the other two names being put forward by outside bodies. His discretion is further limited by the need to balance the claims of the different communities, Chinese, Indian and British. Finally the Governor presumably has to look for evidence of ability, willingness to serve the public interest and capacity to represent some side of public opinion. The result is that the choice has to be made from a restricted class in society and from those who have proved themselves in the Urban Council or in other public work.

In some ways the fact that there are nominated unofficials at all makes them representative, in the sense that members of the general public will discuss their grievances and present their views only to those whom they believe to have influence with government and so are in a position to help.

Public Opinion and Administration

The unofficial members of the Legislative Council are officially acknowledged as representatives of public opinion in the Colony in the matter of legislation. In day-to-day administration, the

Government is assisted by advisory bodies on which other members of the community serve and make their influence felt. The Urban Council with its eight nominated and eight elected members is the most important of these. The Civil Service List for 1962 gives the names of 67 advisory 'Councils, Boards and Committees etc.' with their composition. Of these, thirty-seven are statutory bodies in which the membership is wholly or partly determined by ordinance and which carry out statutory duties. Three are set up in accordance with regulations made under the authority of an ordinance. Nineteen are appointed by the Governor to advise the head of a department and keep him in touch with local opinion, and which he consults as much or as little as he finds advisable. The remaining eight are without indication of the constituting authority, though some appear to be of purely domestic interest to the Government's internal working.

These advisory bodies are an important and characteristic feature of Hong Kong's constitution. They are of bewildering variety in function, membership, powers, origin and influence and the list does not exhaust their number. Some are large representative bodies advising a department over the whole of its work, some are *ad hoc* bodies advising on a special aspect. The membership may be prescribed, in whole or part, by ordinance; there are *ex officio* members by virtue of positions occupied in the community, while others are appointed at the Governor's discretion. It is unnecessary to deal with all these bodies individually, a few examples will suffice to show the system at work.

In the Education Department, for instance, a Board of Education, set up by ordinance, advises the Director of Education, who is its *ex officio* chairman. Its twenty members, of whom ten are Chinese, comprise representatives of the main religious bodies interested in education, and of the chief communities, together with individuals qualified by experience and attainment to advise. There is a statutory Appeals Board, to which appeal may be made against the refusal of the Director to register a school, a manager or a teacher, with eight members, of whom three must be registered teachers, under an independent chairman. There is also a British Universities Selection Committee, appointed by the Governor, with the Director or his Deputy as chairman and seven other members such as representatives from the University of Hong Kong, the British Council, and an Assistant Director of Education. The

Social Welfare Department has a Social Welfare Advisory Committee appointed by the Governor with the Director as *ex officio* chairman, the chairman of the Hong Kong Council of Social Service, the chairman of the Hong Kong Council of Women, the chairman of the Standing Conference of Youth Organizations, and the Chairman of the Tung Wah Hospitals Board of Directors, all as *ex officio* members, and six other members selected for their experience of social welfare work.

Among the bodies looking after the interests of the Chinese is the Chinese Permanent Cemetery Board of Management with the Secretary of Chinese Affairs as chairman, the Director of Public Works, the chairman of the Urban Council, seven Chinese members of the Executive or Legislative Councils, present or past, one of whom is vice-chairman, and seven other Chinese members. Another is the Chinese Temples Committee, a statutory body consisting of the Secretary for Chinese Affairs, the Chinese members of the Executive and Legislative Councils, the Chinese nominated members of the Urban Council, the chairman of the Board of Directors of the Tung Wah Hospitals, the chairman, Po Leung Kuk[1] Committee, a director of the Tung Wah resident in Kowloon, and one member appointed by the Governor. The Chinese Recreation Grounds Committee has the Secretary for Chinese Affairs as chairman and seven Chinese members of one or other of the Executive and Legislative Councils. The Po Leung Kuk Permanent Board of Directors is a statutory body, with the same government official as chairman, and six Chinese members chosen from one or other of the two Councils, plus seven other Chinese, and has statutory powers in connection with the welfare of women and girls. The Tung Wah Hospital Advisory Board is a statutory body supervising the work of the Tung Wah Group of Chinese charity hospitals, with the Secretary for Chinese Affairs as chairman and fourteen prominent Chinese as members.

The Marine Department has two statutory bodies, the Mercantile Marine Assistance Fund Committee consisting of the Director of Marine, a clergyman, the divisional superintendent of Marine Police and two other members drawn from shipping companies, and a Pilotage Board of six members including members of the Marine Department, an officer of the Royal Navy and two master mariners. There are also three advisory bodies appointed by the

[1] The Society for the Protection of Virtue, i.e. to protect women and girls.

Governor. The Port Committee consists of the Director of Marine as chairman, Director of Public Works, Manager and Chief Engineer of the Kowloon-Canton Railway, Commissioner of Labour, the Commodore of the Naval Base, and four representatives of shipping interests; the Port Executive Committee consist of the Director of Marine as chairman, a naval officer, and six representatives of shipping interests; the Port Welfare Committee has an independent chairman and eleven members chosen from the Marine Department, the religious organizations working in the Port, and representatives of shipping companies. The Director of Medical and Health Services is *ex officio* chairman of no less than eight bodies; five of them are professional and statutory bodies, the Dental Council, the Medical Council, the Midwives Board, the Nursing Board and the Pharmacy Board, and their members are chosen from those with appropriate professional qualifications. The Medical Advisory Board appointed by the Governor has six members all *ex officio*, of whom two are government officials, two are senior officers in the armed forces, and two represent the profession. The Hong Kong Examination Board, Royal Society of Health, has seven *ex officio* members, all officials of government. A Radiation Board, under the same chairman, has as members the Commissioner of Labour and Director of Commerce and Industry, both *ex officio*, the Superintendent of Mines, a senior specialist (Radiology), a government law officer, the head of the Physics Department at the University, a medical practitioner and two scientists. One important statutory body is the Hong Kong Housing Authority set up under the Housing Ordinance which has already been referred to.

Two further examples are given to show the variety. The Advisory Committee on Corruption has an unofficial member of the Executive Council as chairman, with three other unofficial members of the Executive and Legislative Council, the Deputy Commissioner of Police and the Establishment Officer. The Public Services Commission set up under ordinance has three members, all independent of the Government and of the Executive and Legislative Councils.

Also in the above list is a Cotton Advisory Board set up as a result of the problems created over the renewal of an agreement made between Lancashire and Hong Kong cotton manufacturers by which the latter voluntarily and reluctantly accepted a temporary ceiling on exports of cotton goods to Britain. There was also pressure from the United States for a similar restriction. The Hong Kong Government proposed the formation of a Cotton Advisory Board to the cotton manufacturers who accepted it subject to certain reservations, and the Board came into being in July 1961, having as its terms of reference: 'arising out of the exceptional issues which the cotton industry in Hong Kong faces, to advise the Government on any matter which directly affects the cotton industry in Hong Kong'. The Board, under the chairmanship of the Director of Commerce and Industry, was to be composed of two representatives each from the Hong Kong Cotton Spinners Association, the Federation of Hong Kong Cotton Weavers and the Hong Kong Weaving Mills Association, and one representative each from the Chinese Manufacturers Association, the Federation of Hong Kong Industries, the Hong Kong General Chamber of Commerce, the Hong Kong Garments Manufacturers (for the U.S.A.) Association and the Dyeing and Finishing Industry. The Cotton Spinners Association refused to join the Board but the way was left open to it to nominate its two representatives later when it felt it could co-operate. Provision was also made for the later appointment of an independent vice-chairman. The Board provides an excellent illustration of the method of consultation used by the Government in policy making. The Board has advisory status only, but having been set up, the Government would find it difficult to ignore its advice.

There is also the Advisory Committee on Public Transport set up by the Governor in October 1961, consisting of an independent chairman, with the District Commissioner New Territories, the Director of Public Works, the Commissioner of Police, the Director of Marine and the Deputy Economic Secretary as official members, and five unofficial members. Its terms of reference are to keep under continuing review the routes, frequency, capacity and fares of all public transport services having regard to distribution of population, existing roads, piers, etc., the requirements of the public and the interests of the companies operating the services; to examine all complaints and suggestions and to make recommendations regarding the long-term development of the public transport services. This is quite a different body from the Traffic Advisory Committee.

These advisory bodies are mostly permanent standing bodies, but they vary in number and composition from year to year, some disappearing and new one being added as occasion demands, making the system quite flexible.

But consultation with the public goes further than this, for there also exists a number of *ad hoc* committees to advise on specific projects or problems, whose span of life is long or short as the nature of the project dictates. A list is not readily available, and there is little publicity beyond occasional references in the press or in government announcements. No important official project is without its advisory committee containing usually both official and outside members. It acts as the liaison between the Government and the interests affected and helps to ensure that difficulties are ironed out at an early stage and that those likely to be adversely affected are able to make themselves heard. The process can be illustrated with reference to the building of the new airport of which the runway jutting out into the harbour was completed in 1958.

A Kai Tak Progress Committee was set up on 15 December 1954 to watch over the general progress of the scheme to recommend any modifications suggested by the consulting engineers or the Director of Civil Aviation to make recommendations on the design and layout of the terminal building and the equipment and personnel required to operate the airport with particular reference to the financial aspect.

It is difficult to evaluate this mass of permanent and *ad hoc* committees as evidence of consultation with the general public without a complete list over the years with terms of reference, mode of appointment and membership. They are all technically administrative in scope, but in so far as policy-making often arises from administrative difficulties, they do have some bearing on government policy. Besides it may be assumed that the Government would not establish them if they did not fulfil their main purposes of providing useful advice. In this way they help bridge the gap between the Government and the People.

Public opinion is given other opportunities of making itself felt. As in Britain, use is made of commissions or committees of enquiry, on which members of the community with appropriate experience are asked to serve, when legislation on some important topic is contemplated. Their reports are published, often accompanied by a White Paper giving the Government's view of the findings and proposals. A Committee of Enquiry into Chinese Law and Custom in Hong Kong was appointed in 1948, consisting of the Solicitor-General as chairman, the District Officer, New Territories, a Chinese official from the Secretariat of Chinese Affairs, and four Chinese. More recently there has been an enquiry into the validity of Chinese customary marriages, following a petition for the abolition of concubinage. A report by the Attorney-General and the Secretary for Chinese Affairs was issued on 14 March 1961, and copies, together with an intimation that it did not necessarily represent Government policy, were sent to the press, to all the unofficial Justices of the Peace, to thirty-two women's organizations, to a number of leading Chinese and welfare bodies, to the Bar Association, Law Society and the Heung Yee Kuk. Members of the general public were also invited to give their views. This may well have been a piece of government stonewalling but the Government has clearly shown it would not embark on any contentious legislation without full enquiry and opportunity for public discussion. Again, letters critical of official action appear in the press and are noticed and replied to, by the head of the department concerned, or by a press release from the Government Information Services Department.

In these many ways, public opinion has ample opportunities of being listened to and consulted. Government action is sifted in one or more of a mass of committees and thus public opinion plays no small part in Hong Kong both in the determination of official action and in the implementing of plans already decided. The system of consultative committees works well in a small compact community like Hong Kong, and might not be so efficacious in a larger state.

Summing up, though the government of Hong Kong remains the responsibility, through the Governor, of the Secretary of State in London, who is responsible to the Parliament at Westminster, the evidence of the Government's desire to associate members of the community with the governing institutions of the Colony is undeniable. The result is reasonable contentment, because action is not taken in the face of opposition. Chinese prejudices and customs are safeguarded and the Chinese do not feel themselves oppressed or slighted; all are free to pursue their lawful avocations, with reasonable security for person and property.

The system serves a community in which the ends of government are accepted without cleavage, and provides an efficient administration within an accepted social and economic framework, bound up with a laissez-faire economy. It tends therefore to be based on the maintenance of the *status quo*.

CHAPTER XV

EPILOGUE

THE evolution, form and practice of the constitution having been described in the foregoing chapters, it only remains to look at the prospects.

The British declared policy of preparing the colonies for self-government within the Commonwealth continues unchanged. This was confirmed in regard to Hong Kong by the Colonial Secretary at the first reading of the Urban Council (Amendment) Bill of 1956, which increased the number of its elected members from four to eight. He said on that occasion 'such a balanced increase in the proportionate representation of elected members, accords with the policy of Her Majesty's Government for a steady but gradual advance in the constitutional field and the Government has accordingly accepted these proposals'.[1] But the implementation of this policy has been held up by abnormal conditions.

Hong Kong could not defend itself, and to set up self-governing institutions to which Britain's present responsibilities could be transferred, is clearly impracticable. It is extremely doubtful if it would be economically viable without the currency link with sterling and the advantage of Commonwealth preferences; for example, there is understandable anxiety over Britain's possible membership of the European Economic Community.

The refugee influx has put back the clock. The 1961 Census gave the number of immigrants since September 1947 as 827,222 or 26·43% off the total population. If there is added the estimated balance of immigration for 1961 of 10,000, and that for 1962—an exceptional year—of 208,000, then at the end of the year 1962, some $1\frac{1}{4}$ million out of an estimated total of $3\frac{1}{2}$ million were immigrants. There is the added complication of factional rivalry between supporters of the Chinese People's Republic and those who, for various reasons, look to the Republic of China in Taiwan.

One further point has to be made. The Peking Government has shown marked sensitivity over frontier relations with its neighbours. The reason is clear. The Chinese, whether Communists or Nationalists, have never been reconciled to the territorial and other

[1] Hong Kong *Hansard* 1956, p. 30.

concessions which they were forced to yield under the so-called Unequal Treaties during the period of their national weakness. It would be clearly unrealistic to imagine that the demand for boundary revision will stop at the Shum Chun River.

These considerations point to the impracticability of any far-reaching constitutional change in Hong Kong, and to the continuance of special relations with Britain, which in the absence of political agitation appears to be not unacceptable, or with some other external authority such as the United Nations. On the other hand, they do not point to the impossibility of any change at all. There seems no reason why constitutional progress should be frozen at the present stage of its evolution.

The British tradition of free political institutions is too firmly rooted to be disregarded, except for compelling reasons; and the British people can have little satisfaction in being asked to turn their backs on that tradition particularly in face of a resurgent Asia. Lord Lansdowne, the Minister of State for Colonial Affairs, on his visit to Hong Kong in September 1963, was reported to have defended the form of government here as a 'workable system, taking all circumstances into account'. This cannot be denied. The judgment, however, rests on the assumption that being 'workable' is the sole criterion and ignores the fact that in the long term government can be based only on the alternatives of popular consent or the security forces.

The problem is how to modify the constitution so as to reconcile administrative efficiency with the legitimate claims of responsible citizenship. Efficiency cannot be an end in itself, for government is made for man and not man for government. A government, however exacting the tests by which its personnel is recruited, which is not rooted in the loyalty of responsible citizenship is unlikely to survive an onslaught in which fifth-column techniques are employed. It is argued that the apathy shown in the Urban Council elections and the conspicuous absence of political agitation demonstrate clearly that no demand for constitutional change exists. One reason for this political quiescence is awareness of the fact that important decisions affecting the future of Hong Kong will be taken in various world capitals rather than in Hong Kong itself. So far as the Chinese majority are concerned there has been no tradition of popular government among them. In the dominant Confucian system, ethics and politics were closely bound up and good government was founded on good human relations. The state was the family writ large, and obedience to the state was an extension of filial piety. The state interfered little with the daily lives of the people, because it was based not so much on law, as on each individual carrying out his moral obligations. The Chinese therefore did not look to the state as the instrument of social betterment, but rather relied on the family and generally asked only to be left alone. The Chinese concept of state government was that of a moral order for which no man-made law could be a substitute, and that the same moral order that made for happy family life applied to the state, which was regarded as an enlarged household. They were thus unreceptive to a Western order based on respect for law, for law was meant only for peoples who lacked the moral basis which alone made civilized life possible. To Europeans, this appears to be anarchy, but to the Chinese, law cannot be an adequate substitute for the moral obligation. So the Chinese in Hong Kong have shown a natural hesitation in adopting Western ideas of law and administration, which should not be confused with apathy. With regard to the Europeans, so few are permanent residents, that there is little incentive for interest in constitutional change.

It is also true that the local people, Europeans, Chinese, Portuguese and Eurasians, whose families are rooted in Hong Kong which is their home, have not demanded self-government. The probable reason is that they feel more secure under the existing régime. In addition, Government would be unlikely to introduce a franchise sufficiently restricted to give them control and make them a privileged aristocracy, and with a broad franchise, their influence would be lost. The answer is that little can be done unless the bulk of the people living in Hong Kong regard it as their home. Talk of constitutional progress is idle in the absence of a community, conscious of its own identity, demanding its own way of life, and willing to share fully in its defence. Such a community would be neither Chinese nor European but Hong Kong. Hong Kong is rapidly changing but few would claim that such a community already exists. Indeed, it still has many communities differing in race, creed and social customs, and tending to draw themselves apart socially but to be brought together by economic factors. One difficulty in integrating people into one community is that Western influences by which the traditional Chinese life is being eroded, appear to operate with diminishing force as one goes down the social and economic scale. Such a Hong Kong community could come into being, given sufficient time and freedom from external pressures to allow it to develop along its own lines.

Two further assumptions have to be made. First, the liberal character of the present régime must be maintained. The police admittedly have stronger powers than normal because of the extent and seriousness of crime, but freedom of speech, of the press, of conscience, of association, protection against arbitrary arrest given by the writ of habeas corpus, equality of all before the law, give freedom to the law-abiding citizen to go about his business in security. Secondly, Hong Kong must be able to offer to its people a reasonable standard of living through industry and trade, backed by opportunities in the educational system for those who can benefit by them.

These considerations, point to the dilemma facing British policy in Hong Kong of deciding what to do in an admittedly difficult situation without repudiating constitutional principles which the British have given to the world. Assuming the necessity for continued association with Britain, then constitutional advance must be gradual and evolutionary. Experience elsewhere shows that the hope of early self-government creates tension, a jockeying for political influence, and ultimately generates a cataclysmic rush towards the final transference of power.

Discussion of contitutional change naturally focuses attention on the Legislative Council and the extent to which it represents or could be made to represent public opinion. Of the eight unofficial members, six are nominated by the Governor and one each by the the Chamber of Commerce and unofficial Justices of the Peace. In the absence of any broad electoral system, the justification for nominated members as argued by Sir Man Kam Lo in 1949, remains, for it is the only way by which the representation of important sections of opinion or important minorities can be assured. A system containing a nominated element must therefore continue. To suggest that the field from which nominated members are chosen should be widened is no criticism of the present nominated members. On the contrary, their devotion to the public service and to the interests of Hong Kong must be acknowledged. Many would agree that other bodies exist in Hong Kong, free from external affiliation or control, which might claim to express important sections of opinion, besides the two already enfranchised. The University Convocation consisting of graduates, the Federation of Hong Kong Industries, the Heung Yee Kuk, the unofficial members of the Urban Council, or, what almost amounts to the same thing, the Urban Council electoral body and the Kaifongs. There could be little of a revolutionary nature about this if the existing arrangements were retained whereby members had to be British subjects and nominations remained technically those of the Governor.

The sphere of local government centred around the Urban Council might provide opportunities of constitutional advance. This was the basis of the abortive Young Plan. Here again, tribute must be paid to the unofficial members of the Council for accepting an office with a heavy burden of committee work. With the rapid growth of population, the efficacy of one Urban Council to reflect and deal with the needs of over three million people, must sooner or later be questioned. The growth of existing and projected satellite towns at Aberdeen, Shaukiwan, Shatin, Tsuen Wan, Castle Peak, Yuen Long and Kwun Tong might give the opportunity for a new look at local government with the object of keeping Government in closer touch with the People. The rioting in Kowloon of October 1956, due perhaps to economic and social factors, clearly revealed the existence of an underlying malaise, and, it may be, an unbridged gap in communication between the Government and the People. The interest of the people in their own immediate and local problems such as hygiene, public amenities, housing and water supply, etc., might be enlisted through a number of local councils, from which the Urban Council might then be partly recruited by indirect election. If the present Urban Council's administrative powers were interpreted broadly to include policy making, then, it might conceivably develop into the lower house of a bicameral legislature with powers restricted to that area of administration covered by the present Urban Services Department, the Legislature remaining unicameral in the remaining fields of legislation. This is not the place to examine in detail the consequent problems of devising electoral machinery and liaison with government departments, but of course they would be considerable.

This brief review of principles cannot be closed without pointing out that any constitutional change, however seemingly minor, must have considerable repercussions in the economic and political fields. On the economic side, Hong Kong must continue to rest, as it has done in the past, upon the maintenance of its trade relations with the rest of the world. Latterly it has become an important centre for the movement of capital, of which it is a net importer. Constitutional change may involve a lessening of confidence in its economic and financial stability.

On the political side the existing system of government rests on a delicate poise which at least works. Public proceedings in the Legislative Council appear formal, but real debate takes place in private. Public debate of government action and policy would certainly carry with it the necessity of seeking a new equilibrium within the constitutional set-up.

Whether these risks are taken depends on the importance attached in Hong Kong to those values which underlie political life in the West.

ARMORIAL BEARINGS OF HONG KONG

Armorial bearings were presented to Hong Kong on behalf of Her Majesty the Queen by H. R. H. the Prince Philip, Duke of Edinburgh, when he visited the Colony in March, 1949. The crest consists of a royal lion wearing the imperial crown and holding a pearl, representing Hong Kong as the 'Pearl of the Orient'. The shield carries pictures of a naval crown symbolizing the Colony's link with the Navy and Merchant Navy, battlements indicating the Battle of Hong Kong in 1941, and two Chinese junks to indicate trade on the seas surrounding the Colony. A royal lion and Chinese dragon support the shield and crest, symbolising the British and Chinese aspects of the Colony. They stand on a green mount surrounded by water, an allusion to Hong Kong Island. [From The Hong Kong *Annual Report 1959*, with permission.]

APPENDICES

A. *Changes in the Constitution of the Executive Council*

Year	Number of Official Members exclusive of the Governor	Number of Unoffiial Members
1843	3	—
1844	4	—
1845	3	—
1865	3 [All *ex officio*]	—
1872	4 [3 *ex officio*]	—
1875	5 [3 *ex officio*]*	—
1884	6 [4 *ex officio*]	—
1896	6 [4 *ex officio*]	2
1926	6 [4 *ex officio*]	3
1928	6 [5 *ex officio*]	3
1946	7 [5 *ex officio*]	4
1948	6 [5 *ex officio*]	6

*A special additional appointment because the Senior Military Officer refused to attend Meetings of the Council.

B. *Changes in the Constitution of the Legislative Council*

Year	Number of Official Members exclusive of the Governor	Number of Unofficial Members
1843	3	—
1844	5	—
1845	3	—
1850	3	2
1857	5	3
1858	6	3
1865	5 †	4 [including 1 official]
1884	6	5
1896	7	6
1929	9	8
1946	9	7
1947	8	7
1951	9	8
1964	12	13

† From 1865 onwards, five officials hold their seats *ex officio*.

C. *List of Unofficial Members of the Executive Council, 1896–1941*

ARRANGED IN CHRONOLOGICAL ORDER

Catchick Paul Chater	1896–1926	Broker
James Jardine Bell-Irving	1896–99, 1901–02	Jardine, Matheson & Co.
James Johnstone Keswick	1899, 1900–01	Jardine, Matheson & Co.
Charles Wedderburn Dickson	1902–06	Jardine, Matheson & Co.
Thomas Henderson Whitehead	1902 (temporary)	Chartered Bank of India, Australia and China
Charles Stewart Sharp	1902 (temporary)	Gibb, Livingston & Co.
William Jardine Gresson	1904, 1905, 1908 (temporary)	Jardine, Matheson & Co.
Edbert Ansgar Hewett	1906–1915	P. & O. Steam Navigation Co.
Henry Keswick	1908, 1910 (temporary)	Jardine, Matheson & Co.
Sir Henry Spencer Berkeley, K.C.	1908 (temporary)	Barrister
Henry Ernest Pollock, K.C.	1911, 1912, 1921–41	Barrister
Ernest Hamilton Sharp, K.C.	1916–22	Barrister
David Landale	1916, 1918 (temporary)	Jardine, Matheson & Co.
N. J. Stabb	1919 (temporary)	The Hongkong and Shanghai Banking Corporation
Percy Hobson Holyoak	1920, 1921, 1923, 1924–26	Reiss & Co.
Edward Victor David Parr	1920 (temporary)	Mackinnon, Mackenzie & Co.
Alexander Gordon Stephen	1922–24	Jardine, Matheson & Co.
Charles Montague Ede	1924 (temporary)	Union Insurance Society of Canton
Archibald Orr Lang	1925, 1926–27	Gibb, Livingston & Co.
Sir Shouson Chow	1926–1936	
Dallas Gerald Mercer Bernard	1927 (temporary)	Jardine, Matheson & Co.
William Edward Leonard Shenton	1928–36	Solicitor
Arthur Cecil Haynes	1928 (temporary)	The Hongkong and Shanghai Banking Corporation
John Owen Hughes	1930, 1931 (temporary)	Harry Wicking & Co.
Charles Gordon Stewart Mackie	1930, 1931, 1933, 1934, 1935	Gibb, Livingston & Co.
Robert Hormus Kotewall	1932, 1934, 1935, 1936–41	Hong Kong Mercantile Co., Ltd.
John Johnstone Paterson	1936–41	Jardine, Matheson & Co.
William Henry Bell	1936 (temporary)	Asiatic Petroleum Co. (South China) Ltd.
Stanley Hudson Dodwell	1936, 1937, 1938, 1939, 1940	Dodwell & Co.

D. *List of Unofficial Members of the Legislative Council, 1850–1941*

ARRANGED IN CHRONOLOGICAL ORDER

C = Elected by the Chamber of Commerce.
J = Elected by the unofficial Justices of the Peace.

David Jardine	1850–1857	Jardine, Matheson & Co.
James Frost Edger	1850–1857	Jamieson, How & Co.
Joseph Jardine	1857–60	Jardine, Matheson & Co.
George Lyall	1857–61	Lyall, Still & Co.
John Dent	1857–60, 1866–67	Dent & Co.
Alexander Perceval	1860–64	Jardine, Matheson & Co.
Angus Fletcher	1860–62	Fletcher & Co.
Francis Chomley	1861–66	Dent & Co.
Charles Wilson Murray	1862–64	Birley & Co.
James Whittall	1864–67, 1872–75	Jardine, Matheson & Co.
Thomas Sutherland	1864–65	P. & O. Steam Navigation Co.
Hugh Bold Gibb	1860–70, 1879	Gibb, Livingston & Co.
Phineas Ryrie	1867–92	Turner & Co.
Francis Parry	1867–68	Birley & Co.
William Keswick	1867–72, 1875–86	Jardine, Matheson & Co.
James Banks Taylor	1868	Smith, Archer & Co.
James Pender Duncanson	1868	Gibb, Livingston & Co.
H. J. Ball	1863, 1869–73	Judge of the Summary Court sitting as unofficial
Richard Rowett	1869, 1871–75	Holiday, Wise & Co.
Henry Lowcock	1872, 1875–80	Gibb, Livingston & Co.
William Hastings Alexander	1872–1876	Registrar of the Supreme Court, sitting as unofficial
John MacNeile Price	1877–1884	Surveyor General, sitting as unofficial
Ng Choy	1880–1882	
Francis Bulkeley Johnson	1878, 1881–84	Jardine, Matheson, & Co.
Emanuel Raphael Belilios	1881, 1892–1900	Belilios & Co.
Frederick Stewart	1883–4	Registrar-General, sitting as an unofficial
Thomas Jackson	1884–1886 (C)	The Hongkong and Shanghai Banking Corporation
Frederick David Sassoon	1884–1887 (J)	David Sassoon Sons & Co.
Wong Shing	1884–1890	
Alexander Palmer MacEwen	1886, 1887–90 (C)	Holiday, Wise & Co.
John Bell-Irving	1886, 1887–89	Jardine, Matheson & Co.
Catchick Paul Chater	1887, 1888–1906 (J)	Broker
Bendyshe Latyon	1888 (C) and 1889	Gibb, Livingston & Co.
James Johnstone Keswick	1889, 1890–96 1899–1901	Jardine, Matheson & Co.
Ho Kai	1890–1914	

Thomas Henderson Whitehead	1890–1902 (C)	The Chartered Bank of India, Australia and China
James Jardine Bell-Irving	1892–93, 1895, 1896–99, 1901–02	Jardine, Matheson & Co.
Alexander MacConachie	1894 (C), 1895	Gilman & Co.
Wei Yuk	1896–1914	
Henry Edward Pollock	1896, 1903–41 (C and J)	Barrister-at-Law
Herbert Smith	1900 (C)	Butterfield & Swire
Roderick Mackenzie Gray	1900–01	Reiss & Co.
John Thurburn	1900 (C), 1901–02	Chartered Mercantile Bank
Charles Stewart Sharp	1902–1904	Gibb, Livingston & Co.
Charles Wedderburn Dickson	1902–1906	Jardine, Matheson & Co.
Robert Gordon Shewan	1902–1906 (C), 1918–1920	Shewan, Tomes & Co.
Gershom Stewart	1903, 1904–07	Bill Broker
William Jardine Gresson	1904, 1906–10	Jardine, Matheson & Co.
Edward Osborne	1906–07, 1907–13	H.K. & Kowloon Warf and Godown Co.
Edbert Ansgar Hewett	1906–1915 (C)	P. & O. Steam Navigation Co.
Henry Keswick	1907–1908, 1910–1911	Jardine, Matheson & Co.
Murray Stewart	1908–09, 1912 (C)	Stewart Bros.
Sir Henry Spencer Berkeley, K.C.	1908	Barrister-at-Law
Henry Adolphus Warre Slade	1908–1909	Gilman & Co.
Charles Henderson Ross	1911–1913	Jardine, Matheson & Co.
Charles Montague Ede	1911, 1913, 1924	Union Insurance Society of Canton
John Whyte Cooper Bonnar	1912 (C)	Gibb, Livingston & Co.
Edward Shellim	1913–1918	David Sassoon & Co.
David Landale	1913–1919	Jardine, Matheson & Co.
Lau Chu Pak	1913–1922	
Percy Hobson Holyoak	1915–1926 (C)	Reiss & Co.
Charles Edward Anton	1916	Jardine, Matheson & Co.
Ho Fook	1917–1921	
Herbert William Bird	1918, 1921, 1922–1927	Architect, Palmer & Turner
Chan Kai Ming	1918	
Stanley Hudson Dodwell	1918 (C), 1919, 1920–21, 1936–41	Dodwell & Co.
John Johnstone	1919–1921	Jardine, Matheson & Co.
Chaloner Granville Alabaster	1919, 1924, 1925	Barrister-at-Law
Edward Victor David Parr	1919 (C), 1920–23	Mackinnon, Mackenzie & Co.
Arthur Rylands Lowe	1920, 1922, 1923	Lowe, Bingham & Matthews
Alexander Gordon Stephen	1921–23	Jardine, Matheson & Co.
Archibald Orr Lang	1921 (C), 1922–23, 1923–27	Gibb, Livingston & Co.

Chau Siu Ki	1921, 1923, 1924	
Chow Shouson	1921, 1922–1931	
Ng Hon-tsz	1922–1923	
Robert Hormus Kotewall	1923–1935	H.K. Mercantile Co., Ltd.
Dallas Gerald Mercer Bernard	1926–1928 (C)	Jardine, Matheson & Co.
Wilfred Miller Vincent Koch	1926	Medical Faculty, University
Arthur Cecil Haynes	1927–29	The Hongkong and Shanghai Banking Corporation
John Owen Hughes	1927–31 (C), 1934	Harry Wicking & Co.
William Edward Leonard Shenton	1927, 1928–36	Solicitor
Jose Pedro Braga	1929–1937	Braga & Co.
Ts'o Seen Wan	1929–1937	
Benjamin David Fleming Beith	1929 (C), 1930–33,	Jardine, Matheson & Co.
Charles Gordon Stewart Mackie	1930–31 (C), 1932–35 (C)	Gibb, Livingston & Co.
Paul Lauder	1930, 1933, 1934	Union Insurance Co. of Canton
John Johnstone Paterson	1930–33, 1934–39 1940, 1941	Jardine, Matheson & Co.
Charles Gordon Stewart	1931	Mackinnon, Mackenzie & Co.
Chau Tsun-nin	1931–39	
William Henry Bell	1931 (C), 1933, 1934, 1935–36 (C)	Asiatic Petroleum Co. (South China) Ltd.
Lo Man Kam	1935–41	Solicitor
A. F. B. Silva-Netto	1936	Silva-Netto & Co.
Marcus Theodore Johnston	1936, 1937–38 (C)	Mackinnon, Mackenzie & Co.
Edgar Davidson	1936, 1937	Solicitor (Hastings & Co.)
Arthur William Hughes	1936–37 (C)	Union Insurance Society of Canton Ltd.
L. d'Almada e Castro	1937–41	Barrister-at-Law.
Li Shu Fan	1937–41	Medical Practitioner
Andrew Lusk Shields	1938–41 (C)	Shewan, Tomes & Co.
John Keith Bousfield	1939	Asiatic Petroleum Co. (South China) Ltd.
Li Tse Fong	1939	
Thomas Ernest Pearce	1939–41	J. D. Hutchison & Co.
William Ngartse Thomas Tam	1939–41	

E. *Governors of the Colony of Hong Kong*

Capt. Charles Elliot	Administrator	January–August 1841
Sir Henry Pottinger	Administrator	August 1841–June 1843
	Governor	June 1843–May 1844
Sir John Francis Davis		May 1844–March 1848
Sir Samuel George Bonham		March 1848–April 1854
Sir John Bowring		April 1854–May 1859
Sir Hercules George Robert Robinson		September 1859–March 1865
Sir Richard Graves MacDonnell		March 1866–April 1872
Sir Arthur Edward Kennedy		April 1872–March 1877
Sir John Pope Hennessy		April 1877–March 1882
Sir George Ferguson Bowen		March 1883–December 1885
Sir George William Des Vœux		October 1887–May 1891
Sir William Robinson		December 1891–January 1898
Sir Henry Arthur Blake		November 1898–November 1903
Sir Matthew Nathan		July 1904–April 1907
Sir Frederick John Dealtry Lugard		July 1907–March 1912
Sir Francis Henry May		July 1912–February 1919
Sir Reginald Edward Stubbs		September 1919–October 1925
Sir Cecil Clementi		November 1925–February 1930
Sir William Peel		May 1930–May 1935
Sir Andrew Caldecott		December 1935–April 1937
Sir Geoffry Alexander Stafford Northcote		November 1937–May 1940
Sir Mark Aitchison Young		September 1941–May 1947
Sir Alexander William George Herder Grantham		July 1947–December 1957
Sir Robert Brown Black		January 1958–April 1964
Sir David Clive Crosbie Trench		April 1964

F. *A Select Bibliography*

OFFICIAL GOVERNMENT SOURCES

Colonial Office Records (Public Record Office, London)

Series CO 129 Governors' Dispatches and Replies from the Secretary of State.

Series CO 130 Hong Kong Ordinances.

Series CO 131 Minutes of the Hong Kong Executive and Legislative Councils.

Series CO 132 Hong Kong Government Gazettes.

Series CO 133 Annual Blue Book of Statistics.

Series CO 809 Confidential Prints.

Series CO 403 Dispatches from the Secretary of State to the Governors of Hong Kong.

Series CO 323 Commissions, Warrants and various Documents.

Foreign Office Records (Public Record Office, London)

Series FO 17, FO 223 and FO 228.

Hong Kong Government Publications.

Hong Kong Government Annual Reports 1946 onwards.

Hong Kong Sessional Papers 1884 onwards.

Hong Kong Administrative Reports (called Administration Reports after 1931) 1909–1939.

Hong Kong Hansard (Printed Proceedings of the Legislative Council), 1890 onwards.

Hong Kong Civil Service List.

Historical and Statistical Abstract of the Colony of Hong Kong 1932.

NEWSPAPERS

Canton Register, 1827–43 continued as the *Hong Kong Register* 1844–63.

Canton Press, 1835–44.

Chinese Repository, 1832–51.

Dixon's Hong Kong Recorder, 1850–59.

Friend of China, 1842–61.

Hong Kong Telegraph, 1881–1916.

China Mail, since 1845.

South China Morning Post, since 1903.

REFERENCE BOOKS

ALLEN, G. C. and DONNITHORNE, A. G., *Western Enterprise in Far Eastern Development*, London 1954.

COLLINS, SIR CHARLES, *Public Administration in Hong Kong*, London 1952.

COSTIN, W. C., *Great Britain and China 1833–1860*, Oxford 1937.

DAVIS, S. G. (ed.), *Symposium on Land Use and Mineral Deposits in Hong Kong, Southern China and S. E. Asia*, Hong Kong University Press, 1964.

DENNISON, F. S. V., *British Military Administration in the Far East 1943–46*, London 1956.

EITEL, E. J., *Europe in China*, the History of Hong Kong from the Beginning to the Year 1882, Hong Kong 1895.

ENDACOTT, G. B., *A History of Hong Kong*, Oxford 1958.

FAIRBANK, J. K., *Trade and Diplomacy on the China Coast, the opening of the treaty ports 1842–1854*, Cambridge, Mass. 1953.

FELDWICK, W. (ed.), *Present Day Impressions of the Far East and prominent Chinese at home and abroad*, London 1917.

FURNIVAL, J. S., *Colonial Policy and Practice*, Cambridge 1948.

GULL, E. M., *British Economic Interests in the Far East*, London 1943.

HARRISON, BRIAN, (ed.), *The University of Hong Kong, the First 50 Years 1911–1961*. Hong Kong University Press, 1962.

HERTSLET, GODFREY E. P., *China Treaties*, 2 vols., H.M.S.O., London 1908.

HONG KONG GENERAL CHAMBER OF COMMERCE, *Annual Reports*.

INGRAMS, HAROLD, *Hong Kong*, H.M.S.O., London 1952.

JEFFRIES, SIR CHARLES, *The Colonial Office*, Oxford 1956.

MA, RONALD A. and SZCZEPANIK, E. F. *The National Income of Hong Kong 1947–1950*. Hong Kong University Press, Hong Kong 1955.

MAYERS, W. F., *Treaties between the Empire of China and Foreign Powers*, 5th edition, Shanghai 1903.

NORTON-KYSHE, J. W., *The History of the Laws and Courts of Hong Kong*, 2 vols, London and Hong Kong 1898.

ORANGE, JAMES, *The Chater Collection, Pictures relating to China, Hong Kong, Macao, etc. 1655–1860*. London 1924.

SAYER, G. R., *Hong Kong: Birth, Adolescence, and Coming of Age*, Oxford 1937.

SMITH, REV. G., *A Narrative of the Exploratory Visit to each of the Consular Cities of China and to the Islands of Hong Kong and Chusan*, London 1847.

SZCZEPANIK, EDWARD, *The Cost of Living in Hong Kong*, Hong Kong University Press, Hong Kong 1956.
The Economic Growth of Hong Kong, Royal Institute of International Affairs, London 1958.

TREGEAR, T. R., *Land Use in Hong Kong and the New Territories*, Regional Monograph 1 in the World Land Use Survey, edited by L. Dudley Stamp, Hong Kong University Press, 1955.

TREGEAR, T. R. and BERRY, L. *The Development of Hong Kong and Kowloon as told in maps*, Hong Kong University Press, 1959.

VŒUX, SIR WILLIAM DES, *My Colonial Service*, 2 vols, London 1903.

WIGHT, MARTIN, *The Development of the Legislative Council, 1606–1945*. Faber and Faber 1946.

WRIGHT, A. and CARTRIGHT, H. A. (ed.), *Twentieth Century Impressions of Hong Kong, Shanghai and other Treaty Ports*, London 1908.

YAP, P. M., *Suicide in Hong Kong*, Hong Kong University, 1958.

INDEX